———— TEJANO RELIGION AND ETHNICITY ————

TEJANO RELIGION AND ETHNICITY

San Antonio, 1821–1860

†

TIMOTHY M. MATOVINA

UNIVERSITY OF TEXAS PRESS

AUSTIN

Library of Congress Cataloging-in-Publication Data

Matovina, Timothy M., date
Tejano religion and ethnicity : San Antonio, 1821–1860 /
Timothy M. Matovina. — 1st ed.
p.   cm.
Includes bibliographical references and index.
ISBN 0-292-75170-2
1. Mexican Americans—Texas—San Antonio—Ethnic identity.
2. Mexican Americans—Texas—San Antonio—Religion.
3. San Antonio (Tex.)—History.   4. San Antonio (Tex.)—Church history.
I. Title.
F394.S2M39   1995
976.4'3510046872073—dc20   94-10617

to Marie Orr,
my loving grandmother

CONTENTS

†

PREFACE

†

U.S. Latino theologians have argued that the assimilationist melting-pot image ought to be replaced by that of the stew pot. Just as in a stew pot each ingredient enriches and is enriched by the other ingredients, so too in our society the different cultures should be mutually enriching and should not overpower one another. These theologians also suggest that resistance to the melting pot is manifested in popular expressions of faith. To the extent that popular expressions of faith continue to be practiced among their people, group resistance to assimilation will tend to be fortified.

These claims about the stew pot and Hispanic faith expressions, along with my own experiences teaching and working with Latino communities, are the genesis of this study. This volume adds to the emerging body of literature on Hispanic Catholics in the United States by providing historical analysis of ethnicity and religion in one nineteenth-century Spanish-speaking community. It also substantiates claims about Latino resistance to assimilation and illustrates that public celebrations like those for the feast of Our Lady of Guadalupe can reinforce the religious and cultural heritage of Hispanic communities.

This investigation elucidates the religious and ethnic identity of a people who did not cross a border to enter the United States but had the border cross them during U.S. territorial expansion. As such it provides a perspective for the study of religion and ethnicity in American life distinct from that of European immigrants. This perspective reveals that theories of unilateral assimilation are inadequate for understanding the Tejano experience. It also suggests that pluralism does not necessarily entail a dominant group at a society's center tolerating some degree of diversity on the periphery. Rather, pluralism can also result from various groups in the same society who have not reached a consensus on which group is dominant and normative.

In addition, this book advances the study of Tejano history. It provides data for an era of San Antonio Tejano history not previously treated in a major work and highlights religious and ethnic identity as crucial issues for understanding the Tejano experience. More importantly, it examines a Tejano community which remained vital under the governments of Spain, Mexico, the Republic of Texas, and the United States and explicates significant elements of continuity in the life and identity of this enduring community.

The introductory chapter of this volume presents its methodology, sources, terminology, and historical background. For clarity, I have sectioned chapters 2 to 4 into three chronological divisions: the Mexican period (1821–1836), the period of the Texas Republic (1836–1845), and the period following annexation into the United States in 1845. Each of these chapters begins with a physical description of San Antonio from contemporary observers, along with a demographic and economic profile of the local population. This contextual data is followed by an exposition of Tejano life in San Antonio for the given time spans. Key elements in this analysis include Tejano national loyalties, participation in military conflicts, political activities, religious feasts and other public celebrations, response to Protestant initiatives, and interactions with Anglo-Americans and other immigrants to Texas. This analysis, along with an examination of written sources and other public statements from Tejano leaders, probes Tejano identity as it evolved under these three governments. The final chapter assesses the relevance of the San Antonio Tejano experience for the study of religion and ethnicity in American life, particularly for examining the issues of assimilation and pluralism.

This book stems from a dissertation written at the Catholic University of America in Washington, D.C. Dr. William Dinges directed the dissertation, and the readers were Dr. Margaret Mary Kelleher and Dr. Christopher Kauffman. Other faculty members offered guidance during discussions of this project and related topics. Scholars who address the religious practices and culture of U.S. Latinos in their research also shaped my thinking and this work, especially the faculty at the Mexican American Cultural Center in San Antonio, various Tejano historians, and members of the Academy of Catholic Hispanic Theologians of the United States. In particular, Father Virgilio Elizondo, rector of San Fernando Cathedral in San Antonio, has been both friend and mentor for my reflection on U.S. Hispanic Catholics for over a decade.

The staff at the University of Texas Press helped produce this book from the original dissertation. I am especially grateful for the patience and efficiency of executive editor Theresa J. May and for the insightful editorial comments of copy editor Sarah Buttrey.

A number of archivists and librarians assisted with historical research. These include those charged with the care of collections at the Center for American History, University of Texas, Austin; Catholic Archives of Texas, Austin; Library of Congress, Washington, D.C.; Incarnate Word Archives, Incarnate Word Generalate, San Antonio; University of Notre Dame Archives, South Bend, Indiana; Houston Public Library; San Antonio Public Library; Catholic Archives at San Antonio, Chancery Office, Archdiocese of San Antonio; City Clerk's Office, San Antonio; Béxar County Archives, San Antonio; National Archives, Washington, D.C.; Archivo Matritense C.M., Madrid; Vincentian Archives, St. Mary's of the Barrens, Perryville, Missouri; United Methodist Church Southwest Texas Conference Archives, Travis Park United Methodist Church, San Antonio; Daughters of the Republic of Texas Library, San Antonio; Rare Book Collection, the Catholic University of America, Washington, D.C.; General Land Office, Austin; Texas State Archives, Austin. I would also like to thank Henry and Mary Ann Noonan Guerra of San Antonio, who generously allowed me to use their private collection of works on local history.

The directors of the Cushwa Center for the Study of American Catholicism at the University of Notre Dame awarded a dissertation fellowship in the history of U.S. Hispanic Catholics to support this work. Their generous assistance afforded me time to write and enhanced the quality of this essay.

My uncle, Terry Orr, assisted me with his computer expertise. He, his wife and daughters, and a number of friends and family members provided personal support while I was writing my thesis and later converting it into this book. In this regard, I would especially like to thank Ed and Mary Schmidt and their family, Anne Marie Dalton, Teresa and Harry Post, Mike and Ann Malone, Jaime and Genoveva de la Isla, Joe and Ann Elwood, Mike and Liz La Fortune, Rosendo Urrabazo and the staff at the Mexican American Cultural Center, Chris Megargee, Martha Ann Kirk, Gayle Armstrong, and members of the Congregation of Saint Basil, particularly Paul Walsh, Paul Rennick, Al Sinasac, John Reddy, Raphael O'Loughlin, and Tom McReavy. My grandmothers, parents, sister, and brothers stood by me in good times and in bad. To them especially, I offer my deepest gratitude.

T. M. M.

TEJANO RELIGION AND ETHNICITY

†

ONE

INTRODUCTION

Historical studies of Spanish-speaking populations in Texas and other former territories of northern Mexico have tended to focus on economic, political, and institutional ecclesial issues and not on the interplay between religious and ethnic identity.[1] While scholarship of economic, political, and ecclesial developments are important, they do not offer a complete analysis of how these communities evolved before and after they were incorporated into the United States.

The dearth of studies on religious and ethnic identity in what is now the Southwest is also reflected in the literature on religion and ethnicity in American life. This work has tended to focus on European immigrants and has not dealt adequately with the experience of Spanish-speaking populations who were incorporated during U.S. territorial expansion. As a result, scholars of religion and ethnicity frequently assume that the European immigrant experience is normative for the movement of new peoples in the United States. For example, in their 1921 work, *Old World Traits Transplanted,* Robert E. Park and Herbert A. Miller wrote the following:

> There is in the state of New Mexico a Mexican community about three hundred years old, of peculiar interest to our study because it shows how long an alien group may remain on American soil without change or improvement if it brings a low level of culture, no leaders, no institutions for preserving and developing its characteristic culture or appropriating the surrounding American culture, no channels of communication with the culture of the mother country, which in this case is also low.[2]

Despite their statement that this New Mexican community was some three hundred years old, Park and Miller labeled them "an alien group . . . on American soil," thus illustrating their assumption that ethnic groups in the United States are comprised of immigrants who must adapt to life in a foreign land. While these authors recognized that this New Mexican community did not fit the pattern of assimilation they were presenting, they reasoned that the community's lack of "improvement" stemmed from a substandard culture, a lack of effective leadership, and inadequate institutions.

This volume explores the history of religious and ethnic identity of Tejano[3] Catholics in San Antonio during a critical period when that city shifted from Mexican to U.S. political and economic control. It also addresses the relevance of their experience for the study of religion and ethnicity in the American milieu.

METHODOLOGY AND SOURCES

Primary data for this study is taken from contemporary sources for 1821–1860 San Antonio, such as diaries, journals, memoirs, reminiscences, travelogues, correspondence, newspaper accounts, census data, city-council minutes, and other official documents. Critical exposition and analysis of these sources provide a basis for examining religious and ethnic identity for the period under consideration. Analysis of primary sources is augmented by pertinent secondary literature, including reference to works on religion and ethnicity in American life that enhance an assessment of the San Antonio Tejano experience from 1821 to 1860.

Most extant primary sources were written by immigrants to Texas from the United States. These documents must be interpreted in light of the frequent conflicts between the advancing Anglo-American and native-born San Antonio populations. The majority of primary sources from San Antonio Tejanos were written by prominent male citizens. Of these, the two most important sources for this work are the papers of native San Antonians Juan Nepomuceno Seguín and José Antonio Navarro. Both Seguín and Navarro held political office under three separate governments during this period: Mexico, the Texas Republic, and the United States. As will be seen in the chapters which follow, their prominence in public life frequently placed them in the position of spokesmen for the Tejano community. Two other San Antonio Tejanos also wrote memoirs which deal with the period under study: José María Rodríguez and Antonio Menchaca.[4]

While few mid-nineteenth century Tejanos left written records, their collective behavior helps illuminate their shifting religious and ethnic identity. Tejano collective behavior can be observed in areas such as demographic and marital patterns, religious feasts and other public celebrations, participation in military conflicts and local politics, shifting national loyalties, denominational affiliation, and their interactions with Anglo-Americans and other immigrants to Texas. However, like written documentation, which is obviously limited by the bias of its author, collective behavior has its limitations as a source for historical inquiry. It illuminates general trends in the development of group identity, but by no means does it allow for general application to all members of the group under study. While this study articulates shifting Tejano religious and ethnic identity from written sources and collective behavior, these findings indicate the general pattern of Tejano identity, not a perception of self-identity held universally by San Antonio Tejanos.

ETHNICITY AND RELIGION

In exploring the collective identity of a group that has a common sense of peoplehood,[5] scholars frequently employ the term *ethnicity*. Common characteristics such as language, customs, behavior patterns, political and economic interests, religion, race, and ancestral heritage lead to the perception that certain persons form a group distinct from others. While based in part on these elements of group commonalty, ethnicity is also shaped by interaction with other groups. Such interaction enables a group to overcome "pluralistic ignorance" and become aware of their own tradition as distinct from other traditions. This awareness is enhanced when the contact between groups is characterized by prejudice, conflict, and an imbalance in the distribution of power.[6]

As used in this study, then, ethnicity is a dynamic concept. Tejano ethnic identity was based on their common language, enemies, economic and political interests, and religious and cultural heritage. But that identity was molded and formulated as they came into contact with Anglo-Americans, other immigrants to Texas, and local Native American populations.[7]

Conflicting group perceptions sharpened the Tejano sense that they comprised a group distinct from Anglo-Americans and others. On the one hand, Anglo-Americans frequently bemoaned the alleged inferiority of Tejanos. For example, an Anglo-American who visited San Antonio and other Mexican settlements in the late 1820s went so far as to state that people of Mexican descent were "scarce more than apes." On the other hand, Tejanos were also critical of Anglo-American newcomers to Texas. In 1842, Juan Seguín resigned the San Antonio mayoral office and fled to Mexico under threat of Anglo-American persecution. Later, he described his persecutors as "American straggling adventurers" and "fugitives from their own country, who found in this land an open field for their criminal designs." While Seguín was careful to state that not all Anglo-Americans were evil, such perceptions undoubtedly heightened the sense that San Antonio Tejanos formed a group distinct from the "criminal element" which had invaded their city.[8]

Religion is a crucial component of ethnic identity. Although the meanings of the term *religion* are diverse, as used in this study religion refers to two distinct elements of collective behavior: public ritual practices and denominational affiliation. While they do not define the inner core of the Catholicism Tejanos professed and lived, they are observable patterns of collective behavior which elucidate Tejano religious practice and identity.

In probing Tejano ritual practices and denominational affiliation as collective behaviors, it must be kept in mind that these behaviors stemmed from an inner faith that molded Tejano life. Even without historical data, it is a truism that Tejanos' Catholic faith was an integral part of their everyday life. Although European Catholic clergy frequently described Tejanos as ignorant of their faith, and Protestant ministers decried Tejano religious practice as debased and superstitious, other new arrivals to Texas were deeply impressed by the profound devotional life of Tejanos. John J. Linn, an Irish Catholic who moved to Texas in 1830, observed the morning devotions of a south Texas shepherd and his family. The elderly husband and wife, along with their three children, awoke before dawn to recite their prayers and sing a hymn. Linn was moved by the fervent homage they offered to God, and he later commented that "this little episode made a lasting impression on my mind."[9]

Some twenty years later, Father Emanuel Domenech, a diocesan priest from France, recorded in his journal the virtues of "Rodríguez [who] is an old man of primitive faith and piety; and his high sense of justice and honor is proverbial." Rodríguez and his twelve sons frequently returned stray cattle to their owners in the San Antonio area without expecting compensation. Annually his sons took turns going alone to the woods for extended retreat days of prayer and fasting. Rodríguez himself was noted for singing hymns at Mass "in a voice full of tenderness and feeling." When he sang these hymns at San Fernando Church in San Antonio, he "was generally accompanied in church by the whole congregation." These two examples illustrate the fervent religious practice of Tejanos.[10]

Two important issues for understanding religion and ethnicity are assimilation and pluralism. No clear consensus exists among scholars on these issues. In the broadest terms, assimilation entails not only the loss of cultural traits, but also the integration of one ethnic group into the dominant group's political, civic, economic, religious, social, and particularly marital realms. As a process, then, assimilation admits of varying degrees. A given group might take on the cultural behavior patterns of another (cultural assimilation) without significant intermingling in primary relationships (structural assimilation). When distinct religious or ethnic groups come into contact and assimilation is absent or retarded in any one of these areas, some degree of pluralism results. This does not necessarily entail a state of stagnation, however, since the religious and ethnic identities of two (or more) groups can change without one group assimilating the identity of another.[11]

TEJANO IDENTITY IN EIGHTEENTH-CENTURY SAN ANTONIO

The San Antonio Tejano experience from 1821 to 1860 is rooted in the earlier history of that settlement. Recent scholarship has suggested that during the eighteenth century the experience of the settlers in San Antonio de Béxar led to the emergence of a Tejano regional identity.[12] Spain's first establishments in the area were a military *presidio* (garrison) and Mission San Antonio de Valero in 1718. By 1731, Franciscan friars had added four more missions. That same year, immigrants from the Canary Islands founded the Villa de San Fernando. Although all were to serve the same Church and king, these military, civilian, and missionary settlers frequently competed for land, water rights, political offices, and Native American labor. As the century progressed, other factors influenced local residents: the incorporation of some Native Americans into their community, relationships with tribes which were not missionized, and further immigration, particularly from adjacent provinces in northern New Spain.

The various groups of settlers found themselves isolated on the frontier, with common Native American enemies and the need to develop farming, ranching, and trade for the economic good of all. In time their group interests coalesced around the mutual need for survival and the common desire for prosperity. This is seen, for example, in the shifting concerns of the town council from the civil settlement's founding to the end of the eighteenth century:

At first the Canary Islander-controlled *cabildo* [town council] served the political interests of that group, but, in time, as others in the community gained economic or social influence, they too participated in the *cabildo*. By the final third of the century the city's ruling council no longer represented the interests of an ethnically defined *Isleño* [Canary Islander] group, but rather the interests of the region's farmers and ranchers, regardless of ethnic background, against the encroachment of Crown authority.[13]

Common interests, enemies, and hardships helped shape a sense of regional independence and identity among the various settlers at Béxar. Cultural exchange, social interaction, and intermarriage between members of the various groups also contributed significantly to the formation of a distinct Tejano regional spirit and self-understanding. This regionalism consisted of "a strong impulse for autonomy, based on the community's relative self-sufficiency."[14]

Eighteenth-century Béxar Tejano regional identity is also evidenced in the emergence of a Catholic ritual calendar which gave precedence to the settlement's patrons. The 1691 expedition of Domingo Terán de los Ríos named the place the Native Americans called Yanaguana for San Antonio de Padua, who later became the patron of the area's *presidio* and first mission. Canary Islanders named the *villa* they founded in 1731 San Fernando to honor a relative of Spain's monarch, later Ferdinand VI. The patronesses of the first parish church at the Villa de San Fernando were those of the civilian settlers and soldiers in the area: Nuestra Señora de la Candelaria and Nuestra Señora de Guadalupe. In celebrating the four patronal feasts of San Antonio, San Fernando, Nuestra Señora de la Candelaria, and Nuestra Señora de Guadalupe, local residents followed the Spanish custom of designating patrons deemed to have a particular relationship with a town or village.[15] While other feasts like the Immaculate Conception, Christmas, Holy Week, and Corpus Christi also were celebrated, Béxar's particular combination of patronal feasts marked it as distinct from other settlements in New Spain.

Town-council members and other prominent citizens organized these religious feasts in conjunction with their clergy. Local leaders also worked with their priests to plan ceremonies for events like the announcement of a new Spanish monarch, peace treaties, and the installation of a new town council. Thus a strong tradition of local initiative in public celebrations and Catholic ritual was established by the 1821 proclamation of Mexican independence at Béxar.[16]

†

TWO

SHIFTING REGIONAL IDENTITY: THE MEXICAN PERIOD, 1821–1836

San Antonio de Béxar was a struggling frontier settlement during its fifteen years as part of Mexico, resembling, as an 1828 visitor commented, "a large village more than the municipal seat of a department."[1] The population of Béxar experienced a slow but steady decline after Mexican independence. This downward trend reflected a struggling local economy. Despite this lack of progress under the Mexican Republic, the loyalty of Béxar residents to their new nation and to its official Catholic religion was illustrated at the 1821 proclamation of independence at Béxar, as well as in local affairs during the years that followed. At times, these loyalties to Catholicism and the Mexican nation placed Béxar residents in conflict with the Anglo-American population in Texas, as Béxar leaders were caught between Anglo-American demands and the authority and procedures of Mexican officials. Consequently the relationship between Béxar Tejanos and Anglo-American immigrants to Texas was marked both by cooperation and compromise during this period. At the same time, Tejanos responded to local concerns at Béxar in a way that reflected their Mexican Catholic heritage.

BÉXAR, 1821–1836:
A DEMOGRAPHIC AND ECONOMIC PROFILE

At the time that Mexico won independence, San Antonio de Béxar was comprised of three different communities: the remains of the five Franciscan missions, the military *presidio,* and a civilian settlement. Secularization of the missions, which had begun in 1793, was completed in 1824, placing the mission communities under the political authority of the town. Census reports indicate that the total population of Béxar declined steadily from almost two thousand in 1820 to 1,634 in 1832. Later reports by visitors to Béxar suggest a subsequent increase in population by the outbreak of the Texas revolt in 1835. The population was overwhelmingly Tejano throughout the Mexican period. Official reports from 1828, for example, indicate that Anglo-Americans comprised less than 2 percent of the town's population at that time. Right up to the outbreak of the war for Texas independence, visitors to Béxar noted that the population was comprised of "almost all Mexicans."[2]

Visitors and residents also noted the existence of class divisions among the local populace, a prevalent element of life at Béxar since the early stages of its settlement. The majority of local residents engaged in farming. Béxar census figures for 1830 showed that 60.3 percent of employed persons were farmers, while 16.6 percent were artisans, 14.8 percent laborers, and 8.3 percent merchants. These figures reflect a largely agrarian economy, with a local elite controlling mercantile interests.[3]

Economic distress was a consistent concern of Béxar residents. Their financial situation was strained by the national government's decreased fiscal support of the local military *presidio* during the Mexican period. Ranching and farming in the fields surrounding the town were hampered by conflicts with Native Americans and remained at a subsistence level. The commercial enterprises of local artisans and merchants were still at a nascent stage. Béxar leaders promoted the town as a trade center, fostering links with Louisiana and northern Mexican regions such as Coahuila, Chihuahua, and New Mexico. Mexican laws aimed at protecting the native economy inhibited some of these efforts but did not prevent Béxar leaders from realizing some profit in both legal and contraband trade.[4]

BÉXAR AT THE OUTSET OF MEXICAN INDEPENDENCE

On July 19, 1821, the governor, town officials, clergy, soldiers, and citizenry of Béxar took an oath of allegiance to Mexican independence and acknowledged Colonel Agustín de Iturbide as the new nation's leader. The first to pledge allegiance were Governor Antonio Martínez, *Alcalde* (Mayor) José Angel Navarro (a brother of José Antonio Navarro), and other members of the *ayuntamiento* (town council) in a private economy at six o'clock that morning. This leadership group then proceeded to the town plaza where the troops and townspeople had been asked to assemble. Governor Martínez addressed the crowd, explaining the purpose of their gathering and requesting that the transition from Spanish to Mexican rule be made in an orderly fashion. Addresses were also given by *Alcalde* Navarro and Father Refugio de la Garza, pastor of the settlement's parish. Father de la Garza then received the allegiance oaths of the military officers, who pledged before a crucifix and bible to defend the Catholic faith, Mexican independence, and the public order of Mexico. Following this, the same oath was taken before an upraised crucifix by members of the *ayuntamiento,* the clergy, and the civilian population. Next, the military officers administered the oath to the soldiers and dismissed them. Father de la Garza led the governor, *ayuntamiento,* and townspeople into the parish church for religious services, which were followed by an extended ringing of the church bells and the firing of several artillery salutes in the plaza.[5]

From a political perspective, the actions of Spanish governor Martínez, Béxar town-council members, and Father de la Garza during this time of transition were pragmatic. Although loyal to the Spanish crown, Martínez was shrewd enough to recognize that the tide had turned irreversibly in favor of independence, especially when his immediate superior officer, Commandant General Joaquín Arredondo, capitulated to Iturbide's Plan of Iguala on July 13 in Monterrey. Memories of cruelty and bloodshed from the 1811–1813 revolutionary battles in Béxar were undoubtedly another factor influencing the decision for a peaceful shift of allegiance.[6]

Within this political climate, the allegiance ceremony of July 19 provided a forum for local residents to express their assent to Mexican independence. This ceremony built on a long-standing local tradition of public ritual in which national and Catholic identity were intertwined. The combined efforts of military, civic, and religious leadership in this ceremony enabled leaders and the general populace to transfer their loyalties in a public, communal declaration. They pledged their willingness to defend the Catholic faith, Mexican independence, and public order in their new country. Like other newly declared members of the Republic of Mexico, they do not appear to have seen their loyalties to Catholicism and the Mexican Republic as two separate allegiances. For them being Mexican necessarily included being Catholic, and vice versa.[7]

But the national loyalty of Béxar residents also continued to have a regional flavor. While their Mexican and Catholic loyalties were closely bound, these were declared from a Tejano perspective, a perspective formed by their local political and economic interests, common enemies and hardships, frontier heritage, and a ritual calendar which marked them off as distinct from those who made a similar declaration at other sites in the Mexican Republic.

BÉXAR TEJANOS AND ANGLO-AMERICAN COLONIZATION

The most significant change in Texas during the Mexican period was the colonization by immigrants from the United States. Mexican officials awarded Texas colonization grants to *empresarios* (literally, managers) who were then responsible for recruiting immigrants and distributing land to them. *Empresarios* also were to ensure that immigrants became Mexican citizens and obeyed Mexican laws. The first Anglo-American colonization grant was approved in 1821. Within a few years, Mexican visitors reported that "the majority of inhabitants" in Texas were North Americans. Census reports indicate that, by 1832, the Anglo-American town of San Felipe de Austin was more than three times the size of Béxar. An official sent by the Mexican vice president to visit Texas in 1834 reported that the residents in the predominantly Anglo-American departments of Brazos and Nacogdoches accounted for more than 80 percent of the Texas population.[8]

This shift in population represented more than mere demographic change, since Anglo-American immigrants came with their own expectations for the social, political, economic, and religious life of the colonies they founded or joined. Such an immense shift in population inevitably led to change and adjustment as Tejanos and Anglo-Americans came into contact. This contact resulted in cultural exchange between the two groups, as well as significant interaction in the political and religious realms.

Cultural Contact between Tejanos and Anglo-Americans

Although the focus of this work is the Tejano residents of Béxar, it is important to realize that Anglo-Americans also adapted to the new situation in which they found themselves. In the area of religion, for example, Anglo-Americans moved from a society that proclaimed religious freedom to one in which Catholicism was the official religion of the land. Historian Howard Miller has pointed out that

the prospective [Anglo-American] colonists could have seen their situation as reversing directly that of the Pilgrims. Whereas those original Founding

Fathers had fled religious persecution for a land in which they hoped to find religious freedom, these later colonists contemplated leaving the "land of liberty" for one dominated by the church most closely associated in the nineteenth-century American mind with religious intolerance.[9]

Although Protestant ministers were active in Texas throughout the period of the Mexican Republic, official structures of Protestant churches were effectively prohibited until after Texas independence. This is a clear indication that the laws proscribing all religions except Catholicism had some effect.[10] Apparently the shock of emigrating from a nation of religious pluralism to Catholic Mexico did not change Anglo-Americans' minds about freedom of religion; the 1836 Constitution of the Republic of Texas provided for religious liberty. Still, the Mexican prescription of Catholicism meant that Protestant religious activities were conducted outside of the law, and the lives of Anglo-American immigrants were shaped accordingly by their contact with Mexican society. Anglo-Americans were also influenced by their contact with Tejano forms of municipal government, social structure, and ranching practices.[11]

Apparently the Anglo-American presence also caused some changes in the lifestyle of Tejanos. A Mexican observer at Nacogdoches in 1828 noted that residents there had adopted many North American customs and habits, to the point that "they are not Mexicans except by birth, for they even speak Spanish with marked incorrectness." In that same year a visitor to Béxar wrote that

trade with the Anglo-Americans, and the blending in to some degree of their customs, make the inhabitants of Texas a little different from the Mexicans of the interior . . . In their gatherings, the women prefer to dress in the fashion of Louisiana, and by so doing they participate both in the customs of the neighboring nation and of their own.

This visitor also commented that religious customs and practices were the same throughout the Mexican Republic "with the exception of the towns situated on the coasts or on the frontiers of the United States of America." There is some evidence, then, that the Anglo-American presence influenced local customs and practices among Béxar Tejanos. Though few in number, marriages between Anglo-American men and Tejanas account in part for the initial Anglo-American influence on Tejano customs and practices. For example, Philip Dimmit, John W. Smith, James Bowie, Erasmus "Deaf" Smith, and Horatio A. Alsbury were five

Anglo-American men who settled at Béxar and married Mexican women during the period of the Mexican Republic.[12]

Tejanos, Anglo-Americans, and Regional Politics

Anglo-Americans who sought to establish settlements in Texas needed the support of Béxar officials to secure their colonization grants and to assist in other negotiations with the Mexican government. This tended to build friendly alliances. For their part, the Tejano population saw increased colonization as necessary to address the Native American threat and the region's economic development. Since there were few new arrivals from within the Mexican Republic itself, Anglo-American immigrants were seen as a needed asset for the future of Texas.

The interaction between Stephen F. Austin, the most noteworthy leader of the early Anglo-American colonization in Texas, and the prominent Seguín family of Béxar illustrates Anglo-American and Tejano alliances. Erasmo Seguín, father of Juan Nepomuceno Seguín, assisted Austin in receiving official sanction to fulfill a colonization contract that Austin's deceased father had procured. He also lent his support to Austin's legislative endeavors, opened his home to Austin whenever the latter visited Béxar, and housed Austin's younger brother when he was studying Spanish at Béxar from 1822 to 1823. In turn, Austin secured for Seguín a cotton gin and advised him of Anglo-American legislative efforts.[13]

Austin's relationship with José Antonio Navarro, another leading citizen of Béxar, was also mutually beneficial. As a representative to the state congress of Coahuila y Tejas, for example, Navarro promoted legislation which Austin deemed necessary for the growth and development of his colony. For his part, Austin assisted Navarro in purchasing goods at New Orleans and in securing a land claim. Both Austin and Navarro kept one another informed of political events that were of mutual interest. Such alliances between Béxar Tejanos and Anglo-Americans led them to joint efforts on several political issues perceived as being significant for the future of Texas, most notably colonization laws, administrative reform, and the slavery question.[14]

Despite such cooperation, Tejano leaders did not hesitate to counteract Anglo-American efforts which could be interpreted as an affront to Mexican officials and their procedures. In 1828, for instance, the Anglo-American *ayuntamiento* of San Felipe de Austin sent a proposal to Ramón Músquiz, the *jefe político* (political chief) at Béxar and highest ranking Mexican official in Texas at the time. This proposal presented a law to protect the practice of bringing "servants or hirelings" to Texas from "foreign countries." Músquiz directed the San Felipe proposal to Miguel Arciniega and José Antonio Navarro, the two Texas representatives at the state legislature. But he also wrote Austin advising him that the Mexican Constitution reserved the presentation of such proposals to members of the state government. Thus while Músquiz promoted the San Felipe proposal, he also insisted that Mexican procedures be followed in presenting it.[15]

Nor did the cooperation between Tejanos and Anglo-Americans inhibit Tejano attempts to check increasing Anglo-American influence. In October of 1832, for example, Anglo-Americans held a convention at San Felipe de Austin and drafted a petition for officials in Mexico City.[16] No Tejanos were among the fifty-eight delegates present, although afterward the Tejanos of La Bahía (later Goliad) approved the petition's resolutions. Béxar Tejanos were unwilling to give such approval, however, despite general agreement with the specific grievances outlined in the San Felipe document.

Stephen F. Austin initiated discussion of the San Felipe petition at Béxar. Austin realized that a statement lacking the approval of Béxar officials would not be well received in Mexico, thus his trip to their town seeking the support he needed. In response, Béxar leaders drafted their own petition which was signed on December 19. This document treated many of the major issues raised at the San Felipe Convention, for example the need for reforms to deal with Native American attacks, poor local government, the burden of import duties, and inadequate schools and colonization laws. Unlike the San Felipe delegates, however, the Tejanos of Béxar did not request that Texas be separated from Coahuila to become a separate state.[17]

Jefe político Músquiz sent the Béxar petition along with an accompanying letter to the governor of Coahuila y Tejas. In his letter, Músquiz claimed that some of the problems in Texas were caused by the disorderly conduct of Anglo-Americans. He also stated that Béxar Tejanos did not endorse the Plan of Veracruz as Austin had suggested (which involved overthrowing Anastasio Bustamante, the president of Mexico) and that the local populace had refused to cooperate with the "illegal" San Felipe Convention.[18]

The reticence of Béxar Tejanos to endorse the cause of Texas statehood, the Plan of Veracruz, and the San Felipe Convention indicates their awareness of the Tejano political situation. Alliances were needed at the state and national levels to offset the Tejano loss of political clout in Texas to an Anglo-American population that had vastly eclipsed them in size. Texas statehood would have nullified the advantage Béxar leaders enjoyed from their political contacts with state officials of Coahuila y Tejas. Support of the controversial Plan of Veracruz or the illegal San Felipe Convention could have endangered those political contacts. But the Béxar petition also endorsed most of the calls for reform outlined by the San Felipe delegates, as Béxar leaders realized that their political and economic future necessitated overcoming regional problems common to Anglo-Americans and Tejanos alike.

Led by Stephen F. Austin, the *ayuntamiento* of San Felipe de Austin persisted in its requests that the Béxar *ayuntamiento* support the cause of Texas statehood and even suggested that this course of action be pursued with or without the consent of Mexican officials. Their petitions were answered by Béxar leaders in a letter sent to Austin in October, 1833: "It is certainly very deplorable that you breathe out sentiments so contrary and so opposed to those of every good Mexican, whose constitution and laws prohibit in the most terminant manner this class of proceedings . . . Therefore this corporation . . . prays you to cease from sending it messages concerning this idea." Béxar leaders also advised Mexican officials of Austin's aspirations for Texas statehood. These officials then imprisoned Austin for over a year in Mexico City.[19]

Tejanos, Anglo-Americans, and the Religion Question

Anglo-American Protestant ministerial efforts, which violated Mexican laws, placed Tejano leaders in the difficult position of offending their Anglo-American neighbors by enforcing the law or upsetting Mexican officials by ignoring illegal religious activity. While no official structures of Protestant denominations were established in Texas during the Mexican period, sporadic Protestant ministries were extant. Services in private homes and camp meetings date from before Mexican independence, and itinerant preachers were active in Texas throughout the 1820s and 1830s. At least thirty-one Anglo-American ministers came to Texas from the United States during the period of the Mexican Republic, among them Methodists, Baptists, and Presbyterians. They held services, distributed bibles and tracts, and organized Sunday schools, camp meetings, and local congregations.[20]

Although most Protestant efforts were conducted in Anglo-American settlements, later recollections of early Anglo-Americans report that at least two Protestants preached at Béxar during the Mexican period. One of those who preached was Presbyterian Sumner Bacon. Later he became the first colporteur commissioned by the American Bible Society to distribute Spanish bibles and testaments in Texas. In 1836, Bacon reported that he had "succeeded in placing a Bible or Testament in the hands of every Mexican I have met that could read[,] and when they have money they willingly pay for them."[21]

Many Protestant activities were conducted away from the scrutiny of Mexican authorities, but in other instances open conflict occurred. After preaching and conducting prayer meetings at Béxar in 1830, for example, Sumner Bacon left the town when local officials threatened him with reprisal.[22]

A similar incident involved Methodist layman David Ayers, who settled with his family at San Patricio (south of Béxar) in 1834. Upon his arrival he presented the local priest, Father John Thomas Malloy, with several testimonial letters he had procured from Catholic clergymen in New York. This won him the curate's esteem. Soon afterward Father Malloy visited Ayers' cabin and expressed his satisfaction with the library he found housed there, including a Spanish testament which he deemed a "correct edition." Ayers presented the priest a copy of the testament as a gift and proceeded to offer other San Patricio inhabitants the same. This work of bible distribution progressed well until Father Malloy arrived one day at Ayers' door protesting the circulation of "that *damnable* book" among the people. Malloy then threatened Ayers with imprisonment and the confiscation of his property and seized a quantity of tracts which were burned in the public square by order of the *alcalde*. Later the priest demanded that San Patricio residents present to him the testaments they had received. Some did not do so or secretly requested an additional copy from Ayers. In the end, Ayers and his family moved from San Patricio because of the conflicts they experienced among the "ignorant Catholic population" there.[23]

Such conflicts no doubt fueled Anglo-American resentment of the Mexican Catholic system under which they lived. Even Austin, who in many instances upheld among his own colonists the prescription of Catholicism as the law of the land, opined, "Rome! Rome! until the Mexican people shake off thy superstitions & wicked sects, they can neither be a republican, nor a moral people." Protestant ministers who came to Texas during Mexican rule expressed similar sentiments, for example Baptist Z. N. Morrell: "Here was a semi-savage, Mexican government, administered by a tyrant, himself under the tyranny of Catholicism, demoralizing in its character, and but one step in advance of the most degrading heathenism." Methodist minister Orceneth Fisher opined that, before its independence from Mexico, Texas had been "the prey either of savage heathenism, or of Romish superstition and bigotry." Reverend W. P. Smith, also of the Methodist Church, described the Mexican period as a "day of darkness, iniquity and religious intolerance" due to the "persecuting spirit of Catholicism."[24]

Others directed this general critique of Mexican Catholicism at the Catholicism of Béxar Tejanos specifically. An Anglo-American visitor to Béxar in 1828 concluded that the inhabitants were "completely the slaves of Popish Superstition and despotism—distinguished for their knavery and breach of faith" and that "the religion of this place is understood by very few if any as a gracious affection of the heart and soul but a mere requisition of personal mortification in [the] form of penances[,] etc."[25]

Although these statements were not made in public forums, such attitudes undoubtedly influenced the interactions of Anglo-Americans and Tejanos. Like the response at Béxar to political initiatives such as the 1832 San Felipe Convention, however, official Tejano response to the religion question conformed to Tejano interests. Public illegality like Sumner Bacon's ministrations at Béxar and David Ayers' distribution of tracts at San Patricio often led to reprisal by civic or religious authorities (or both); services, Sunday schools, and camp meetings held in less conspicuous places were frequently ignored. Tejanos at Béxar and elsewhere seemed to walk a thin line between offending their new Anglo-American neighbors, whose presence was a potential boon for Texas, and offending national and state officials by a lax enforcement of Mexican statutes.

In 1824, Erasmo Seguín, at the time a representative from Béxar to the Mexican National Congress, wrote that

> with regard to the requirement that all emigrants be Christians [Catholics], I find no reason to convince me; since, under the previous administration, religious toleration was permitted in the province, I do not believe that this can be prohibited. One thing to which I cannot agree is to allow them [Protestants] the right of public worship, for, according to the constituent act in force, there must be no other public worship than the Roman Catholic.[26]

Seguín's liberal interpretation of Mexican law in allowing for religious toleration would, of course, have drawn criticism from many of his contemporaries. But his position is clearly that of a Béxar Tejano, combining his desires to appease the religious sensibilities of Anglo-American colonists while not offending Mexican officials who frowned on public Protestant worship as a blatant affront to existing laws.

LOCAL CONCERNS AT BÉXAR

While compromise with the political and religious aspirations of Anglo-Americans at San Felipe de Austin and other settlements was possible and even desirable, the town council and everyday affairs at Béxar were still in the hands of local leadership. Despite cultural exchange with Anglo-Americans in areas such as dress and other customs, affairs at Béxar continued to be conducted with the Tejano style that had developed over the settlement's first century of existence. This Tejano approach was marked by a pattern of intertwined Mexican and Catholic loyalties, as evidenced in the 1821 allegiance ceremony conducted at Béxar. The presence of Anglo-Americans who sought Mexican citizenship but were not Catholic does not seem to have shaken the sense at Béxar that being Mexican and Catholic were both part of the Tejano birthright. Béxar's isolation from Anglo-American settlements, along with its overwhelmingly Tejano population, helped facilitate the continuing unified effort of "cross and crown" as the modus operandi for responding to local concerns at Béxar.

The Béxar Public Free Primary School

The founding of a public school at Béxar is indicative of how local affairs were conducted. In 1827, a statewide system of education was mandated in the state constitution of Coahuila y Tejas. At Béxar, collections for a school had been in progress since the previous year. Revenue sources included donations from military companies and individual citizens, proceeds from the local Mexican Independence Day celebration of 1827, and some tax fees designated for the school project. Military and civic leaders and local citizens formed a *junta patriótica* (patriotic council) to establish a school fund and assist in the institution's ongoing fiscal support. The town council was ultimately responsible for the school's operation and was to oversee expenditures, examine written reports from the school teacher, and have council members make weekly inspections of the school. An ordinance was drawn up to govern the operation of the new "public free primary school." As in several other aspects of the school's operation, one local leader included in the preparation of this ordinance was the local curate, Refugio de la Garza. Early in 1828, Béxar officials opened the local school.[27]

Besides basic instruction, the Béxar school ordinance had the clear intention of instructing local youth to be loyal Catholics and good citizens. Its first article declared that the patron of the school would be the Christ Child and that the school teacher would be responsible for planning a worship service and other festivities each year on December 25. Plans for this celebration were to be presented to the town council for official approval, and the parents of the school children were to be invited in writing to make a contribution for this feast. Annual holidays were set for the week after Christmas and Holy Week, but school was to be held per usual on minor feast days. The teacher was also responsible for opening and closing school days with prayer. Memory lessons would consist of three Christian doctrine questions in the morning and three more in the afternoon. Students were to learn proper behavior in church and, on Fridays and Sundays during Lent, recite the Vía Crucis (Way of the Cross) and attend a doctrinal discourse. The local curate was to be consulted regarding these discourses, and the teacher was to arrange with the priest for the students' Lenten confessions and for periodic pastoral visitations to the school. Students were also to gather at the school an hour before Mass on all Sundays and observed feast days so they could process to and from Mass together. In these processions, they were to "go praising God by means of some devout song in which the teacher shall instruct them, seeing that all of those who can carry some book in which shall be explained the unspeakable mysteries of this august sacrifice."[28]

These provisions for the Catholic instruction of the youth were paralleled by other statutes aimed at good citizenship. By ordinance the pupils were to address one another as "Citizen So-and-so." Besides suitable behavior in church, they were to be taught to conduct themselves with propriety in their homes, on the streets, and in all dealings with their elders. The student body was divided into two groups, the Romans and the Carthaginians, each having a president, six captains, and six corporals. Holders of these posts were selected on the merit of meeting specific requirements, among them knowledge of the Mexican Constitution. Members of the two groups were assigned colors, and the rank of the officers was appropriately designated. Monthly academic contests between the groups were mandated and regulated with stringent rules of decorum. The groupings had the practical effect of allowing a single teacher to deal with a large group of pupils through the assistance of student officers; they also enabled students to learn by example the need for structure and order in society. This, and the lessons of greeting one another as citizens, respecting elders and the public order, and learning the Mexican Constitution, added to the religious dimension of education at Béxar the dimension of good citizenship in the Mexican Republic.

The Béxar public free primary school was not an overwhelming success, as apparently only a fraction of the settlement's children attended with any consistency. Finances were an almost constant problem, and the town council was lax in fulfilling its obligation of weekly inspections. The school was by no means a complete failure, however, as it provided education for a number of local children. In some cases it even helped incorporate newcomers into the local Tejano community. One such newcomer was John Duff Brown. Brown was about eight years old when his family moved to Béxar in 1832. Shortly thereafter, he was baptized a Catholic. Although later in life he would observe religious practices learned from his Presbyterian grandmother, for the three years his family lived in Béxar he "was sent to a Spanish school; and every Sabbath [I] marched with the pupils in double file to the cathedral singing full-voiced some Catholic hymn."[29]

Brown's account is not surprising since receiving Catholic baptism and attending the local school were required by law. But considering the number of Anglo-Americans in settlements to the east of Béxar who ignored, resisted, or were unable to fulfill these legal requirements, Brown's experience at the Béxar public free primary school presents a sharp contrast.[30]

Response to Cholera Epidemics at Béxar

Response at Béxar to cholera epidemics in 1833 and 1834 demonstrates further the approach which guided local efforts. The response of Béxar Tejanos combined public health initiatives with the organization of religious processions to invoke divine protection from the malady. As in the school project, the town council, military, clergy, and residents worked together to combat the cholera threat.

The first step taken to counteract the cholera scourge of 1833 was the appointment of a seventeen-member *junta de sanidad* (community health commission) by *jefe político* Músquiz. At a mass meeting early in September, the town was divided into five wards, and three members of the *junta de sanidad* were assigned to each word. An order went out for citizens to sweep the streets and dispose properly of all garbage. Although not a physician, citizen Alejandro Vidal was appointed to oversee the distribution of medicines and the treatment of any cholera cases that might arise. The town council suspended school for the month of October and made plans for distributing mutton to the populace. The latter measure was based on the belief that mutton was a helpful preventive against contracting cholera. On September 19 and again on October 1, processions were held as a "religious invocation to God for preservation from the cholera." By the end of October, the cholera scourge at Béxar had abated.[31]

The return of the cholera epidemic in 1834 was more devastating to

Béxar residents, although their response to the renewed threat of the disease was no less vigorous. News of cholera victims at La Bahía reached Béxar by the end of June. *Alcalde* Juan Seguín immediately issued regulations aimed at thwarting a potential medical emergency. He enacted prohibitions against the sale of spoiled food, the importation of fruits and vegetables, and the sale of liquor (except for medicinal purposes). Citizens were to keep the streets swept and their homes clean. Seguín also asked the local pastor not to ring the church bells for the deceased lest the tolling disturb the settlement's surviving population. *Jefe político* Músquiz authorized the town council to allocate funds for medicine and the care of indigent residents. He then called together members of the *junta de sanidad* to enlist their support in preparations for dealing with the threat of epidemic. The town council requested that Músquiz ask military leaders to dispatch troops along the road from La Bahía to Béxar and prohibit the passage of travelers from that cholera-plagued settlement. They also asked people to fumigate their homes. Alejandro Vidal, who had rendered medical assistance to Béxar residents during the 1833 epidemic, offered the same services to cholera victims during the summer of 1834.[32]

Despite all of these precautions, so many local residents fled to the countryside for safety that the settlement was too depopulated to conduct the annual census. Even *jefe político* Músquiz eventually left for healthier environs.[33] While this mass exodus probably saved many lives, local efforts to combat the cholera undoubtedly averted many fatalities as well. Apparently the rapid spread of disease and abandonment of the town during 1834 precluded elaborate religious processions like those held to intercede for divine protection in 1833.

Feast Days and Communal Celebrations

Yet another example of a continuing Tejano style in the management of Béxar affairs is the way the local community organized public celebrations. Following the heritage developed through the Spanish era and evidenced in the 1821 allegiance ceremony, these celebrations were joint efforts of citizens and the various leaders of Béxar society. As under Spanish rule, Catholic rites were often part of public ritual during national events and holidays.

Official correspondence of the period indicates that Mass was frequently celebrated at Béxar to mark some affair of the nation. In October of 1821, a solemn Mass ending with the Te Deum (a religious chant of praise for God's wondrous deeds) was held to honor the triumphant entry into Mexico City of the Republic's victorious leader, Agustín de Iturbide. That same month, another Mass was offered in thanksgiving for the defeat of James Long, an Anglo-American who had led an expedition which declared Texas independence from Mexico. Governor Martínez requested that the *ayuntamiento* attend this celebration. The *ayuntamiento*'s attendance also marked the 1822 Mass celebrated in honor of Iturbide's patron saint. In June 1823, a solemn Mass and the Te Deum were offered at the reassembling of the Mexican Congress. A celebration in honor of the Mexican missionary and martyr San Felipe de Jesús was mandated in 1827. Public mourning was decreed for the deceased Prince Frederick of York in 1827, and in 1833 government orders for the memorial funeral rites of Juan Martín de Beramendi, vice governor of Coahuila y Tejas, included instructions for a volley fired by thirty militiamen at the conclusion of religious services.[34]

The participation of the military in religious services was not limited to funeral rites, as they also were asked and agreed to assist in Holy Week services. December was known as "la temporada de fiestas" (the season of feasts). Celebrations continued from the feast of the Immaculate Conception (December 8), through Our Lady of Guadalupe (December 12) and Christmas, and did not end until early in the new year. Town-council efforts to tax and control the games and booths set up on the plaza during these feast days illustrate the popularity of the December festivities. At times, the council petitioned militia members to assist in crowd control for the plaza entertainments as well. The planning of festivities for religious feasts at town-council meetings would abruptly cease after Texas independence, but up until the last December before the Texas Revolution, Béxar Tejanos continued their long-standing practice of elected officials' working cooperatively with other local leaders in organizing religious feasts and saint days.[35]

A new tradition which quickly gained prominence in Béxar was the September commemoration of Mexican Independence Day. Overall responsibility for preparing festivities was in the hands of a *junta patriótica*. This group appointed subcommittees to whom they assigned various tasks, for example collecting funds, decorating, and organizing dances and the program of other festivities. The town council worked with the *junta patriótica*, providing financial support and taking on duties such as issuing a formal invitation to the priest, requesting his presence and participation in the celebrations. Military officials and their charges also participated in the processions and Masses connected with the celebration, offering cannon and gun salutes. The priest, usually Father Refugio de la Garza, presided over religious services that formed part of the festivities. On at least two occasions, he also gave a patriotic speech in the plaza.[36]

The shape of these festivities can be glimpsed from the records of Independence Day in 1829. On September 15, the anniversary eve of Miguel Hidalgo's *grito* (proclamation) for independence in 1810, a procession accompanied by music, church bells, and gun salutes wound its way through the streets. The next morning Mass and the Te Deum were offered, followed by an afternoon procession and a speech on the meaning of Independence Day. That evening two dances were held, apparently dividing the more prominent citizens from the general public. The next day the populace dressed for mourning and attended a Mass offered on behalf of the dead.[37]

SUMMARY: SHIFTING REGIONAL IDENTITY

In early December 1835, San Antonio de Béxar was the site of the first major battle of the Texas Revolution. This revolution would have serious consequences for the people of Béxar. Up until armed revolt began, however, the town's Mexican Catholic heritage continued to form local efforts in such areas as education, public health, and communal feasts.[38] Town-council members, military officers, the local pastor, and citizens worked together to found and operate the Béxar public free primary school. The Béxar school initiative reflected the population's Catholic and Mexican loyalties. This initiative continued the long-standing practice of religious and civic authorities' overseeing public responsibilities jointly. The school curriculum reinforced religious and national loyalties by including instruction in Catholicism, the Mexican Constitution, and the exercise of responsible behavior in civic life. Catholic worship was also required. The school project at Béxar thus illustrated the interwoven Mexican and Catholic loyalties of Béxar Tejanos; the initiation of newcomers like John Duff Brown into these loyalties is evidence of their continuing strength during the Mexican period.

Béxar leaders and other residents utilized a range of strategies in combating the 1833 and 1834 cholera epidemics, including public sanitation, medical practice, quarantine from persons and products that might transmit the disease, and communal intercessory prayer in the form of religious processions. Faced with the crisis of cholera, local Tejanos turned to the mode of operation that was most familiar, one in which piety, government decrees, military support, and citizen cooperation were fused into an integrated communal response.

A united communal effort was also evident in local initiatives to organize public celebrations. These included feasts like the Immaculate Conception, Our Lady of Guadalupe, and Christmas, as well as Catholic rites and other ceremonies on the occasion of significant national events. Mass was an integral part of Mexican Independence Day festivities at Béxar, for example, as was prayer for the deceased who were the forebears of the independence Tejanos now enjoyed. These festivities were also marked by remembrance of the *grito,* which initiated the movement for independence, and a patriotic oration which underscored the significance of the *grito* and this historical movement. Like other public celebrations at Béxar, those for Independence Day celebrated and reinforced Tejano national and religious allegiances.

Tejanos at Béxar responded to Anglo-American political initiatives and religious sensibilities by steering a middle course between Anglo-American demands and Mexican legislative directives. In doing so they attempted to support Mexican officials and ordinances while advancing causes which they considered important for the prosperity of their town and region. As the Anglo-American population increased, so did the Tejano dilemma of being caught between Anglo-American demands and the authority and procedures of Mexican officials. By the early 1830s, Tejanos "found themselves caught between succumbing to pressures from Anglo-Americans, who formed the numerical majority in Texas, or remaining loyal to Mexican procedures and traditions. It was a dilemma that Mexicans in Texas would come to understand all too well after Texas won independence in 1836."[39]

The Béxar Tejano regional identity of 1835 was thus different from that of 1821. In 1821, Tejano regional identity was based on an independent frontier spirit developed over years of facing common enemies and hardships, promoting the needs of the area's economy, and celebrating patronal feasts that marked the settlement as distinct. By 1835, Béxar Tejanos frequently found themselves caught between Anglo-American settlers and Mexican officials, and their regional identity was increasingly shaped by efforts to promote Tejano interests in the face of the competing forces they felt on both sides. Still, their Mexican and Catholic loyalties remained strong, especially in local affairs like public education, health, and communal celebrations. But the initial influence of the growing Anglo-American presence would accelerate as the strained conditions of war pressured Tejanos to make an explicit delineation of allegiance to either the Texan or Mexican armies.

†

THREE

BETWEEN TWO WORLDS:
THE PERIOD OF THE TEXAS
REPUBLIC, 1836–1845

The most striking element of life in San Antonio during the period of the Texas Republic was the frequent military conflicts in and near the city. In describing the physical appearance of San Antonio, various travelers commented on the signs of destruction from these hostilities. One visitor remarked:

> The military squares, of which there are two, have been [at various times] heaped with the slain. The houses that surround the square, and the church, which occupies the center[,] are perforated by hundreds of musket and cannon shot . . . numerous heaps of ruins both in the town & neighborhood marke [sic] the places where houses once stood. Ruined walls, hedges, ditches, and artificial channels, some of which are dry, but though many bright streams of watter [sic] trickling along, with here and their [sic] some flowering shrub, or wounded and dying fig or peach tree, standing on these borders, tell us in language not to be mistaken of a once industrious, wealthy, and to a great degree refined and civilized population.[1]

Two major battles of the Texas Revolution were fought at San Antonio, and in 1842 the city was occupied by Mexican forces on two separate occasions. Battles in and near the city caused San Antonio's population to fluctuate widely, as some residents abandoned the city during times of conflict and returned in times of relative calm. These conflicts also adversely affected the local economy, upsetting trade and the harvesting of crops and partially destroying the city's infrastructure.

Military conflicts in their city precipitated a dilemma for local Tejanos. They were native Texans who had consistently promoted regional interests in their dealings with state and national officials. But they were also Mexican Catholics who valued their cultural and religious heritage. To side with the Anglo-Americans of Texas would mean fighting against those with whom they shared that heritage; to side with Mexico might mean expulsion from their Texas homeland. Anglo-Americans and Mexican officials pressured Tejanos to support their respective efforts for control of Texas, further exacerbating the Tejano dilemma of choosing between their opposing armies.

After Texas independence, Tejano representation in the national legislature declined in political clout, and San Antonio Tejanos lost their monopoly on the mayoral office of their city. San Antonio Tejanos also experienced a change in leadership at the local parish, as the two native priests were replaced by European clergy after Texas was removed from Mexican ecclesiastical jurisdiction. Tejano responses at San Antonio to the new political order, the changing ecclesial situation, and the dilemma of allying themselves with Texas or Mexico illustrate their shifting identity during the decade which followed Texas independence.

SAN ANTONIO, 1836–1845:
A DEMOGRAPHIC AND ECONOMIC PROFILE

The 1840 census of the Republic of Texas is the only official census of this period; it lists land holders only and does not indicate the overall population. Travelogues and travelers' accounts vary in their estimates of San Antonio's population but consistently indicate that the city was predominately Tejano. Their estimates range from a high of two thousand to under a thousand. These discrepancies are partly due to differences in perception, but they also reflect the actual population flux during times of peace and hostility. After the Texas Revolution, for example, a Houston newspaper reported that "many of the Mexicans who fled the country at the time of the invasion are returning . . . [They] fled to the settlements on the Rio Grande, not so much on account of hostility to us, as to withdraw their wives and children from the scene of war."[2] The 1850 census confirms that San Antonio Tejanos returned to Mexico during times of conflict. One Tejano household recorded on this census had five minor children, three born in Texas and two in Mexico. The latter two were born in 1837 and 1842, apparently on occasions when the family was waiting in Mexico for a time of peace so they could return to Texas.[3] Other Tejanos repaired from scenes of conflict to the security of ranches in the countryside. For example, a number of them evacuated San Antonio during the 1835 Texan siege of the city; others abandoned the city during the Alamo battle a few months later.[4]

The San Antonio Tejano population was augmented by Mexican citizens who moved to the city even after Texas independence. According to official sources, at least five hundred people with Spanish surnames moved into Texas between the declaration of Texas independence on March 2, 1836, and January 1, 1841. Estimates made by visitors to San Antonio indicate that, around the time of U.S. annexation in 1845, the population continued to be predominately Tejano, numbering some fifteen hundred inhabitants.[5]

As was previously mentioned, battles in and near the city adversely affected the local economy. In times of relative peace, however, trade with Mexico provided a fairly lucrative income. From 1838 to 1840, for example, this trade was estimated to be valued at $100,000 annually, more than double the 1835 figure of forty thousand dollars. Not all of this trade was conducted by Tejano merchants, however, as Anglo-American entrepreneurs achieved an economic success disproportionate to their numbers.[6]

Anglo-Americans also acquired a considerable amount of another local commodity, land certificates. Land grants were issued as certificates, which did not correspond to any particular plot of land until unclaimed land was surveyed and a patent was properly filed with the General Land Office in Austin. From 1837 to 1842, thirteen Anglo-Americans bought certificates for some 1,368,574 acres of land from Tejano sellers in the San Antonio area. By comparison, the fourteen most active Tejano buyers purchased certificates for 278,769 acres over the same period. Although the 1840 census is based on tax rolls and is incomplete, the figures on unclaimed land grants among San Antonians and other Béxar County residents are striking. Local Tejanos, who comprised the vast majority of the population, owned only 11.1 percent of all land grants which had not yet been patented. In 1840, unclaimed land included vast tracts in areas still unsettled by citizens of the Texas Republic. Thus these figures indicate a considerable amount of Anglo-American land speculation.[7]

Tejanos did retain considerable land holdings, however: they owned 85.1 percent of the town lots at San Antonio and 63.8 percent of land claims with completed titles. It is not surprising, then, that despite Tejano losses to Anglo-Americans in land and trade, city residents and visitors continued to note the existence of a local Tejano elite.[8]

THE TEJANO DILEMMA:
FOR OR AGAINST TEXAS INDEPENDENCE?

Events in the years preceding the Texas Revolution had already demonstrated the Tejano dilemma of being caught between Anglo-Americans and Mexican officials. Response at San Antonio de Béxar to the 1832 San Felipe Convention, for example, clearly illustrated Tejano efforts to promote regional interests while remaining loyal to Mexican procedures and administrators. The middle position Tejanos took on this and other occasions was severely strained during the 1835–1836 revolution, as the polarized conditions of armed conflict pressured Tejanos to choose between the two opposing sides. Even after the defeat of Santa Anna and the subsequent withdrawal of Mexican forces from Texas, Mexican leaders refused to accept Texas independence, and hostilities over the control of Texas continued. In 1842, San Antonio was occupied twice by Mexican forces. The Tejano dilemma of choosing between their Texas homeland and the Mexico of their cultural heritage was evidenced by their divided loyalties in the various battles at San Antonio and elsewhere.

Tejanos and the Texas Revolution

At the siege of San Antonio by Texas troops (December 1835), the battle of the Alamo (March 6, 1836), and the decisive battle of San Jacinto (April 21, 1836), citizens of Mexican descent fought on both sides of the conflict. As difficult as the decision to take up arms against one's friends and neighbors must have been, for Tejanos the divisions between family members were undoubtedly more distressing. San Antonio native Gregorio Esparza fought for Texas in the siege of his town and in the Alamo, while his brother Francisco fought on the Mexican side. At the battle of San Jacinto, San Antonio resident Ambrosio Rodríguez fought on the Texas side, while his kinsman Mariano Rodríguez was in Santa Anna's army. Jesús "Comanche" Cuellar and his brother Salvador also fought on opposing sides. Others, such as the Navarro family of San Antonio, did not have combatants enlisted on both sides but remained divided in their loyalties.[9]

Conflicting loyalties resulted in stressful situations for divided families. For instance, after the Alamo battle, Francisco Esparza asked permission to bury his brother Gregorio, who had fallen with Anglo-American and other Tejano defenders. His request was granted, thus saving Gregorio's remains from the incineration ordered for the Alamo defenders by Santa Anna. Francisco and other members of the Esparza family then proceeded to search for Gregorio's remains within the walls of the Alamo. One can easily imagine the anguish of the Esparza family as they examined the faces of various corpses until they found Gregorio's body.[10]

In March 1836, Colonel James Walker Fannin sent Jesús Cuellar into the Mexican camp to plant false information and lead Mexican forces into an ambush. As Cuellar had been fighting on the Texan side for three months, he faced incarceration or possible execution if his false claims of allegiance to Mexico were not believed. His brother Salvador vouched for his good faith, however, saving Jesús from punishment and placing some 350 Mexican soldiers in jeopardy. Salvador's predicament was not an enviable one, as he had to choose between endangering the welfare of his brother or comrades.[11]

A few years after Texas independence, an Anglo-American named Tinsley instigated a fight in San Antonio with local resident Eugenio Navarro, in which each mortally wounded the other. The cause of Tinsley's ire was reportedly related to Navarro's Mexican allegiance during the revolution, although subsequently Navarro had made peace with Texas officials. After the bloody incident with Tinsley, Navarro's older brother José Antonio, a signer of the Texas Declaration of Independence, was in the crowd that gathered at the scene. Despite the shock of finding his deceased brother, the elder Navarro urged this gathering crowd of Tejanos and Anglo-Americans not to engage in retaliatory violence. His conciliatory response to this tragedy does not diminish the anguish these events must have caused him and his family.[12] The acute suffering connected with the Tejano dilemma of choosing sides undoubtedly made this choice all the more agonizing for citizens of Mexican heritage at San Antonio.

The accusations of traitorous conduct directed at Tejanos by both Anglo-Americans and Mexican authorities added to the dilemma Tejanos faced. In December 1835, Governor Henry Smith warned General Edward Burleson not to trust the "false friends" among San Antonio Tejanos during the Texan siege of their city. A month later Doctor Amos Pollard warned Smith from San Antonio about "our most formidable foe—our internal enemy—the Mexican Tory party of the country." Colonel William Barret Travis wrote a letter from the Alamo declaring all San Antonio residents who had not joined him there "public enemies." While Anglo-Americans were making these accusations, Mexican officials wished a "thousand curses on the Mexican who should be dastardly enough to join in that murderous and anti-national plot [the Texas revolt]" and asserted that anyone who did not oppose the loss of Texas was a traitor who deserved death. Those of Mexican descent who sided with the Texas cause were also accused of being traitors to their own people, such as Lorenzo de Zavala and native San Antonians José Antonio Navarro and Antonio Menchaca.[13]

Tejanos and the Post-Revolutionary Era

The accusations and pressures directed at San Antonio Tejanos by both sides continued after the revolution. In November 1836, a press report in a Texas newspaper labeled Tejanos who remained at San Antonio "pretended friends" of Texas. A visitor to the town in 1837 observed that "a small military force is stationed at San Antonio to prevent treasonable intercourse with the inhabitants beyond the Rio Grande." Such "treasonable intercourse" was actively promoted by Mexican authorities, who considered it the duty of all patriotic Mexicans to assist in the reconquest of Texas. Mexican authorities had clandestine negotiations with persons of Mexican descent in Texas, attempting to win their support for a reconquest effort in exchange for the promise of future privileges under Mexican rule.[14]

The continued pressures placed on Tejanos to choose for the Mexican or Texan cause reached a pinnacle in 1842. San Antonio was occupied twice that year by Mexican forces, first in March by an expedition under the leadership of General Rafael Vásquez and again in September by General Adrian Woll. These invasions were preceded by a proclamation from Mexican general Mariano Arista, which promised amnesty and protection to those who did not resist the upcoming invasion and threatened to direct "the sword of justice against the obstinate." Arista's proclamation was distributed to residents of Mexican descent at San Antonio, who would presumably be counted among the "obstinate" if they refused to align themselves with the Mexican cause.[15]

While Arista pressured Tejanos to revivify their Mexican allegiance, Anglo-Americans claimed that San Antonio Tejanos encouraged the Vásquez raid and that one of the primary purposes of Woll's expedition was to escort two hundred San Antonio families who were faithful to Mexico back across the Rio Grande. After Woll withdrew from San Antonio with these two hundred families in late September, a Houston newspaper claimed:

> Some of the most intelligent and respectable citizens of Béxar assert that a petition was forwarded to Santa Anna a few months since. It was signed

by a large number of the Mexican citizens of Béxar, and in it they complained that they were constantly subjected to impositions and exactions by marauding parties . . . They stated moreover that they had never been satisfied with the Texian government, and that they desired to be placed once more under the laws of Mexico.

A week later, the same newspaper directed accusations of disloyalty to Texas at Tejanos who remained in San Antonio: "The Mexicans at Béxar have become quite insolent, and openly declare that Gen. Woll will soon come to their aid and assist them in removing their property to the Rio Grande." Anglo-Americans also accused Tejanos of advising the enemy about the movements of the Texas militia.[16]

Deeds of violence which often accompanied such words of mistrust intensified the pressures placed on Tejanos. One Texas volunteer claimed that General Woll imprisoned a venerable Tejano citizen of San Antonio. This man had a sixteen-year-old daughter, and "his liberation and life were pressed by the enamoured ruffian [Woll] upon the anguished girl, as the reward of her acquiescence in his wishes."[17]

Although Woll's reported criminal behavior must have been devastating, even more disastrous for Tejanos was the formation of a volunteer Texas army to defend the frontier. Catholic bishop Jean Marie Odin described their presence:

The volunteers coming from the United States to help Texas and several Texan individuals to whom the protection of the frontier was entrusted do not cease to commit the most shameful depredations; they steal from the poor inhabitants of the valley of San Antonio all that they possess; corn, animals, nothing is spared. Entire villages have been devastated, several families have had to abandon the land in order to escape the violence of every kind to which they were exposed. Some men were assassinated.

Odin's perceptions were echoed by the Houston press, which stated, "We regret that the government has not the means to station a company of soldiers near that city [San Antonio], to protect the citizens not only from the marauding Mexicans, but even from our own volunteers." An Anglo-American volunteer stated that the soldiers at San Antonio "acted very badly, having ventured to force the Mexican families from their homes, [causing them] to droop about in the woods and seek shelter wherever they could find it. Moreover[,] in order to gratify their beastly lusts [they have] compelled the women and Girls to yield to their hellish desires, which their victims did under fear of punishment and death." Odin summed up the sentiments of these observers when he stated that "one is beginning to believe they [the volunteers] will do more harm to Texas than a Mexican army." [18]

With accusations, threats, rape, murder, and other violent acts directed at them from both sides, the Tejano population of San Antonio responded to the events of 1842 with ambivalence. As in the 1835–1836 struggle for Texas independence, in the 1842 conflicts San Antonians of Mexican heritage were reportedly represented in both the Mexican and Texan military forces. Tejanos also offered assistance to the wounded and captured of both sides. [19] Woll stated that four San Antonio Tejanos went out and asked him to turn back, claiming that if he did not, residents of Mexican descent would be compelled to join Anglo-Americans who were preparing to defend the city. Before they did so, another group of San Antonio Tejanos had already voluntarily joined the Texas militia. This group disbanded at the sight of Woll's numerical strength, however, and were seen a few days later greeting him peaceably. One Tejano defender of the city, Antonio Menchaca, later successfully resisted Anglo-Americans who proposed to burn San Antonio. While Anglo-Americans argued that San Antonio's isolation enabled the Mexican army to plant spies there and easily capture it, Menchaca reminded them that his aging mother and others would be left destitute by their proposed action. In the space of just a few weeks, then, Menchaca defended his home town both against Mexican attack and Anglo-American destruction. [20]

The Case of Juan Nepomuceno Seguín

The dilemma of San Antonio Tejanos during the 1842 conquests is especially vivid in the experience of Juan Seguín. Seguín was mayor of San Antonio at the time of the Vásquez raid in March. By September, he was an officer in Woll's expedition which occupied the city.

Previously, Seguín had consistently demonstrated his allegiance to Texas. At the siege of San Antonio in 1835, he led a troop of Tejano volunteers on the Texas side. He then remained to defend the city from Santa Anna's attack, escaping death within the Alamo only because he was sent through the Mexican lines for reinforcements. At San Jacinto, he and his Tejano troops were commended for their courage. After the revolution, he continued his service to Texas in the military and as San Antonio's representative in the Texas Senate (1838–1840). He was mayor of San Antonio from January of 1841 until his resignation on April 18, 1842. Seguín's strong support of the Texas cause led some Mexicans to label him a rebel and a traitor. [21]

Despite Seguín's impressive civic and military record, Texan accusations of his disloyalty appeared as early as December 1840. In time, these accusations became virulent attacks:

> General Woll had persons in his employment well calculated for spies and pilots, and adepts in robbery and murder. Among the principal of these was Antonio Periz [sic] and Juan M. [sic] Seguín, both of whom had been constantly in the employment of our government . . . In 1836 they had been traitors to that country [Mexico]—the country of their language, laws, religion, and birth—and now, Mexican-like, they sought to reinstate themselves by an act of compound treason upon us.[22]

How was it that Seguín went from his position as mayor of San Antonio to form part of a conquering Mexican army in the space of five months? His own account accused Anglo-Americans of showing no respect for the Mexican citizens of Texas, claiming that "at every hour of the day and night, my countrymen [fellow Tejanos] ran to me for protection against the assaults or exactions of those adventurers." When Seguín heard of the impending Vásquez raid, he called a session of the San Antonio city council and advised the evacuation of the city. During the March occupation, General Vásquez and other Mexican officers started a rumor that Seguín was a Mexican spy. Upon hearing of these rumors, Seguín presented himself to General Edward Burleson of the Texas forces and asked that the issue be settled publicly in a court of inquiry. Burleson declared that there were no grounds for such proceedings. Nonetheless, Seguín was hunted by bands of armed Anglo-Americans and finally had to leave Texas for fear of losing his life. He was imprisoned upon his arrival in Mexican Laredo but later given an opportunity to vindicate himself by accompanying the expedition of General Woll, as he did. Seguín described his predicament vividly:

> Thrown in a prison, in a foreign country, I had no alternative left, but, to linger in a loathsome confinement, or to accept military service. On one hand, my wife and children, reduced to beggary, and separated from me; on the other hand, to turn my arms against my own country. The alternative was sad, the struggle of feelings violent; at last the father triumphed over the citizen; I seized a sword that galled my hand.[23]

There is considerable evidence to back Seguín's claims. San Antonio resident Elizabeth Canterbury confirmed that Seguín called a meeting to warn local citizens of the impending invasion. His warning of his fellow citizens about the invasion is also a matter of public record.[24] The testimony of various persons about Anglo-American violence directed at Tejanos was previously noted. Both Seguín and his father suffered directly from this lawlessness. Other evidence confirms that a lynch mob left for dead a man named Calaveras, who allegedly had hidden Seguín in his home and refused to divulge his whereabouts. This verifies not only the tension between Anglo-Americans and Tejanos, but also Seguín's claim that he was in physical danger because of the false allegations leveled against him. Even after Seguín's departure from San Antonio, President Sam Houston of Texas wrote that he would continue to believe in Seguín's innocence until "the most conclusive evidence" proved otherwise.[25]

Was Seguín guilty of treason against the Texas Republic? If one is to rely on Vásquez' claim, the answer is no. As Seguín himself argued, why would Vásquez announce that the Tejano was spying for his army if that was in fact true? There is a possibility that "Seguín, trying to do business with both sides, lost the confidence of both." While not impossible, this is also questionable. This claim would mean that Seguín was willing to risk losing considerable property, status, livelihood, and contact with his family and lifelong friends in exchange for some bribery money or other concessions from Mexican authorities. Considering the fact that he put his life on the line fighting for Texas independence, such a risk does not seem likely. The fact that Seguín refused to defend the city as he did against all odds in 1836 is not traitorous. Even Anglo-American defenders, who said they would remain to fight Vásquez, left "without firing a shot" when they saw the size of the Mexican force.[26]

The cause of Seguín's shifting allegiance in 1842 was that he was caught between two opposing sides: one which lied to ruin him, the other which accepted the lie and condemned him without trial or jury. Forced to seek refuge in Mexico because of attempts on his life in Texas, he was then given the choice of accepting a Mexican military command or remaining in prison. Seguín was caught between two opposing forces, a Tejano victim of Texan-Mexican animosities.

While Seguín was one of San Antonio's most influential citizens, less prominent Tejanos had similar experiences. Bishop Odin wrote that at least two hundred Tejano families who left San Antonio for Mexico after Seguín's departure were forced out by the Texas militia.[27]

Tejano Strategies for Survival

The response of Seguín and other San Antonio Tejanos to the 1842 conflicts and other battles is in part explained by the instinct to survive.

Local Tejanos experienced violence and mistreatment from both sides and had reason to fear dire consequences if they supported a losing army. The survival instinct accounts for the neutrality which the Houston press noted in local residents: "They [the Tejanos near Victoria, Texas] appear, however, to be inoffensive, and probably temporise with both parties like the Mexicans of Béxar, in order to maintain their homes undisturbed." An Anglo-American who visited San Antonio in 1842 commented that local Tejanos "profess to be friendly to the Texans, but are also obliged, for safety, to make similar protestations to the Mexican soldiery, when they see fit to visit them."[28] The number of families that moved back and forth to Mexico and ranches in the San Antonio area during these turbulent years, as was previously mentioned, is further evidence of Tejano neutrality.

Not all Tejanos were neutral, however, and many participated actively in the cause of Texas or Mexico. Conflicting family loyalties, accusations of traitorous conduct, threats of reprisal, and the violence visited on Tejanos by both Mexicans and Anglo-Americans exacerbated the Tejano dilemma of choosing sides. Whether neutral or active in the Texan-Mexican conflict, San Antonio Tejanos were caught between Mexican and Texan demands. Depending on the circumstances, some Tejanos employed alternately the strategies of neutrality and participation. Others changed sides when they thought it convenient or, as in the case of Seguín, necessary.

TEJANO RESPONSE TO POLITICAL CHANGES

The victory over the Mexican army at San Jacinto won Texas independence and made the Texas Constitution and subsequent legislation the law of the land. San Antonio Tejanos, who constituted only a fraction of Texas' population by the 1830s, had exercised a political influence disproportionate to their numbers under Mexican rule. As might be expected, however, with the advent of Texas independence, Tejano representation in the national legislature declined in political clout. Only two Tejanos were elected to the Texas Senate during this period, Francisco Ruiz (1836–1837) and Juan Nepomuceno Seguín (1838–1840). Two others, José Antonio Navarro (1838–1839) and Rafael Calixto de la Garza (1842–1843), served in the House of Representatives. Despite the declining influence of San Antonio Tejanos, their city remained the stronghold of Tejano political strength, as all four of these congressmen represented Béxar County. On the local scene, only one Tejano mayor was elected during this period, but Tejanos retained control of the city council.

San Antonio Tejanos and National Politics

San Antonio Tejano leaders demonstrated their allegiance to the Republic of Texas in various ways. Senator Juan Seguín, for example, introduced a resolution in 1838 that would allow the government to confiscate the property of collaborators in "the present Indian war." This legislation was directed at participants in the Córdova Revolt, an unsuccessful attempt by Nacogdoches Tejanos and their allies to restore Mexican rule over Texas. Seguín's resolution shows his willingness to oppose fellow Tejanos who did not accept Texas independence. Three years later, José Antonio Navarro served as a commissioner in the Santa Fe expedition, an effort to incorporate New Mexican residents into the Republic of Texas. Navarro was captured along with other members of this ill-fated expedition and subsequently imprisoned for four years in Mexico. While Navarro's rationale for accepting the role of commissioner in this venture is subject to debate, clearly his participation indicates pro-Texas sentiments.[29]

More frequently, however, San Antonio leaders lobbied for the concerns of their Tejano constituency in Texas national politics. They were not always successful in their efforts. In 1836, Senator Francisco Ruiz argued that Tejanos who accepted Santa Anna's offer of pardon after the Alamo battle did so "in the midst of confusion, terror and affright [sic]" and pleaded that the First Congress of the Republic of Texas "adopt some measure which will give them the assurance that they may return without the fear of harm or molestation" to their homes. But no such legislation was passed by the Congress.[30]

One of Senator Juan Seguín's first acts in the 1838 sessions of Congress was to present a bill that would have provided relief for widows and orphans of Tejanos slain in the defense of the Alamo. Despite Seguín's plea, many of these families never received land grants during the Texas Republic. As late as 1860, the Béxar County Court of Claims was still debating the grants due by law to the families of these Tejano veterans; some never received their justifiable claims.[31] In 1840, Senator Seguín asked when the laws of Texas would be translated into Spanish for the benefit of his constituency. Claiming that the lengthy delay in providing these translations was a violation of Tejano rights, Seguín argued that "the Mexico-Texians were among the first who sacrificed their all in our glorious Revolution, and the disasters of war weighed heavy upon them, to achieve those blessings which, it appears, [they] are destined to be the last to enjoy." Despite Seguín's urgent appeal, translations of this legislation were not immediately forthcoming. Seguín also introduced legislation at that Congress to provide national funds for a jail in Béxar County but once again was unsuccessful.[32]

In 1839, San Antonio congressional representative José Antonio Navarro pleaded in vain for the enactment of another piece of legislation; it would have aided San Antonio Tejanos who had no title to their lands, could not speak English, and lacked the finances and familiarity with the legal system necessary for lawsuits. At the Texas Constitutional Convention before U.S. annexation in 1845, Navarro moved that the seat of government for Texas be located in Béxar. He even offered a league of land to encourage this decision, but his motion was defeated.[33]

In some instances, Tejano legislative efforts on the national level were successful. A bill presented by Senator Seguín in 1839 established a mail route from Austin to San Antonio. In 1840, Seguín made a report as chairman of the Senate Committee on Military Affairs. He claimed that the laws to provide military defense for the border settlements of Texas "have been carried out but partially, and that but very limited protection has been afforded to the frontier settlers." The legislation which Seguín endorsed was passed a month later.[34]

At the 1845 Texas Constitutional Convention, there was heated debate about the proposal that suffrage be extended exclusively to the "free white population." A speech made by F. J. Moore of Harris County left no doubt that for some delegates this was meant to disenfranchise Tejanos:

> Strike out the term "white," and what will be the result? Hordes of Mexican Indians may come in here from the West, and may be more formidable than the enemy you have vanquished. Silently they will come moving in; they will come back in thousands to Béxar, in thousands to Goliad, perhaps to Nacogdoches, and what will be the consequence? Ten, twenty, thirty, forty, fifty thousand may come in here, and vanquish you at the ballot box.

José Antonio Navarro contended that including the word "white" in electoral legislation was "odious" and "ridiculous." In the end, the position of Navarro and others held sway, as Tejanos were not denied voting rights in the Constitution of the State of Texas. Perhaps in response to the suffering the Texas army inflicted on Tejanos during the period of the Texas Republic, Navarro also successfully promoted the following statute in the state constitution: "No soldier shall, in time of peace, be quartered in the house, or within the enclosure of any individual, without the consent of the owner; nor in time of war, but in a manner prescribed by law."[35]

San Antonio Tejanos and Local Politics

The influence of the change from Mexican to Texan rule on local affairs at San Antonio, and on Tejano response to those affairs, was demonstrated in a series of events following the Texas Revolution. With threats of a renewed Mexican invasion after the Texas victory at San Jacinto, Colonel Juan Seguín left San Antonio with his troops in June 1836. He also urged local Tejanos to do the same and take their livestock to keep it from any advancing Mexican army. Seguín led his troops back to San Antonio in November at the order of President Sam Houston. Claiming the threat of Mexican attack continued, the Houston press called for the evacuation and destruction of San Antonio, thus preventing enemy use of its resources. General Felix Huston concurred with this strategy and ordered Seguín to abandon and destroy the town. Seguín did not comply with General Huston's orders, however. Instead, he successfully petitioned President Houston to rescind them.[36]

As commander of San Antonio, Seguín encouraged Tejano citizens to cooperate with the Texan defense against a threatened Mexican reconquest effort. But upon receiving an order that was clearly harmful to his home town and its inhabitants, he petitioned the president to join him in defending Tejano interests. His attempt to promote Tejano interests while demonstrating loyalty to his new nation illustrates Tejano political strategy during the period of the Texas Republic.

This strategy is also evident in local elections at San Antonio. Tejanos continued to be the majority population and won the majority of city council seats in all elections held during this period. In the first municipal elections after Texas independence, all but one of the forty-one candidates were of Spanish-Mexican descent. Continuing Tejano control of the city council was reflected in the council minutes, which were kept exclusively in Spanish until 1838 and in both Spanish and English from 1838 to 1844.[37]

Nonetheless, Tejanos accommodated to the reality of an increasing Anglo-American population. Indeed, it is striking that despite the Tejano electoral majority, Anglo-Americans consistently won election to the mayoral office in San Antonio during the Texas Republic. The sole exceptions were the elections of 1841 and 1842, when voters selected Juan

Seguín for mayor. In 1837, John W. Smith, the only Anglo-American in a field of forty-one candidates, was elected mayor![38]

David Montejano has argued that Anglo-American control of Tejano strongholds like San Antonio was consolidated by means of a "peace structure." By "peace structure" Montejano refers to "a general post-war arrangement that allows the victors to maintain law and order without the constant use of force." One of the primary elements in this structure was "an accommodation between the victorious Anglos and the defeated Mexican elite." This accommodation did not substantially alter the traditional authority structures of Tejano society, but rather placed Anglo-Americans atop the existing hierarchy. Often marriages between Anglo-American men and daughters from the elite families of a locale played a key role in this arrangement. These marriages offered Anglo-Americans the advantages of land, inherited wealth, and social status. They offered local Tejanos allies to help protect familial interests and land holdings. After Texas independence, such allies were particularly useful as many Tejanos did not speak English, were unfamiliar with the legal system, and were vulnerable to accusations of disloyalty.[39]

It is not surprising, then, that during this time of transition "at least one daughter from almost every *rico* [rich] family in San Antonio married an Anglo." Several Anglo-American elected officials often had Tejana wives; for example, a daughter of José Antonio Navarro married the adjutant general of the state, while two daughters from the De la Garza family wed the county clerk and the sheriff, respectively. Among the mayors of San Antonio during the Texas Republic, John W. Smith (1837–1838, 1840–1841, 1842–1844) and Edward Dwyer (1844–1845) had Tejana wives.[40]

Other Anglo-American mayors such as Samuel A. Maverick (1839–1840) maintained social contacts with Tejanos. The Mavericks exchanged social calls with prominent Tejano families like the Navarros, Sotos, Garzas, Garcías, Zambranos, Seguíns, Veramendis, and Yturris. Samuel Maverick's wife, Mary, wrote in 1838 that "our only society are Mexicans." The Mavericks participated at local festivities in honor of Our Lady of Guadalupe, including a dance held by "the more prominent families" at the Flores residence, and also attended a dance at the Yturri home given in honor of Mirabeau Buonaparte Lamar, the president of Texas. While Samuel Maverick did not marry a daughter from a local family, his election as mayor was accompanied by his incorporation into the social circle of the Tejano elite. This is consistent with the concept of peace structure outlined by Montejano.[41]

TEJANOS, RELIGION, AND PUBLIC CELEBRATIONS

Despite the fact that religious freedom in the Republic of Texas opened the doors to expanded Protestant ministries, San Antonio Tejanos retained their Catholic allegiance. The replacement of San Antonio's native priests with foreign clergy necessitated increased Tejano initiatives to continue local traditions for feasts like Our Lady of Guadalupe. Tejanos persisted in the celebration of those traditions and even sought to incorporate Anglo-American newcomers in their festivities. But they also gave public expression to their Texas allegiance on such occasions as the burial of the Alamo dead and a visit by the president of Texas to their city.

Tejanos and the Increased Protestant Presence

After Texas independence, Protestant denominations quickly established official structures to coordinate ministries in the new republic. Cumberland Presbyterians organized a Texas Presbytery in 1837; Old School Presbyterians followed by establishing the Brazos Presbytery in 1840. The Methodist Episcopal Church created the Texas Mission District in 1837, and in 1840 formed the Texas Conference, which was divided into two conferences in 1844. Baptists organized district associations during this period, which led to the establishment of the Baptist State Convention in 1848.[42]

Most Protestant activity was in settlements to the east of San Antonio and conducted predominantly among Anglo-American residents. Protestant leaders recognized that the possibilities of success were greater among Anglo-Americans from Protestant backgrounds. Furthermore, a scarcity of resources prevented much initial outreach to Tejano Catholics at San Antonio and elsewhere. As one Methodist missionary wrote in 1838: "I have hitherto [been] prevented from visiting Béxar and its vicinity, as I had intended; but it seems, in some instances, more needful to supply and occupy places which we have explored, than to explore others which we cannot occupy." The danger of Native American attack on the journey to San Antonio was another obstacle; an Episcopalian priest canceled a trip to San Antonio in 1843 because of this threat. Denominational life at San Antonio during the period of the Texas Republic was summarized well by Baptist minister Z. N. Morrell, who claimed after an 1839 visit that Catholicism "reigned without a rival" in the city.[43]

Some Protestant ministers did make pastoral visits to San Antonio, however. Presbyterian William C. Blair, the first Protestant to receive a denominational appointment for the evangelization of Tejanos, expressed his intention "to visit as often as practicable San Antonio and other Mexican towns." Blair was commissioned in 1839 and may be the minister who reportedly preached at San Antonio in May of that year. Like other Protestant ministers who followed him, Blair's official reports suggested that the ultimate missionary objective was evangelizing Mexico and South America. His first annual report to his denomination's Board of Foreign Missions stated: "Although this mission is for the present located in Texas, it is properly a mission to Mexico. The day is not distant when the intolerance of popery will no longer be able to retain in seclusion and darkness the millions of Mexico and South America."[44]

Another Protestant minister who visited San Antonio during this period was John McCullough, a Presbyterian. McCullough first visited the city in 1842, then returned in 1844 to investigate the possibility of ministering among the city's Mexican population through a distribution of Spanish tracts and testaments. On his second visit, McCullough was accompanied by Reverend John Wesley DeVilbiss, a Methodist. Together, they led a Protestant service. DeVilbiss began holding monthly services at San Antonio in the spring of 1845, thus establishing the first consistent Protestant efforts in the city.[45]

Anglo-American visitors to San Antonio made negative assessments of Tejano Catholicism. An 1837 visitor claimed that San Antonio Tejanos

> are taught to read and write at schools under the management of the priests, and it is to be attributed to that source that a religious enthusiasm or by whatever name it should be called gives a strong coloring to the Mexican character and accounts for the powerful influence which the clergy exercise over the minds of the people. Every Mexican professes to be a Catholic and carries about his person the crucifix, the rosary, and other symbols of the mother church. But religion with him, if one is permitted to judge of the feelings of the heart by outward signs, is more a habit than a principle or feeling.

Morrell stated that the religious practices of San Antonio Catholics during his 1839 visit exemplified "the blindest superstition." Presbyterian minister William L. McCalla, who visited San Antonio in 1840, decried the local customs of holy-day festivities and *fandangos* (dances) as evidence of Catholicism's corrupting influence and prayed that Protestant emissaries would reclaim Texas from "the mother and mistress of all churches."[46]

Other Protestant clergy interpreted the independence of Texas as divine sanction for the spread of their missionary influence. Reverend A. B. Lawrence wrote in 1840:

> To Protestant Christians the events of Texas are further deeply interesting, as an indication of Providence in relation to the propagation of divine truth in other parts of the Mexican dominions . . . Viewed then as the beginning of the downfall of Antichrist, and the spread of the Saviour's power of the gospel, the history and relations of Texas must furnish to the mind of the ardent Christian subjects of deep enquiry, delightful contemplation, and fervid thanksgiving.[47]

Along with the pressure of demonstrating their Texas loyalty to suspicious Anglo-Americans and adapting to a new political system, then, Tejanos were also confronted with an Anglo-American approach to religion which saw Mexican Catholicism as inherently inferior and Protestantism as a force that would inevitably conquer the continent. This view of religious "manifest destiny" was reinforced by expanding Protestant ministries in other areas of the Republic. As Catholicism was the prescribed religion at San Antonio de Béxar throughout the Spanish and Mexican periods, these attitudes challenged an assumed element of Tejano life and identity. There are no recorded instances of San Antonio Tejanos becoming Protestants during this period. But their continued practice of Catholicism becomes more significant in light of the Anglo-American assumption that abandoning their Catholic heritage would enable Tejanos to comply with divine providence and improve themselves as a people.

Changes in Catholic Leadership

Within the Catholic Church, other changes influenced the religious life of San Antonio Tejanos. In 1840, Pope Gregory XVI removed Texas from the Mexican diocese of Linares and declared it a prefecture apostolic under the diocese of New Orleans. He appointed Father John Timon, a Vincentian, as prefect apostolic. Since Timon was unable to undertake the responsibility personally because of other duties within his congregation, his French confrere, Jean Marie Odin, assumed the leadership of the Church in Texas as vice prefect apostolic. The following year, the pope elevated Texas to a vicariate apostolic and named Odin the vicar apostolic. Texas remained a vicariate apostolic under the diocese of New Orleans until the establishment of Galveston as the first Texas episcopal see in 1847, with Odin as first ordinary.[48]

This shift in ecclesiastical jurisdiction led to a change in clergy at San Antonio's San Fernando parish. During his first visit to the city in 1840, Odin removed the two native priests at San Antonio, Refugio de la Garza and José Antonio Valdéz, claiming that their ministry was ineffective and that they had broken their priestly vows by having wives and children. In their place, he appointed his Spanish confrere Miguel Calvo as pastor of San Fernando.

Given the frequent conflicts between European immigrants and the U.S. hierarchy over the assignment of native clergy to serve immigrant congregations, the lack of evidence that Tejanos protested against Odin's removal of their two priests is striking. Odin even claimed that John Smith, San Antonio's mayor, sought to reinstate Father Refugio de la Garza as pastor of San Fernando because Odin refused permission to ring the church bells for a Protestant funeral. According to Odin's accounts, no San Antonio Tejanos participated in the public outcry against him. This claim is confirmed by a published complaint against Odin in the *Austin Texas Sentinel;* no Tejanos were among the signers of this complaint.[49]

Some historians have suggested that the Mexican nationalist loyalties of the two San Antonio clerics may in part explain the apparent Tejano silence upon their dismissal. Father de la Garza represented San Antonio de Béxar in the Mexican National Congress in 1824 and, as was previously mentioned, gave patriotic speeches at Mexican Independence Day celebrations during the period of the Mexican Republic. A Mexican soldier claimed that De la Garza also sympathized with the Mexican side during the 1835 siege of San Antonio. Shortly after his dismissal by Odin, De la Garza was arrested for corresponding with Mexican military leaders, an act prohibited by Texas laws.[50] Odin later wrote that, when General Rafael Vásquez occupied San Antonio in March of 1842, De la Garza attempted to have Vásquez install him as pastor. Apparently the curate thought his own reinstatement was possible once Mexican political rule was reintroduced. When General Adrian Woll occupied San Antonio in September of the same year, his official reports described De la Garza as the "parish priest of Béxar and Chaplain of the Rio Grande Company" and related that the priest had escaped from captivity by the Texas army, arriving in the Mexican camp with his arms still bound.[51]

Father Valdéz, the other San Antonio cleric Odin removed, had also shown Mexican nationalist sympathies. During the Texas Revolution, he organized Tejanos to fight for the Mexican side and probably led an attack on Texan forces. He was captured by Colonel James W. Fannin but later freed by the advancing Mexican army.[52]

The nationalist tendencies of Valdéz and De la Garza were undoubtedly unacceptable to many San Antonio Tejanos, who were engulfed in the difficult challenge of reconciling loyalties to their Texas homeland and their Mexican cultural motherland. It is not surprising, then, that when Father Timon conducted an inspection tour of Texas in 1839, Juan Seguín and José Antonio Navarro, both San Antonio congressmen at the time, testified against the San Antonio clergy. While the official charges were that the native priests lived openly with wives and neglected their pastoral duties, political differences (and perhaps personal rivalries) also may have entered into their disapproval of De la Garza and Valdéz. These differences explain in part the apparent silence of San Antonio Tejanos over the loss of their native clergy.[53]

Some foreign priests who encountered Tejanos for the first time opined that their knowledge and practice of the faith were inadequate. Former prefect apostolic Timon stated that "the poor Mexicans would die for their religion, yet they hardly knew what their religion was; how could they? Their faith was rather a divine instinct that grew from their baptism, than a faith of knowledge." Recalling his first years in Texas, Odin later wrote that the Catholic population he encountered "kept no more than a slight vestige of faith."[54]

Catholic clergy were certainly not as critical of Tejano Catholicism as Protestant ministers and other Anglo-Americans were condemnatory of Tejano religious practices. Odin, for example, participated in Tejano religious feasts like the 1841 San Antonio celebration in honor of Our Lady of Guadalupe and, in contrast to his later statement about Tejanos' lack of faith, spoke enthusiastically of the religious zeal demonstrated in these celebrations. Many priests also made heroic efforts to serve the Spanish-speaking segment of their flock. Odin learned Spanish and was insistent that those coming to minister in Texas do the same, including his episcopal successor, whom he said should be "acquainted with the English and Spanish languages." Calvo's Vincentian confreres later claimed that, during his twelve years as pastor of San Fernando (1840–1852), he "consoled and defended the native-born [Tejanos] against the cruelty of the yankees."[55]

Public Celebrations at San Antonio

Even though Odin and others may have been caring pastors, however, their lack of familiarity with local traditions meant Tejano leaders had to assume much of the responsibility for continuing those traditions. While local leaders had organized communal celebrations since the eighteenth century, frequently they had done so in conjunction with clergy like Father de la Garza who were accustomed to Tejano feasts and practices. Odin and Calvo may have been familiar with feasts like Our Lady of Guadalupe,[56] but some local practices in celebrating these feasts were undoubtedly new to them. By Odin's own account of San Antonio's 1841 Guadalupe celebration, Tejano leaders collected funds for purchasing gun powder, which was used in firing salutes as an expression of devotion. He also wrote that Tejanas exercised a leadership role, assisting in the decoration of San Fernando Church and the Guadalupan image used in processions. Odin asserted that he had "seen few processions more edifying" than the one prepared by the local Tejano population. His cooperative approach does not detract from Tejano initiatives to celebrate the feast of their patroness in the customary manner. These initiatives reveal the value of local traditions to the Tejano community.[57]

Two contemporary accounts of the San Antonio Guadalupe celebrations from primary sources are extant. One is Odin's account of the 1841 celebration; the other, taken from the memoirs of Mary A. Maverick, who was Protestant, provides an account of the celebration in 1840.[58]

In both Odin's and Maverick's descriptions the most noteworthy activity mentioned is the Guadalupe processions. Maverick describes one procession, Odin two (one in the afternoon and the other in the evening). Although there are minor discrepancies between the two accounts, there is enough agreement to suggest some general patterns for the ritual performance of the processions. An elegantly adorned image of Our Lady of Guadalupe was the principal ritual object. Odin also mentions a cross, a banner of Mary, and the ornaments offered by local women for the decoration of the church. Priests and the general populace both took part in the processions. Young girls dressed in white and bearing candles (some had flowers, according to Odin) were the immediate attendants of the Guadalupan image. Maverick adds that fiddlers also participated, Odin that sixty members of the militia served as escorts. The rosary was prayed, and according to Odin religious hymns honoring the mother of God were sung. Both observers recall guns being fired off as part of the devotion, and Odin wrote of cannons and bells sounding as well. They also mention religious ceremonies at San Fernando Church in addition to the processions.

These colorful Guadalupe processions exemplified the Mexican heritage of local Tejanos and perpetuated a devotion prevalent in San Antonio from the early years of the settlement's history. As in the Spanish and Mexican periods, the militia, clergy, and general populace participated in the processions. They also joined together in the prayer of the rosary, religious hymns, and services at San Fernando Church. The continued celebration of the Guadalupe feast in the traditional manner showed that Tejano signs of allegiance to the Texan cause did not indicate a rejection of their Mexican Catholic heritage.

Anglo-American participation in the Guadalupan feast showed the strength of local traditions at San Antonio and the Tejano desire to incorporate newcomers into those traditions. As was previously mentioned, the Maverick family attended the 1840 Guadalupe celebration, while Odin wrote that a number of Anglo-Americans from as far away as Austin attended in 1841.

Anglo-Americans also joined with Tejanos in other public events at San Antonio. The popular *fandangos* were attended by numerous visitors to the city.[59] In 1841, both Tejano and Anglo-American residents participated in a twenty-one-gun salute and dance given in honor of visiting Texas president Mirabeau Buonaparte Lamar. The 1837 interment ceremony for the ashes of the Alamo dead also brought Tejanos and Anglo-Americans together. Juan Seguín led the ceremony and was accompanied in procession by other members of the military, civil authorities, clergy, musicians, and the general populace. Seguín gave a speech in which he stated: "The venerable remains of our worthy companions as witnesses, I invite you to declare to the entire world, 'Texas shall be free and independent, or we shall perish in glorious combat.'" While the procession resembled similar communal efforts in the city's past, the rationale for gathering and the sentiment of Seguín's speech demonstrated loyalty to the Texas Republic.[60]

The Mexican background of San Antonio Tejanos was reflected in other communal events. Despite claims to the contrary by Mexican officials, the celebration of Mexican Independence Day continued in San Antonio even after Texas independence. Apparently Tejano separation from Mexico as a political entity did not sever the bonds of national sentiment they held in common with others of Mexican heritage. A British traveler wrote the following in his diary entry for October 1, 1843: "The Maromeros, or Mexican rope dancers are jumping about this evening. Although San Antonio is governed by Texan laws, Mexican customs prevail; rope dancing, tumbling, and plays on a Sunday!"[61]

SUMMARY: BETWEEN TWO WORLDS

When asked in later years if he loved Texas more than Mexico, San Antonio resident Enrique Esparza reportedly stated that he was of mixed

Indian and Spanish blood and "proud of that ancestry." He then added that he saw his father "die for Texas" in the battle of the Alamo and that he was "proud to be a Texan and an American." [62] This statement reflects the Tejano response to the dilemma they faced during the Texas Republic. Caught between demands, accusations, and pressure from both Anglo-Americans and Mexican officials, Tejanos tried to sustain themselves during a series of attacks and counterattacks. Conflicting allegiances among San Antonio Tejanos are indicative of their desire to remain loyal both to their Texan homeland and their Mexican cultural motherland. The choice for neutrality was an attempt to avoid violence and harm by remaining in peace with both sides. In either case, the pressure to choose sides led Tejanos to forge an identity which could resolve the tensions inherent in being caught between two opposing armies. Faced with the dilemma of choosing sides in the Texas-Mexico conflict, Tejanos who chose to remain in Texas increasingly presented themselves as a people of Mexican heritage who were loyal (or at least unopposed) to the cause of Texas.

Diminishing influence in national affairs after Texas independence forced Tejanos to accept a new political reign in which Anglo-American interests consistently won out over Tejano claims. While actions like José Antonio Navarro's participation as commissioner in the Santa Fe expedition supported Anglo-American political aspirations, Tejano legislative efforts more typically promoted their own concerns. The suffrage debate at the 1845 Texas Constitutional Convention is evidence of the Tejano political struggle, as Navarro had to fight for voting rights which never would have been challenged under Mexican rule. Limited potential influence did not deter Tejano representatives from championing the rights of their constituency, however. They respected Texas law and procedures but struggled within that framework to advance the interests of Tejano citizens.

Juan Seguín's response to General Felix Huston's 1836 order for the abandonment and destruction of San Antonio illustrates Tejano political strategy during the Texas Republic. Seguín demonstrated his allegiance to Texas in his efforts to protect the frontier but defended Tejano interests by counteracting his superior's potentially damaging order.

The election of Anglo-American mayors during this period was also part of Tejano accommodation to a new political reality. Tejanos incorporated Anglo-Americans into local leadership by consistently electing Anglo-American mayors. But they also tended to select Anglo-Americans who were aligned by marriage or other ties to local families, while Tejanos themselves retained a majority among the members of the city council. By choosing Anglo-American mayors, San Antonio voters demonstrated that they were not sustaining a Tejano enclave which was hostile to its Anglo-American neighbors. By choosing mayors tied to local families, they gained potential allies in the broader network of a new and unfamiliar political system.

Despite increased religious pluralism in Texas and Protestant inducement to change religious affiliation, the Mexican Catholic identity of San Antonio Tejanos remained intact throughout the period of the Texas Republic. Following the removal of their native clergy, continuing Tejano initiatives perpetuated local traditions for feasts like Our Lady of Guadalupe. The celebration after Texas independence of the Guadalupan feast, Mexican Independence Day, *fandangos,* and Mexican entertainments like the *maromeros* showed that Tejano signs of allegiance to the Texan cause did not indicate a rejection of their Mexican heritage. Anglo-American participation in Tejano celebrations like the Guadalupe feast and *fandangos* demonstrate the vitality of Tejano traditions at San Antonio and the Tejano desire to incorporate newcomers into the celebrations of their religious and cultural heritage. At the same time, ceremonies such as the interment of the Alamo dead and social events like the dance for President Lamar indicated that Tejanos were also loyal to Texas. Intentionally or not, San Antonio Tejanos' religious and other celebrations provided a means to express their emerging identity as a people of Mexican Catholic heritage who were citizens of the Texas Republic.

Tejanos were not merely adapting to outside forces. Faced with a new political system and the establishment of religious pluralism, San Antonio Tejanos attempted to incorporate Anglo-Americans into their local community. Under the Mexican Republic, Anglo-American settlers were required by law to accept Catholicism and the Mexican political system. In large part, Anglo-Americans at San Antonio de Béxar complied with these requirements. Under the Texas Republic, the prescription of Catholicism and the Mexican political system were removed. Lacking legal sanction for incorporating Anglo-Americans into local political and religious life, San Antonio Tejanos attempted to enlist voluntary Anglo-American participation in their community. Tejano activity in the period of the Texas Republic cannot be understood solely as a reaction to outside forces, then, but also as a continuing attempt to incorporate Anglo-Americans into the life of San Antonio Tejanos and their city.

While San Antonio Tejanos continued attempts to incorporate Anglo-Americans, they also severed their loyalties to Mexican officials. Under the Mexican Republic, they had evidenced loyalty to Mexican procedures and administrators; under the Texas Republic, they demonstrated loyalty to their Mexican heritage, not the Mexican government. This is the more critical development in terms of Tejano identity during this period. Cultural differences between Tejanos and Anglo-Americans were apparent during the early stages of contact between the two groups. Tejanos held a common heritage with the people of Mexico, however, even though a particular regional identity had developed over the years since the settlement's founding. Separation from Mexico removed Tejanos from political alliance with others of Mexican heritage and raised the question of whether they would abandon that heritage altogether. As Andrés Tijerina has said, during this period Tejanos "increasingly defined themselves as an entity different from Mexico and separate from the Anglo culture."[63]

The end result of separation from Mexico, then, was an emerging sense of distinct peoplehood or Tejano ethnic identity. Having never been Anglo-American and now dissociated from the Mexican nation as a political entity, Tejanos defined themselves as distinct from both. After U.S. annexation in 1845, the steady influx of European immigrants vastly increased the ethnic complexity of Texas. This made the issue of Tejano ethnic identification in the face of political separation from Mexico increasingly significant.

†

FOUR

EMERGING ETHNICITY:
THE FIRST FIFTEEN YEARS
AFTER U.S. ANNEXATION,
1845–1860

Texas became the twenty-eighth state of the United States on December 29, 1845. By the time of U.S. annexation, Anglo-Americans exerted considerable influence in the political and economic life of San Antonio. But the population of the city remained predominately Tejano and, as one 1846 visitor wrote, it had "somewhat of a foreign appearance, altogether dissimilar to any other Texas city." In 1849, another traveler commented that "San Antonio is a Mexican town but rapidly becoming yankeeized." Five years later, yet another visitor stated that the most striking characteristic of the city was its "jumble of races, costumes, languages and buildings." This ethnic pluralism was evident in the distinct German, Tejano, and Anglo-American neighborhoods which the traveler passed through on entering the city and the mix of architectural styles representing various nationalities around the central plaza. A Tejano resident summed up the changes in San Antonio during this period in his observation that "after annexation, things began to assume a more cosmopolitan appearance." [1]

These shifts in the physical appearance of San Antonio reflect Texas' changing demographic composition from U.S. annexation until the outset of the Civil War. Anglo-American colonization had been in progress since before Mexican independence, along with a much smaller wave of immigration from Europe and Mexico. With U.S. annexation, the threat of Mexican invasion was considerably lessened and all but eliminated after the U.S. defeat of Mexico in the Mexican War (1846–1848). These developments facilitated an increase in Anglo-American and European settlement in Texas. Mexican citizens, many fleeing from sporadic revolutionary activity in their homeland, also continued to cross the Rio Grande and settle in land now under U.S. jurisdiction. After the war, military outposts were formed in San Antonio and several other Texas locations, further increasing the presence of Anglo-Americans and some immigrants who served in the military or worked in civilian occupations necessitated by the military presence. The massive immigration to Texas is reflected in 1850 census figures, which revealed that two thirds of Texas residents were born outside the state.[2]

For San Antonio Tejanos, these population shifts brought dramatic change. Although the city enjoyed increased trade, bolstered by the economic boon of the U.S. military presence, many Tejanos lost land holdings, worked in menial occupations, and earned a livelihood that was "exceedingly meagre."[3] By 1850, Tejanos comprised less than half of the city's population, the first time since the foundation of San Antonio de Béxar that they were not the overwhelming majority.

Tejano and Anglo-American relations were at times marked by conflict, at other times by cohesion, but most frequently by separation between the two groups. The city's first Protestant congregations were established during this period; Protestant ministries included some proselytizing efforts directed at Catholic Tejanos. Tejanos also lost control of the city council after U.S. annexation, and only two San Antonio Tejanos were elected to serve at the state legislature. But Tejano votes remained an important bloc in local elections, and the Tejano community responded in various ways to contemporary political issues. Newly arrived Anglo-Americans wrote accounts of Texas history; Tejanos responded from their own perspective as native Texans. This historical perspective, along with their response to the growing Anglo-American presence, Protestant proselytizing efforts, and changing political realities, reveals shifting Tejano identity during this time of change.

SAN ANTONIO, 1845–1860:
A DEMOGRAPHIC AND ECONOMIC PROFILE

The presence of Anglo-Americans and European immigrants was not a new phenomenon at San Antonio.[4] After U.S. annexation, however, their presence increased dramatically. The first large wave of new arrivals was the military personnel who camped in or near the city during the Mexican War. During 1846, U.S. troops quartered in San Antonio and the environs eclipsed the local civilian population in size. After the war, San Antonio became a major military center and depot for the U.S. Army. An official report of 1853 indicated that eighteen frontier posts received supplies from the San Antonio base; an 1856 report stated that at least 150 civilians were employed by the military in the city.[5]

The increased military presence, comprised predominantly of Anglo-Americans, was accompanied by increased foreign immigration. According to census figures, San Antonio's foreign-born population increased from 39 percent in 1850 to 47.1 percent in 1860. The latter census revealed a total of twenty-two foreign nations represented in San Antonio, including small groups of Poles, Irish, French, English, Swiss, Russians, Italians, and Danes. Anglo-Americans, Germans, and Spanish-surnamed residents comprised the three largest groups in 1860 and throughout the previous decade. The free-population schedule for the 1850 census showed that 42 percent of San Antonio's 3,268 free residents had Spanish surnames, 25 percent were Anglo-American, and 16 percent were of German birth or parentage.[6] Although Spanish-surnamed residents remained among the largest ethnic contingents in the city throughout the 1850s, they no longer comprised a majority of the population. According to the free-population schedule for the 1860 census, slightly less than one third of San Antonio's 7,643 free residents had Spanish surnames.[7]

Migration from south of the Rio Grande continued even after U.S. annexation. Persons of Mexican birth numbered 570 on the 1850 census; by 1860 this number had more than doubled to 1,220. Clusters of entries on the 1850 and 1860 census tracts indicate considerable separation of Spanish-surnamed residents from other ethnic groups in San Antonio neighborhoods. In the 1860 census, for example, the city was divided into four wards. Almost 80 percent of Tejanos and more recently arrived Mexicans resided in two of these four wards. Perhaps noting this physical proximity, many contemporary observers at San Antonio referred to native Tejanos and other residents of Mexican descent as a single group, usually calling them Mexicans. Besides their relatively segregated neighborhoods, most long-standing Tejano residents and new arrivals from south of the Rio Grande shared a common language, culture, religion, and socioeconomic status. Perceptions of a single Mexican ethnic group reflect the initiation of these new arrivals into San Antonio's Tejano community.[8]

Census tracts also indicate a downward trend in the economic situation of San Antonio Tejanos. The 1830 census showed that most San Antonio residents were farmers and only 14.8 percent were laborers. No employment figures are available from the 1840 census. According to the 1850 census, 61.4 percent of the Tejano population were in labor positions. Tabulations from 1860 indicate that this number had risen slowly to 65 percent. While Tejanos were increasingly becoming a working underclass in San Antonio, they also were losing their land holdings. Although incomplete, the census of 1840 showed they owned 85.1 percent of the town lots at San Antonio, along with 63.8 percent of all land acreage titled to local residents. On the 1850 census, they owned only 9.1 percent of real estate values claimed, however, and 7.8 percent on the 1860 census.[9] Given this upward trend in labor positions and the downward trend in land holdings, it is not surprising that only a few observers noted the existence of a Tejano elite after U.S. annexation. An 1855 visitor to the city, for example, wrote that "only 4 or 5 [Tejanos] are received into the circles of the elite."[10]

TEJANOS AND ETHNIC DIVERSITY IN SAN ANTONIO

In 1853, a San Antonio newspaper account reported that

we strolled into a Justices Court the other day, and were reminded of the time when God smote the children of men with a confusion of tongues. A German was complained of by a Mexican, and a Frenchman was the witness. Each one spoke his native tongue only, and yet there were no interpreters. Both Justice and Attorneys understood the four languages [including English].[11]

This incident illustrates San Antonio's ethnic diversity in the wake of demographic changes after U.S. annexation. Public celebrations were another visible reminder of this diversity, as they included Tejano feasts, along with Anglo-American and German holidays. While contact between San Antonio's ethnic groups occasionally marked these celebrations and other elements of social life, the various groups tended to operate independently of one another.

Public Celebrations at San Antonio

After Texas independence, San Antonio's municipal council no longer assisted in organizing Tejano festivities, and Tejanos planned celebrations like those for Our Lady of Guadalupe in conjunction with local clergy. This practice continued after U.S. annexation. Apparently the informal structures which governed the planning of Guadalupan festivities were adequate, as the local Tejano population celebrated the feast of their patroness enthusiastically throughout this period. As in previous years, these celebrations included gun and cannon salutes, extended ringing of the church bells, processions, and large crowds for services such as Mass, vespers, and the rosary.[12]

Tejanos also offered public devotion during the Christmas season. For the nine days preceding Christmas, they lit lamps and placed them on their homes, "in remembrance of the 'Light of the World.'" They began Noche Buena, or Christmas Eve, with a dance. Mass was celebrated at midnight. Afterward, the people filed to the front of San Fernando Church and kissed the feet of "el Santo Niño," the Holy Child. Then they held a grand supper. As in the Guadalupe celebrations, Tejanos incorporated tributes like gun salutes, cannonading, and bell ringing into their Christmas devotions.[13]

Another prominent Tejano celebration was the feast of San Juan (June 24), which consisted of religious ceremonies such as Mass and other festivities. Robert E. Lee stated during his 1860 stay in the city that on this day "the principal, or at least visible, means of adoration or worship seemed to consist in riding horses." Of particular note was a sport called El Gallo Corriendo, the running rooster. A brightly decorated rooster was given to a contestant, whose objective was to ride it on his horse over a given route and across a designated finish line. Meanwhile his opponents rode alongside him and attempted to take the rooster, employing almost any means imaginable. Contestants continued to vie for possession of the rooster until one of them successfully carried it across the finish line. These contests were often run through the principal streets of the city. Sometimes a watermelon was used instead of a rooster. Often an evening dance was also part of the festivities. These observances were also kept on other feast days, such as those for San Fernando, San Antonio, and San Pedro.[14]

Tejano feasts were no longer the only public celebrations in the city. After U.S. annexation, the growing Anglo-American population organized parades, ceremonies, dances, and other festivities for national holidays like the Fourth of July and Washington's birthday. San Antonio residents also commemorated the anniversary of the Texas Declaration of Independence (March 2) from Mexico. In 1859, José Antonio Navarro, a signer of the Texas Declaration of Independence, and Antonio Menchaca, a veteran of the Texas Revolution, were among the honorees at a ceremony to mark this occasion and received enthusiastic applause when introduced. By the late 1850s, the Presbyterian, Episcopalian, and Methodist churches offered special services on Thanksgiving Day, apparently rotating the leadership of the service annually. Protestant leaders also introduced May Day celebrations, which included a public procession and awards ceremony for Sunday-school students. Germans at San Antonio commemorated Schiller's birthday, recalling the life of the noted German poet.[15]

Anglo-American celebrations were not merely an attempt to provide a greater variety of public festivities. Editorials and speeches given on these occasions expressed a presumption of Anglo-American superiority. After the celebration of U.S. Independence Day in 1854, one editorialist asked rhetorically: "When we contemplate these glorious annual re-unions of the American people, native and adopted, as a common brother-hood, to commemorate the event that gave existence to a nation of freemen, we are led to exclaim, 'Who would not be an American?'" Even at the 1859 celebration of Texas Independence Day, in a speech which praised the heroism of honorees José Antonio Navarro and Antonio Menchaca, orator I. L. Hewitt claimed Texas' winning of independence from Mexico demonstrated that "no enemy however countless in their numbers can force the bold Anglo Saxon to yield to a tyrant's decrees." A Thanksgiving editorial interpreted the events since Texas independence as a sign of divine favor: "From being oppressed by a half savage people, we are the fondled, and likely to be the happy and petted sister of the union, the most powerful that has ever held sway upon the earth . . . why should'nt [sic] we be happy and return thanks to the Almighty Being who has so powerfully wrought in our favor?"[16]

Presumptions of superiority led some Anglo-Americans to envision Tejanos and others joining them in their national sentiments. A report published in the *San Antonio Ledger* after Fourth of July celebrations in 1851 stated: "We have many foreigners among us who know nothing of our government, who have no national feeling in common with us . . . Let us induce them to partake with us in our festivities, they will soon partake our feelings, and when so, they will be citizens indeed."[17]

Tejano public rituals were also criticized and, in some cases, altered because of the Anglo-American presence. An 1853 letter to the editor of the *San Antonio Ledger* deplored the Tejano practice of funeral processions with open coffins, deeming it "a heathen or Indian practice" which "has been very offensive to a larger [sic] portion of our community, and should be prohibited by the city authorities." Another Anglo-American quipped that, during the early 1850s, the local Catholic celebration of Christmas "was carried out in a semi-barbaric style." The correspondence of Sister Mary Patrick Joseph, an Irish Ursuline, revealed that cannonading and bell ringing for the 1852 Guadalupe festivities took place on Friday rather than Sunday, the actual day of the feast. This was done in order "not to disturb" the Sunday "methodistical devotion" of the

Anglo-American population. In another letter, she claimed that Guadalupe processions were canceled because Anglo-Americans found them uncivilized.[18]

Tejano and Anglo-American Relations at San Antonio

Differences between Tejanos and Anglo-Americans were not limited to their perspectives on public celebrations. In 1858, for example, Béxar County elected officials instituted a program of teacher certification for public schools, decreeing that public funds would be available solely for the salaries of certified teachers in schools where the principal language was English. This law was contested by José Ramos de Zúñiga. Zúñiga was the editor of *El Correo*, a local newspaper. He contended that, when limited to speaking English in school, Spanish- (and German-) speaking children ended up speaking neither language fluently.[19]

A more conspicuous form of conflict between Tejanos and Anglo-Americans derived from their frequently opposing stances on *fandangos*. Taxes on *fandango* licenses, which were levied in both the Mexican and Texas Republic periods, continued after U.S. annexation. During 1847, for example, 560 *fandango* licenses were issued by the city council at one dollar each. Sarah Brackett King, who moved to San Antonio in 1846, later recalled the Tejano attitude with regard to their dances: "There was a great deal of dancing—even on Sunday—for the Mexicans argued that God gave them legs and arms to use as well as heart and soul and that there was no sin in gaiety and pleasure."[20]

Newcomers to San Antonio did not hold Tejano dances in such high esteem. Newspaper editors deemed them a "great nuisance." Father Claude Marie Dubuis, who became pastor of San Fernando parish in 1852, desired "to discourage dancing among the Mexicans, as it becomes a real passion with them." Some San Antonio residents presented petitions to the city council requesting the abolition of *fandangos*.[21] In one council discussion of this issue, *fandangos* were reportedly described as "nothing but a heterogeneous mass of rottenness." After enacting legislation to ban *fandangos* in 1849, Mayor James M. Devine stated in an address to the council that "all the murders and outrages" committed in San Antonio during the Mexican era and since "have flowed directly and indirectly from their [*fandangos'*] toleration." Continuing conflicts resulted in numerous city-council ordinances, and at different times during the fifteen years after U.S. annexation, *fandangos* were taxed, restricted, banned, and reinstated again.[22]

Tejanos resisted laws which curtailed or prohibited *fandangos*. In

1853, city-council member Angel Navarro, a son of José Antonio Navarro, attempted to defend the practice by legislative means. At the February 1 meeting of the council, citizens presented a petition requesting that *fandangos* be suppressed. Navarro was on the committee that responded to this petition. The committee did not endorse the abolition of *fandangos* as requested by the citizens' group, however. Three weeks later, Navarro presented an ordinance which required that *fandangos* be licensed, secured by the presence of police officers, and restricted to certain sections of the city. This ordinance was passed, but the following day council voted to reconsider the measure. On April 14 the ordinance was unanimously adopted. That same day Navarro introduced a separate bill which outlawed gambling at *fandangos,* perhaps as a concession for the continuance of the dances within the city limits. Two months later, the *fandango* ordinance was repealed, however, and *fandangos* were banned. That same day Navarro submitted his resignation from the council.[23]

Another Tejano mode of resistance was simply to ignore municipal statutes aimed at regulating their dances. According to newspaper reports, *fandangos* were held even during periods when they were banned by the city council. On at least one occasion, Tejano resistance reached the point of violence. Shortly after newly elected Know Nothing city council members voted to ban *fandangos* in January 1855, two men of Mexican descent reportedly assaulted the local constable when he appeared at their dance.[24]

Such conflicts were undoubtedly exacerbated by the negative attitude some Anglo-Americans held about the Tejano population. Even the local press referred to Tejanos with the racist slur "greaser."[25] Commenting on people of Mexican heritage, one Anglo-American stated that they "are as bigoted and ignorant as the devil's grandchildren." Another described San Antonio Tejanos as "ignorant, cunning, treacherous, thieving, bigoted, superstitious . . . [and] infamously cowardly." Contemporary Protestant newspapers added to the wholesale attacks on the Tejano character. Quoting an Anglo-American correspondent, the *Texas Presbyterian* described persons of Mexican descent in 1848 as "useless, worthless, abandoned, yet with a happy self-sufficiency that renders them blind to every disgrace and indifferent to every disaster." Sometimes racial tensions led to potentially volatile situations. For example, on one occasion the lynching of a Tejano accused of horse theft nearly resulted in a riot between Anglo-Americans and San Antonio's Tejano population.[26]

Interaction between Tejanos and Anglo-Americans was not always marked by conflict, however; some events in San Antonio illustrated efforts at cohesion between them. Native San Antonian José María Rodrí-

guez escorted his sisters to social gatherings attended by U.S. Army officers during this period. Other social events brought together Tejanos,
Anglo-Americans, and the growing German population of the city. In
1855, Tejanos, Anglo-Americans, and Germans celebrated Mexican Independence Day. As was previously mentioned, the Texas Independence
Day ceremony of 1859 honored Tejanos and others who had been citizens of the Texas Republic. More recently arrived Anglo-Americans and
other immigrants accompanied them in the celebration. On another occasion, plans were made to give Fourth of July orations in different languages. The participation of the general populace at one U.S. Independence Day gathering led a local editorialist to remark that "English, Irish,
German, Spanish, all joined with the Americans as one brotherhood, and
seemed to vie with them in public show of devotion to our common
country."[27]

Such exuberant praise for San Antonio's ethnic unity was tempered by
the comments of other observers. One newspaper article stated that "the
higher grades of German and Mexican families, in social intercourse,
mingle freely with the same class of [the] American population."[28] While
the general populace participated in some of the aforementioned ethnically mixed events, in other cases Tejano and Anglo-American cohesion
was accompanied by the exclusion of the lower classes. José María Rodríguez and his family were prominent in the city, for example, and their
participation in military balls does not indicate that Tejanos (or others)
of lesser social status were invited.

Marriages between Tejanas and Anglo-Americans were also dispro-
portionately linked to upper-class status. According to historian Jane
Dysart, civil marriage records from 1837 to 1860 indicate 906 marriages
at San Antonio between two partners of Mexican descent and eighty-
eight marriages between Mexican women and Anglo-American men. Of
these eighty-eight mixed marriages, almost half "involved women from
high status families." Most of the children born from these unions received Catholic baptism and were given Spanish names. Because their
fathers were by and large immigrants whose extended families resided
elsewhere, kinship associations such as baptismal *padrinos* (godparents)
tended to be with the mother's relatives.[29]

Despite these links with their mothers' families and heritage, Dysart
claims that "the vast majority of these upper-class children of mixed marriages established identity with their father's ethnic group rather than
that of their mother." This identification resulted in large part from
Anglo-American presumptions of racial and cultural superiority, frequent contact with Anglo-American neighbors, and the marked tendency

of these children to attend English-speaking schools, including board-ing schools and colleges in other states. Evidence of their identification with their father's ethnic group includes the choice of many to anglicize their given names by the time they reached adulthood and their almost universal choice of a non-Mexican marriage partner. In addition, at least three of these families joined predominately Anglo-American Prot-estant churches while five others affiliated with the English-speaking Catholic congregation of St. Mary's parish, which opened at San Antonio in 1857.[30]

To be sure, only 8.8 percent of recorded marriages involving Tejanas in San Antonio during this period were mixed, and only about half of these involved wealthy Tejanas whose children tended to identify more readily with their fathers' ethnic group. But within these families a cer-tain ethnic cohesion was achieved by the gradual acceptance of Anglo-American cultural identification as predominate.

While at times cohesion or conflict marked relations between Tejanos and Anglo-Americans at San Antonio, frequently these groups (and oth-ers) simply remained separate from one another. On one Friday night in 1854, for example, it was reported that a German dance had taken place at the Vauxhaul Gardens, a number of Spanish-speaking residents had gathered for a private party at the Navarro home, and the predominately Anglo-American Youth Debating Club had also met. An 1853 newspaper editorial stated:

> Among those who assume to be the guide of tone, Mexican as well as American, there is at the present time but little, if any, social intercourse. Once or twice, perhaps, in the course of a year, a public ball will summon the fair representatives of both nations to terms of amity. But then ceases all social intercourse. The German has his soiree attended by his Teutonic friends; the Mexican party is rarely visited even by the American male; and in private American assemblages the fair señorita is no longer visible. The breach seems to be widening.

An 1858 report stated that Tejanos lived at the perimeter of the city and kept "pretty much to themselves." Methodist bishop George F. Pierce wrote of the city during an 1859 visit that "the old and the new live side by side—different races, unlike in origin, government, education, reli-gion, domestic habits and national destiny, constitute the population—neither materially affecting the other; each perpetuating the customs pe-culiar to them while separate."[31]

Tejano social gatherings and public celebrations tended to be frequented exclusively by the Spanish-speaking population. This stands in marked contrast to similar events during the period of the Texas Republic. During that earlier period, for example, Anglo-American and other newcomers to San Antonio frequented *fandangos;* after U.S. annexation such intermingling virtually ceased, and new arrivals even attempted to suppress the popular Tejano dances. Before Texas statehood, Mary Maverick and her family attended San Antonio Guadalupe festivities and the ball given for the president of Texas at the Yturri home. They also entertained Tejanos at parties in their own home, exchanging social calls with prominent Tejano families. Mrs. Maverick and her children fled from San Antonio during the Vásquez raid of 1842 and did not return until 1847. Her *Memoirs* record no instances of social contact with Tejanos after the family's return, nor attendance at Tejano feasts. While some of the Mavericks' earlier social circle no longer lived in the city, another reason for this change was the availability of a sufficient number of Anglo-Americans to maintain their own social circle.[32]

Apparently Anglo-American participation in Guadalupe celebrations during the early 1840s also ceased after U.S. annexation. Editors from local newspapers seemed at a loss to know what the Tejano population was doing around December 12, once mistaking their cannonading as a tribute to the editor of a local paper upon his marriage, another time speculating that bell ringing the days before December 12 was for the imminence of Christmas and the mayoral elections.[33] All reports of San Antonio Guadalupe celebrations from 1845 to 1860 mention the sole participation of the Tejano population.

SAN ANTONIO TEJANOS AND PROTESTANT MINISTERIAL INITIATIVES

Increasing ethnic diversity in San Antonio was accompanied by the establishment of denominational pluralism. San Fernando was the city's only church in 1845. By 1860 a second Catholic parish had been formed, along with Old School Presbyterian, Episcopalian, Lutheran, Baptist, and two Methodist congregations (one English-speaking and the other German).[34] A Cumberland Presbyterian minister visited San Antonio, but no local congregation was founded by this denomination in the antebellum period. An 1859 visitor to the city claimed that an independent African-American congregation was also holding services in the city; other reports indicate public ritual activity among members of the Jewish faith.[35]

Catholicism remained by far the city's largest denomination. In 1855,

Father Francois Bouchu wrote that San Antonio had a population of ten thousand, nine thousand of whom were Catholics. Four years later, Reverend R. F. Bunting, pastor of San Antonio's First Presbyterian Church, claimed there were eight thousand Catholics in the area and considerably fewer Protestants. That same year a Baptist minister who visited the city estimated that "probably half the population are Catholic." Presbyterians formed San Antonio's largest Protestant congregation in 1860, numbering 146 members. Although Bouchu and Bunting's estimates of the Catholic population may have been high, these figures illustrate that San Antonio's Catholic population was far larger than other denominational groups. Census results from 1860 indicated that the aggregate seating capacity for the city's two Catholic parishes, San Fernando and St. Mary's, was thirteen hundred. Protestant churches had a total seating capacity of 680, with 250 in the Methodist church, 150 in the Presbyterian, 150 in the Lutheran, and 130 for the Episcopalians, who met in the Masonic hall. While seating capacities do not reveal weekly attendance, the great disparity between Catholic and Protestant edifices reflects their relative sizes.[36]

Within the local Catholic community, the overwhelming majority of parishioners were Tejanos. Bishop Jean Marie Odin noted in 1853 that there were "7,000 Catholics in the city [San Antonio] and the environs, Mexican for the most part." Two years later, Father Bouchu estimated that, among some nine thousand local Catholics, two to three hundred were English-speaking, seven to eight hundred were German, and the rest were of Mexican descent.[37]

Although Presbyterians were the only Protestant group to commission a minister for work among San Antonio Tejanos during this period, Methodists, Episcopalians, and Baptists all received Tejano members into their congregations. Protestant affiliation among Tejanos was minimal, however. The aforementioned Baptist visitor to San Antonio commented in 1860: "The Mexican population is Catholic. There has never been a convert from Catholicism to Protestantism, except a few cases owing to intermarrying."[38] Continuing Tejano allegiance to Catholicism during the antebellum period resulted from the weakness of Protestant proselytizing efforts, the vigorous Catholic response to the Protestant presence, and the Tejano propensity to retain their Catholic beliefs and practices.

Tejanos and Protestant Denominations at San Antonio

Around the time of U.S. annexation, Reverend John McCullough was commissioned by the Presbyterian Board of Foreign Missions to begin a ministry at San Antonio, with special attention to the Tejano population. McCullough, who had visited San Antonio in 1842 and again in 1844, returned to the city in June 1846 and shortly thereafter began to distribute copies of the New Testament. He also established a Sunday school. Four children of Mexican descent were among the early students, but afterward their parents prevented them from attending. Anglo-American children comprised the student body. McCullough also founded a day school, at the time the only one in the city. His official progress report for 1847 indicated that some fifty students attended the school, "two thirds of whom are Mexican." By 1847, an adobe church was erected, the first Protestant church in San Antonio. Official records indicate that the congregation was exclusively Anglo-American, except for one African-American slave.[39]

After establishing himself at San Antonio, McCullough prompted the Evangelical Society of New York to sponsor Ramón Monsalvage, a converted Spanish monk, in a ministry among local Tejanos. While McCullough's day school apparently did not incite the ire of Catholic leaders, the presence of Monsalvage drew a quick response. McCullough reported in 1848:

> The Catholic bishop has recently been here, devising means to prevent his [Monsalvage's] influence. The priests are afraid to manifest the Catholic spirit towards American Protestants, but have not failed to show the spirit of papacy towards the Spaniard, by warning the Mexicans against him publicly and in private. They have become alarmed for the safety of Catholicism here, and have contracted for the building of a large nunnery and school.[40]

Monsalvage soon left San Antonio for Brownsville. When McCullough's wife died in 1849 and his own health began to fail, he moved to Galveston. After McCullough's departure, the newly founded congregation became inactive. Ensuing efforts by other Presbyterian ministers resulted in a permanent foundation at San Antonio with the arrival of Reverend R. F. Bunting in 1856, but there is no evidence of further ministries among Tejanos during the period under study.[41]

Methodist John Wesley DeVilbiss was the first Protestant minister to hold regular services in San Antonio, beginning monthly visits in the spring of 1845. After U.S. annexation, he moved to San Antonio and began to preach on a weekly basis. He also established a Sunday school and opened a small day school in his home. A series of twelve Methodist ministers served at San Antonio over the following fifteen years. The first Methodist church in the city was completed in 1853.[42]

Although no Methodist ministers were assigned to work exclusively among the Tejano population, a few Tejanos reportedly joined the Methodist Church as early as 1851. Reverend H. G. Horton wrote that in 1859 "the Navarro's [sic], a wealthy and distinguished Mexican family of San Antonio, became interested in Protestant services, and finally fully identified themselves with our church. Two of the young ladies of the Navarro family were teachers of classes of Mexican children in our Sunday-school in San Antonio in 1861 and 1862."[43] In a later account Horton identified these two young women as the daughters of José Antonio Navarro and claimed that Navarro himself converted to Methodism. José Antonio Navarro had only one surviving daughter at the time, however, and his Catholic funeral and burial ten years later cast aspersion on his alleged "conversion."[44] Nonetheless, it is clear that at least some San Antonio Tejanos participated in the local Methodist congregation by 1860.

Both the Episcopalians and Baptists had Tejana members who were married to Anglo-Americans. An Episcopalian clergyman resided at San Antonio as early as 1850, but it was not until 1858 that the organization of a permanent parish was effected under Reverend Lucius H. Jones. The cornerstone for St. Mark's Church was laid the following year. At least two Tejanas who married Anglo-Americans were early members of St. Mark's. Baptists preached at San Antonio as early as 1855, but the First Baptist Church of San Antonio was not organized until early in 1861 under the pastorship of John H. Thurmond. Angela María de Jesús Cooke (nee Navarro), a niece of José Antonio Navarro, was reportedly among the thirteen charter members of this church.[45]

In 1852, Reverend P. F. Zizelmann became the first Lutheran pastor stationed at San Antonio. Zizelmann left after only eight months due to failing health but returned to found St. John's Lutheran Church in 1857. Ulrich Steiner, who was appointed to San Antonio in 1856, was the first Methodist minister assigned to serve the city's German population. By the close of the decade, German services and a German Sunday school were held weekly. As might be expected, there is no evidence of Tejano membership in either of San Antonio's two German congregations during this period.[46]

The dearth of Tejanos in San Antonio's Protestant congregations was caused in part by the lack of funds and personnel for Protestant outreach in the city. Old School Presbyterians were the only Protestant denomination that assigned a minister to work specifically among San Antonio

Tejanos. When John McCullough left after three years in this post, how-ever, no one was sent to replace him. As was previously mentioned, Epis-copalians and Lutherans also had aborted attempts at San Antonio foun-dations before permanent congregations were founded. In both cases, a lack of ministers and financial support were key elements in the decision to abandon early efforts. In 1859, the Rio Grande Conference of the Methodist Church called for a ministerial appointment to San Antonio Tejanos. But the San Antonio appointment was never filled, and the 1860 session of the conference did not list any appointees to Tejano missions. Cumberland Presbyterian minister Amos Stone was sent to San Antonio in 1860 but soon left due to a lack of finances and his disenchantment with city life. Baptist plans to form a congregation at San Antonio were delayed for over two years as four successive ministers declined to accept an appointment there![47]

When Protestant congregations were established, negative attitudes to-ward Catholicism and its Tejano adherents undoubtedly rendered Prot-estant denominations less attractive to potential Tejano members. A few years after U.S. annexation, for example, an article in the *Texas Wes-leyan Banner* stated:

> We have often heard and read of the moral depravity of San Antonio, and that this depravity, instead of being checked and subdued by Romanism, had been encouraged and promoted thereby, especially by the example of the Roman priests, who had been more devoted to the pleasures of the card-table and the billiard room, than to the appropriate duties and func-tions of their high office. Under the influence of a religion of pompous and superstitious ceremonies, with a secular and corrupt priesthood, what other result could be anticipated, but that of the universal depravity of the people.

An 1858 letter to the editor of a San Antonio newspaper criticized the practice of crowning a Sunday school student as May Queen, since U.S. citizens lived "in a republic opposed to Monarchy, and consequently [were] opposed to all kings and queens." But in the course of opposing this Protestant practice, the correspondent taunted May Day practition-ers by associating them with "priest ridden" Catholics.[48]

At times such critiques were directed at specific Tejano devotional practices. One editor of a San Antonio newspaper wrote in 1854 that he had observed an image of the Virgin Mary in a tree near a Tejano *jacal* (hut). Upon inquiry, he discovered that the image was placed there to intercede for rain. He commented that it was "deplorable to think that human beings will place their dependence on an image for the necessaries of life." Amazed, however, he also admitted that "it actually did drizzle a little"![49] As was previously mentioned, Anglo-Americans also criticized Tejano public celebrations on feasts like Christmas and Our Lady of Guadalupe.

Apparently anti-Catholic sentiment motivated a rock-throwing incident in which local youths assaulted students and faculty of St. Mary's Institute, a Catholic school founded at San Antonio in 1852.[50] Such incidents and the attitudes which motivated them undoubtedly deterred Tejanos (and other Catholics) from embracing the denominations of newly arrived Protestants.

Some Protestant ministers did not evidence such negative attitudes, but their efforts were handicapped in other ways. John McCullough, who made the most concerted Protestant outreach effort among San Antonio Tejanos during the antebellum period, wrote in an 1847 report that he was studying Spanish and "hope within a year to be able to speak to them [Tejanos] in their own language."[51] After almost two years of work among San Antonio's Spanish-speaking population, McCullough hoped to develop conversational skills in their language within the coming year!

Like other Protestant ministers, McCullough, in his official reports, expressed an interest in evangelizing Mexico which rivaled his attention to the Tejano population. He wrote from San Antonio in his 1847 report: "I consider this a very important point for communicating with Mexico, and what means I have shall be used for sending Bibles and tracts into that country." When Methodist bishop Pierce visited San Antonio in 1859, he noted the need to begin ministries in Spanish there, as "proper efforts will not only do local good, but will help us to extend the Gospel into the several States of Mexico." Shortly after founding the First Baptist Church of San Antonio, John H. Thurmond wrote that "whenever a permanent and self-sustaining church shall have been established here, then it will become a mighty auxiliary to the spread of the gospel west of this place, and after a while into Mexico." The focus of Protestant attention on Mexico as a more desirable target for proselytizing efforts may have inhibited efforts among Tejanos at San Antonio and elsewhere.[52]

Tejanos and the Catholic Church

Catholic clergy and religious promoted Tejano allegiance to Catholicism, further inhibiting Protestant efforts to attract Tejano members. San Fernando parish had Spanish-speaking priests throughout this period, for example, and Spanish was one language of instruction in the two Catholic schools founded in the city during the 1850s. Spanish Vincentian Miguel Calvo, who was appointed pastor of San Fernando parish in 1840, remained in that post until 1852. Calvo was replaced by Father Claude Marie Dubuis. After Calvo's departure, Bishop Jean Marie Odin made an extended visit to San Antonio because Dubuis did not yet know sufficient Spanish to administer the sacraments to the dying. Odin did not leave the city until a priest who spoke Spanish arrived to assist Dubuis. Dubuis learned Spanish and remained in San Antonio for the rest of the decade. Other priests who could speak Spanish joined him in his apostolic work with the Tejano community.[53] When Dubuis left San Antonio to visit his native France in 1857, a Spanish-speaking priest was secured to replace him during his absence. The Ursuline Academy and St. Mary's Institute, founded at San Antonio in 1851 and 1852 respectively, included Spanish as one language of instruction for their course of study.[54]

Catholic leaders did not minister exclusively to the Tejano community, of course. As early as 1844, Bishop Odin initiated catechism classes at San Antonio in Spanish, English, German, and French; pulpit announcements were made in the same languages in the early 1850s. Priests who spoke these languages, as well as Polish, were available at San Antonio throughout most of the 1850s. English and French were used as languages of instruction in the city's Catholic schools, and German was taught as a course.[55] In 1852, Odin purchased land for the construction of a second parish in the city, principally for English- and German-speaking parishioners. The following year, the *San Antonio Ledger* reported that "the American Catholics desire a building in which the word of God may be constantly expounded in their own tongue." No further action was taken until 1855, however, when Father Dubuis advised Odin that it was "impossible to wait any longer" before beginning construction. When St. Mary's Church was dedicated two years later, San Fernando parish retained Mexican, Italian, French, and Polish Catholics, while the new parish primarily served Irish, Anglo-Americans, and Germans. Polish and German Catholics went on to found their own national parishes in the following decade.[56]

With the removal of English- and German-speaking Catholics to St. Mary's parish in 1857, Tejanos were an overwhelming majority at San Fernando, as the Italian, French, and Polish contingencies were relatively small. The efforts of Catholic priests to offer their ministrations in Tejanos' native tongue at San Fernando, the long-standing Tejano parish, provided a continuity with Tejano religious life that was difficult for Protestant ministers to break.

Besides serving San Fernando's Tejano parishioners in their native tongue, Catholic leaders undoubtedly also communicated to Tejanos their negative perceptions of Protestant religions. Most of the priests and religious in San Antonio during this period were French and received their training in the seminaries and formation houses of post-revolutionary France. Vigilant anti-Protestantism was a consistent element of their approach to the apostolate. Writing to his sister just before leaving for the United States in 1822, future bishop Odin stated: "My dear Benoite, how moving is the pitiful state to which the poor inhabitants of America find themselves reduced! Included in the sole diocese to which I am summoned [the diocese of Louisiana and the Floridas] are millions of idolators and Protestants, everyday these wretched souls fall into hell, and only fifty priests can lend them any assistance." Sister Mary Patrick Joseph wrote from San Antonio in 1852 that Methodists "make regular fools of those who allow themselves to be duped by them" at camp meetings. She went on to add: "Oh! it moves the soul to sorrow and compassion to hear of beings who have immortal souls purchased at such a price, as the precious blood of the Lord Jesus, thus acting and debasing themselves." French priest Emanuel Domenech held similar views of Methodist camp meetings and also wrote that "the greater part of the Methodist, Presbyterian, Baptist, and other ministers of Texas, and the west of the United States, are as ignorant as their disciples." Shortly after his appointment to San Antonio, Father Dubuis founded a society for young people called the Archconfraternity of the Immaculate Heart of Mary; one purpose of this organization was to form "a strong barrier both against Protestantism and against moral laxity." On at least one occasion the attitude of Catholic clergy toward Protestants led to public debate. This occurred in 1858, when a visiting priest reportedly labeled preachers from a recent Methodist revival meeting in the city "false teachers," drawing Protestant response in the secular press.[57]

Catholic leaders also warned their members about public and Protestant sectarian schools, which they claimed were established specifically to oppose Catholic education. After St. Mary's Institute opened at San Antonio in 1852, Bishop Odin expressed his confidence that it would be "a powerful bulwark against the efforts of Protestantism." Father Dubuis declared that one purpose of the archconfraternity he founded was to fight "against the efforts of the public schools." Although he wrote that he would not declaim the public schools from the pulpit, he also stated that "it is in the families themselves that we will strengthen our Catholics in the true sentiments that they should hold in educating their children." While public schools had no denominational attachment, Dubuis obviously thought they were sufficiently under the control of Protestant or secular leaders to pose a danger for his parishioners.[58]

The stern warnings given by Catholic leaders about Protestant influences apparently had some effect on San Antonio Tejanos. As was previously mentioned, John McCullough's Sunday school initially had four Tejano students, but later their parents prevented them from attending. According to McCullough, the apostolic efforts of Ramón Monsalvage were also completely stymied by a vigorous Catholic response. Apparently McCullough's assessment was accurate. In an 1849 letter Bishop Odin stated:

> The Bible Society of New York is going to great lengths to poison the minds of the poor Mexicans still living in Texas. It is sending with its ministers all the Spanish apostles it can procure, paying them enormous salaries in order to have them give a free education to all children of Mexican origin. When, last September, I visited San Antonio, I found, to my regret, several schools supported by funds from the Bible Society . . . So I borrowed 20,000 francs for the building of two schools.[59]

At times, Catholic priests and religious inadvertently supported negative Protestant perceptions of Tejano religious practice. For instance, they decried Tejano Catholicism as lax and inadequate. Father Domenech described the population of Mexican descent as lacking instruction in the faith, claiming that "the religion of the great majority is very superficial, the great truths of the faith are overlooked, and the most essential duties of a Christian neglected." Irish Ursuline sister Mary Augustine Joseph wrote from San Antonio in 1852 that "we are most anxious to speak Spanish, so as to be able to instruct these poor people, and to preserve the children from the danger of imitating the bad example of their parents." Bishop Odin echoed these sentiments in arguing that Catholic education was needed at San Antonio "to regenerate the poor Mexican population." Such perceptions at times led to open conflict, as in 1858 when members of the Mexican-Texan Society, a literary group for young men, were reportedly "denounced from the pulpit by one of the Catholic clergymen of this city [San Antonio], as corrupt and atheistical."[60]

Foreign clergy were also unfamiliar with some Tejano ritual practices. One such practice surrounded funeral processions for deceased infants. Children dressed in white, fiddlers playing, gun salutes, and the Tejano community accompanied these processions. These festive elements were signs of the community's confidence that the deceased infant was experiencing the joy of heaven, since in Catholic belief a baptized child who dies is sinless and therefore goes directly to heaven. When Father Dubuis participated in one of these processions shortly after being assigned to San Antonio, it put his "gravity to the test" as he was "unaccustomed to such a display."[61]

Despite such responses and criticisms, Dubuis and other Catholic clergy continued to participate in Tejano processions like this child's funeral. They presided over religious services for feasts that were significant to the local Tejano community, such as Our Lady of Guadalupe, San Juan, San Fernando, San Antonio, San Pedro, and Christmas Eve. The foreign clergy's participation in Tejano feasts and processions suggests that they saw them as valuable public manifestations of Tejano allegiance to Catholicism. Their objective of preserving Tejano Catholic loyalties coalesced with Tejano efforts to continue practicing their Mexican Catholic traditions.

SAN ANTONIO TEJANOS AND
THE SHIFTING POLITICAL SCENE

Tejano political influence, which had declined dramatically after Texas independence, was depleted further after U.S. annexation. Only two San Antonio Tejanos were elected to the state legislature from 1845 to 1860: José Antonio Navarro was a representative in the Senate (1846–1848) and his son Angel served in the House of Representatives (1857–1860). There were no Tejano mayors or representatives in the U.S. Congress during these years. Five of the eight city-council members were Tejanos in 1845, but in 1860 not a single Tejano served in that capacity. Tejano electees to the city council accounted for 24.2 percent of the total during these fifteen years, while they were 73.2 percent during the period of the Texas Republic.[62]

The case of Juan Seguín, the last Tejano mayor during the period under study, illustrates the loss of Tejano political power at San Antonio during these years. Seguín resigned the mayoral office when he was forced out of Texas by Anglo-American threats of violence in 1842. After the U.S. war with Mexico, he returned and was elected justice of the peace in 1852 and 1854. He was also president of his electoral precinct and was influential in the founding of the local Democratic Party. But the former mayor and national senator never regained these more influential offices after his return from exile.[63]

While Tejano representation on the San Antonio city council and other elected bodies declined after U.S. annexation, Tejanos continued to comprise a significant number of voters. The voting power of Anglo-Americans, Germans, and other groups also increased, but Tejano votes remained an important bloc in elections at San Antonio.[64] Tejano response to shifting political realities is elucidated in their voting patterns and their stance on issues like U.S. expansion and slavery.

Tejanos and U.S. Expansion

The first issues of import during this period were U.S. annexation and the war with Mexico. In both cases, Tejano support of U.S. aspirations was minimal at best. Even San Antonio Tejanos who had united with Anglo-Americans in forming the Texas Republic opposed annexation. Francisco Antonio Ruiz, the mayor of San Antonio during the Texas Revolution, was against Texas' entry into the Union. He opined that those who had participated in the Texas Revolution should decide the issue of annexation. When Texas became a state, he chose to live with the Native Americans on the frontier rather than submit to U.S. rule. Writing from his exile in Mexico, Juan Seguín told Texas president Anson Jones shortly before U.S. annexation: "I know that the true happiness of Texas, according to the general direction its question has taken, consists in preserving its independence from any other power other than Mexico."[65]

Some San Antonio Tejanos obviously feared undesirable consequences from Texas statehood. When war broke out with Mexico just months after annexation, Colonel William Selby Harney issued a proclamation at San Antonio which confirmed the validity of such fears: "Hostilities having been commenced by Mexico against the United States, it becomes necessary that all who owe allegiance to the government of Mexico, should leave the state of Texas without delay. If any such, therefore, are found on the east side of the Rio Grande, after the 5th inst., they will be treated as enemies to the United States." A contemporary witness testified that Harney even threatened to hang Anglo-American merchants who traded with Mexican citizens. Harney's orders were rescinded by General John E. Wool because they violated a treaty between the United States and Mexico, but not until almost four months later. In the interim, "many Mexican inhabitants had left the city and had crossed to the other side of the Rio Grande in order not to live in the land of the enemy of their nation during the war between their compatriots and the hated Yankees."[66]

While directed at Mexican citizens and not Tejanos, apparently the anti-Mexican attitude reflected in this proclamation affected the Tejano community. Some contemporary commentators claimed that Tejanos welcomed American rule because the U.S. Army offered them protection from the Native Americans, but others observed a more conflictive relationship between Tejanos and the advancing army. Sarah L. French, who moved to San Antonio in 1846, later recalled that local Tejanos were "insulted and angered" by U.S. troops who sang anti-Mexican verses to the tune of "The Maid of Monterrey," a popular Mexican song.[67]

The Tejano viewpoint on the Mexican War is expressed by their participation in the armed forces. While Texas had some six thousand volunteers in the U.S. forces, only twenty soldiers with Spanish surnames were among the U.S. ranks. This figure is all the more striking when compared to the significant participation of Tejanos in the Texas Revolution a decade earlier; at least 140 Tejanos received land grants as veterans from that conflict.[68] Clearly, Tejano sentiments were not supportive of an effort which, following so quickly upon the annexation of Texas, must have seemed an act of U.S. aggression against their cultural motherland.

The Know Nothing Party in San Antonio

The Know Nothing, or American, Party emerged in the United States as European immigration increased in the early part of the nineteenth century. Perceiving the increased immigrant presence as a threat, especially the influx of Catholics who allegedly owed their first allegiance to the pope, Know Nothings adopted an anti-immigrant, anti-Catholic stance. They often operated in secret and acquired the Know Nothing label from members' retort that they "knew nothing" when questioned by outsiders about the party and its activities.[69]

Know Nothings achieved their first Texas victory in the San Antonio municipal elections of December 1854, gaining control of the mayoral office and the city council. Apparently Know Nothing supporters adhered to the practice of secrecy before these elections, as the presence of Know Nothing candidates was not mentioned in the local press. The first two legislative actions of the newly elected council, both promulgated within a week after they took office, undoubtedly revealed the political leanings of the electees, however. They repealed a law requiring the city secretary to translate ordinances and other matters into Spanish and French and, as was previously mentioned, banned *fandangos*.[70]

After the 1854 city elections, and perhaps in response to actions of the new city council, the presence of the Know Nothing Party in the city became the major issue for statewide elections the following year. Three newspapers began publication at San Antonio between the 1854 Know Nothing victory and the state canvass of August 1855. Two of these, the *San Antonio Herald* and *The Sentinel,* supported the Know Nothing Party. The other was a Spanish publication, *El Bejareño.* This paper was owned and edited by a Frenchman and an Anglo-American and encouraged its readership to vote for Democratic candidates.

As election day drew near, the Know Nothing press reported that "a Catholic priest has been among the Mexican ranches using his influence to induce the people to vote against the American party." On July 7 at San Antonio, John A. Wilcox gave a speech, which was subsequently published in *The Sentinel.* Perhaps fearing an anti–Know Nothing Tejano bloc vote, Wilcox addressed himself to his "Mexican friends," claiming that "the American party has been misrepresented to you" and that it would "defend and maintain all of your vested rights." He then added:

> One more word to you Mexican gentlemen: whenever the skulking demagogue comes among you, and charges the American party with a design to desecrate your Church, or interrupt you in the slightest degree, in the worship of your God as it best suits you, tell him for me, he lies; that the united valor of Americans and Mexicans achieved the liberty and independence of Texas; that you were friends in the dark struggles of the country, and friends in peace; and that you have no fears from American gentlemen.[71]

Reports in the Know Nothing press drew forceful response from the *San Antonio Ledger* and *El Bejareño.* The *Ledger* defended San Antonio's Catholic clergy against Know Nothing accusations and argued that Tejano supporters of the Democratic Party were outstanding citizens: "The citizens of Spanish origin, both native and adopted, have . . . shown themselves an industrious, peaceable, and worthy class." The Democratic press also accused Know Nothings of prejudice against Catholics and of lying to Tejanos about this prejudice in order to win votes.[72]

In response to Know Nothing opposition, the Democratic Party of Béxar County sustained a vigorous organizing effort during the 1855 campaign. At mass meetings in San Antonio on June 23 and July 3, local Democrats condemned the Know Nothing Party as opposed to the Constitution, the Declaration of Independence, and the spirit of U.S. laws and institutions. They also vowed to support candidates only if they made public denouncements of secret political organizations.[73]

Spanish-speaking San Antonians held a series of "Democratic Meetings of Mexican-Texan Citizens of Béxar County." They convened the first of these meetings on June 28. Participants adopted the resolutions of the Béxar County Democrat meeting five days earlier, condemned the Know Nothings as intolerant and anti-Catholic, and declared that "as children of Texas, members of the Catholic Church, and citizens of the United States, we will always oppose all secret political associations." Tejanos also stated that, as Catholic citizens, they wanted no more nor less than the rights of all other citizens and accused Know Nothings of desiring to make them "political slaves" solely because they chose "to worship God according to the dictates of our conscience and the ritual of our ancestors." Claiming to be the true native citizens of Texas, Tejanos also declared:

> Our sole sentiment and desire is to be witnesses of the honor, glory, and prosperity of the country in which we were born, and the land of our affections; at the same time we contrast our obedience to the law, our interest in the well being of Texas, with that of those who attempt to take away our imprescriptible rights, and who, for the most part, are strangers to this land, with four years, or less, of residence in our State.[74]

At a following meeting on July 12, Tejanos reinforced their intention to unite with the Democratic Party. Several influential Tejanos made speeches to this effect. An open letter to Tejanos by José Antonio Navarro was also read and subsequently published in both the English and Spanish press. Navarro reminded Tejanos that their Hispanic-Mexican ancestors founded their city and built the church in which they worshipped God. Citing Know Nothing anti-Catholic attitudes, he also reminded his hearers that "the Mexico-Texans are Catholics, and should be proud of the faith of their ancestors, and defend it inch by inch against such infamous aggressors." He urged them not to let others abuse their "Hispanic-Mexican generosity" and loyalty, nor to make them "traitors" to their political party and the Catholic faith they inherited from their ancestors.[75]

The staunch defense of their Catholic heritage against Know Nothing attacks undoubtedly united Tejano sentiments with those of their Catholic clergy. At the outset of Texas' Know Nothing controversies in 1854, Bishop Odin wrote from Galveston: "God, I hope, will thwart their [the Know Nothings'] sinister projects. This unfortunate society already produces a very sad effect on minds. It embitters souls and completely divides our small community." In a letter to his parents, Father Dubuis reportedly wrote during an 1857 drought that "God seems to desire the chastisement of this country for the crimes committed during the Know Nothing persecutions." A biographer of Dubuis states that the San Antonio curate gave a "public discourse" on the Know Nothing movement "in which the nature of its errors was exposed charitably and in a scholarly way."[76] The moral support of Catholic clergy could easily have reinforced Tejano opposition to the Know Nothing Party.

Democrats won the 1855 state elections. Among Béxar County voters, Democratic candidates bested their Know Nothing opponents by almost three to one. This victory initiated the decline of Know Nothing Party influence in Texas, although some individual members continued in political life and accusations of Know Nothing allegiances continued to be leveled during political campaigns.[77]

The Democrats' success at San Antonio was followed by a barrage of protest from the defeated Know Nothings. One newspaper report stated: "The worst passions and the silliest fears of the deluded horde of Mexican peones [sic] who populate to such a dangerous extent the county of Béxar, have been appealed to by a squad of black robed villains, who exercise over the minds of their miserable followers a despotism more absolute than that of any Turkish nobleman over those who people his seraglio." Other editorials in the San Antonio press echoed this interpretation of Béxar County election results and even claimed that Tejanos, "being native American Mexicans, if left to themselves, would have preferred the American side of the question." John A. Wilcox wrote from San Antonio that the city's Catholic clergy threatened with damnation anyone who voted for the American ticket, thus attributing the Know Nothing defeat in part to the conscripted votes of Tejano Catholics.[78]

Know Nothing accusations were contested by San Antonio's pro-Democratic newspapers. These journals defended the Catholic clergy by stating that Tejano and other Catholic votes were not cast under duress, but reflected sentiments against a political party which sought to bar Catholics from the full rights of citizenship.[79]

While this election was obviously contested between two opposing camps, both sides evidenced striking agreement in identifying the Tejano population as staunch Catholics and native Texans. In his speech supporting the American Party, John A. Wilcox appealed to Tejano voters by promising that Know Nothings would protect their rights of citizenship and respect their Catholic faith. Wilcox also praised these native-born inhabitants of Texas for aligning with Anglo-Americans in the struggle for Texas independence. At the same time, Know Nothing allegations centered on Tejano voters' corruption because they were enslaved to the dictates of their clergy.

The Democratic press defended their supporters on precisely these points, arguing that native-born Tejanos were outstanding citizens and that Tejano and other Catholic votes were cast without undue clerical influence. They also accused Know Nothings of anti-Catholic bias against Tejanos and their co-religionists.

Tejanos themselves perceived the election as one in which the Catholic faith they had received from their ancestors had to be protected from attack. They also defended their rights as the true native citizens of Texas, most Know Nothing adherents having been in the state only a short time.

The Slavery Issue

After Know Nothings were removed from the city council in the 1855 municipal elections, slavery and secession became the central issues in San Antonio politics. Like their counterparts in the North, Southern Catholics tended to adopt the local point of view on these issues. Jean Marie Odin, bishop of Galveston until 1861 when he was named archbishop of New Orleans, typified the stance of Southern Catholic leaders. Before Odin was assigned to Texas, he served from 1822 to 1840 with his Vincentian community in Missouri and Arkansas. The Vincentians had slaves, and Odin seemed to accept slavery as a fact of life. In the first of his annual Lenten pastoral letters as archbishop of New Orleans, he invited the faithful to pray for the success of the Confederacy: "Although we look with perfect confidence on the result of this conflict [the Civil War] in which justice is on our side, we ought not to cease raising our supplicant hands to heaven." Even after Union forces occupied New Orleans, Odin was bold enough to place St. Rose of Lima parish under interdict and publicly suspend the local pastor, Reverend Claudius Pascal Maistre, "a Unionist and an abolitionist who incited Negroes against the whites." [80] Apparently Odin was more concerned about upsetting the sensibilities of his Southern Catholic faithful than risking reprisal from occupying Union forces.

San Antonio Tejanos did not embrace the Southern approach to slavery as readily as their clergy and co-religionists in Texas. While some Tejanos purchased slaves during Spanish and Mexican rule, a far greater number secured the labor of servants under the peonage system. Although sometimes compared to slaves in the Southern United States, peons differed from Southern slaves in that they were not legally slaves, did not inherit their condition, were not all of the same race, and in theory could upgrade their social status by paying off their debt. The Mexican government outlawed slavery, although Tejano officials supported Anglo-American efforts to circumvent these laws. But their actions stemmed primarily from Tejano attempts to induce Anglo-American immigration, not from widespread Tejano acceptance of slavery as an inherited, racially determined, and irreversible condition.[81]

After U.S. annexation, many Anglo-Americans perceived Tejanos as being staunchly antislavery in their sentiments. Abolitionist Frederick Law Olmsted, who visited San Antonio in 1854, wrote that local Tejanos "consult freely with negroes, making no distinction from pride or race. A few, of old Spanish blood, have purchased negro servants, but most of them regard slavery with abhorrence . . . They are regarded by slaveholders with great contempt and suspicion, for their intimacy with slaves." Anglo-Americans at Seguin and Austin drove citizens of Mexican heritage out of their area in 1854 and later out of Colorado and Matagorda counties. One justification they offered for their actions was that Tejanos abetted the escape of slaves. A meeting was held in San Antonio on August 29, 1854, to provide "additional guarantees" for protecting slave property, principally by offering a five-hundred-dollar reward for information leading to the conviction of anyone assisting in a slave escape. San Antonio residents were warned by the local press to beware of Tejanos in the city who had recently been run out of Seguin because of slave escapes there.[82]

Accusations of Tejano attempts to abet slave escapes continued to appear with some regularity in the San Antonio press during the 1850s. In a few instances, Tejanos were applauded in Texas newspapers for returning runaway slaves to their masters, but they reportedly assisted escaped slaves with far greater frequency. A San Antonio Herald correspondent wrote in 1858: "We know that they [Tejanos] are of mixed blood themselves, low and degraded, and consort with the negro on terms of equality . . . How many instances have occurred of Mexicans persuading or guiding slaves away to Mexico, which have never been published? . . . this population are enemies of slavery, and are constantly aiding the escape of our negroes."[83]

Although slavery was legal under U.S. rule, Tejanos owned relatively few slaves. The 1860 census reveals that only nineteen slaves had Spanish-surnamed owners at San Antonio; this figure represented only 3.2 percent of the 591 San Antonio slaves reported.[84] While these figures reflect the diminished economic status of San Antonio Tejanos, they also suggest that many Tejanos persisted in the local attitude toward slavery despite the laws introduced under U.S. rule.

CHANGE IN SAN ANTONIO: ANGLO-AMERICAN
AND TEJANO PERSPECTIVES

Political changes in San Antonio, along with its transformation into a city of multiple nationalities and religious denominations, were accompanied by Anglo-American and Tejano attempts to interpret these changes. Anglo-Americans tended to interpret their presence in San Antonio as initiating an era of progress; Tejanos emphasized their contributions to San Antonio history before Anglo-Americans had ever arrived, and corrected notions that the Anglo-American presence brought only peace and prosperity to the city.

In 1851, Francis Baylies published a book about General Wool's campaign during the Mexican War. Baylies applauded the Franciscans who worked in the San Antonio missions during the eighteenth century, although he incorrectly identified them as Jesuits. He then added:

> After the expulsion of the Jesuits [sic], everything went to decay. Agriculture, learning, the mechanic arts, shared the common fate; and when the banners of the United States were unfurled in these distant and desolate places, the descendants of the noble and chivalric Castilians had sunk to the level, perhaps beneath it, of the aboriginal savages; but it is to be hoped that the advent of the Saxo-Norman may brighten, in some degree, the faded splendor of the race which has fallen.[85]

Similar views of Tejano demise followed by Anglo-American progress appeared in the San Antonio press. Even Anglo-Americans who "defended" the Tejano population against public criticism ascribed to the view that Tejanos were victims of a morally and intellectually impoverished heritage, and that Anglo-American influence offered a means to redeem that heritage. Concerned that a *San Antonio Ledger* article attacking the character of local Tejanos might discourage further Anglo-American and European immigration to the city, for example, a correspondent responded in another local newspaper:

> It is lamentably true that our Mexican population, generally, do not occupy as high a position in the scale of morality and intelligence as is desirable; yet every one who knows their former condition, and will take into consideration their former mode of life, as well as the demoralizing effect of the Government under which they lived previous to the establishment of

the Texas Republic, must admit that they are reforming as rapidly as could have been expected, under the circumstances by which they have been surrounded.[86]

Contemporary Tejano writers objected to Anglo-American renderings of their history. José Antonio Navarro wrote a response to a *San Antonio Ledger* account of local history, in which the *Ledger* claimed that "for one hundred years after the expedition of Alonzo de León, the history of San Antonio, as well as of all Texas, is but the dreary register of petty territorial squabbles, barbarous feuds and feats of monkish strategy." According to this article, it was not until the arrival of Anglo-Americans that San Antonio "was baptized in the blood of heroism personified, and consecrated Liberty and imperishable renown."[87]

Navarro's initial response was published in December 1853 and began by stating: "In the issue of the San Antonio Ledger of date the 17th [*sic*] of September last, I perused a historical sketch of the foundation and early events of the City of San Antonio de Béxar. Having been an eye witness of nearly all the occurrences therein detailed, I cannot forbear the temptation to correct many substantial errors contained in such narration." His account went on to describe Mexico's struggle for independence from Spain, particularly the valor of local Tejanos during battles between revolutionaries and royalist forces in 1813. Navarro's contention was that San Antonio had an honorable citizenry with aspirations for a free system of government long before Anglo-Americans arrived and that these "noble citizens of Béxar sacrificed their lives and fortunes and performed prodigies of valor" in the cause of Mexican independence.[88]

Four years later, Navarro published another narrative in three installments of the *Ledger,* in which he described the 1811 efforts for independence by San Antonio de Béxar citizens. One purpose of this account was so that "our American people may know how unworthily some amongst us, under mean and miserable pretexts, seek to extirpate from this classic soil its legitimate lords, the descendants of those men who, half a century ago, poured forth their blood in the conquest of that liberty of which we now make our boast." At the conclusion of these three installments, Navarro stated:

To complete the picture of their [the San Antonio martyrs for Mexican independence] misfortunes, their few descendants yet surviving in San Antonio, are disappearing, the victims of assassination, in sight of a people which claims the blazon of justice and grandeur as theirs "par excellence" ... Heaven grant that the perusal of these historical fragments may stir the hearts of the generous, and induce them to treat with more indulgence this race of men who, legitimate lords of this country, lost it with their lives and their hopes in following on the traces of the very people who now enjoy it in the midst of peace and abundance.[89]

A similar defense appeared in *El Correo* during July of 1858. Previously another local newspaper, the *Texan,* had alleged that San Antonio Tejanos were disgruntled with recent violent outrages committed against Tejano cartmen. Cartmen were laborers who transported goods. Tejanos engaged in this work were attacked by their competitors in retaliation for underbidding them. According to the *Texan,* a number of San Antonio Tejanos planned to relocate in Mexico because of these attacks. The *Correo* response to this claim defended Tejano citizenship rights "in this country which witnessed their birth and for which they and their ancestors shed their blood and sacrificed their fortunes."[90]

Other Tejano statements challenged the thesis that the Anglo-American presence had brought only prosperity to the area. Juan Seguín published his memoirs in 1858. As was previously mentioned, Seguín returned to San Antonio and local politics after the Mexican War. His memoirs were motivated by a desire to vindicate his name after his departure from Texas in 1842. Nonetheless, Seguín also outlined Tejano contributions to Texas independence and the Republic of Texas and opined that the increased presence of Anglo-Americans was not a pure boon of progress for Tejanos, but in fact made him (and others) "a foreigner in my native land."[91]

Tejano legends recalled the heroism of early settlers in the San Antonio area. Lifelong San Antonio resident Antonio Menchaca related two of these legends to Charles Merritt Barnes. One was about the origin of the San Antonio River, which local residents claimed had miraculously sprung from the earth in response to the fervent prayers of Venerable Antonio Margil de Jesús, a Franciscan missionary who founded San Antonio's Mission San José y San Miguel de Aguayo in 1720. Another legend narrated a miraculous escape from Native American attack by Venerable Margil and his companions, whose prayers for deliverance were answered when their attackers were changed into harmless deer. Such legends recounted that the origin of San Antonio preceded the Anglo-American presence by over a century and that divine aid had blessed the efforts of Tejanos' ancestors who founded the settlement.[92]

SUMMARY: EMERGING TEJANO ETHNICITY

The presence of other nationalities, Protestant denominations, and a new political order in San Antonio after U.S. annexation served to sharpen rather than diminish Tejano identification with their cultural and religious heritage. For Tejanos, one consequence of San Antonio's increasing ethnic diversity was that their Mexican heritage was no longer the only cultural heritage of the city. During the years of the Texas Republic, Anglo-Americans exercised considerable political and economic influence in the city. But Tejano public celebrations and forms of entertainment prevailed, and Tejanos even attempted to incorporate Anglo-Americans and others into their festivities. After U.S. annexation, San Antonio celebrations included parades and ceremonies for U.S. and Texas Independence days, Washington's birthday, Thanksgiving, the Protestant festivities of May Day, and the German commemoration of Schiller's birthday. The variety of languages used in judicial proceedings and other local activities was another visible sign that San Antonio was no longer a city with one clearly predominate culture. As other nationality groups became more visible in San Antonio, Tejanos' cultural heritage was less an identifying mark of their city and more a mark of their cultural group as differentiated from others within the city.

Despite Anglo-American inducements to accept U.S. holidays as universal and despite criticisms of their religious practices, Tejanos continued to celebrate enthusiastically the principal feasts of their Mexican Catholic heritage. Tejano devotion included practices such as gun salutes, cannonading, bell ringing, processions, Christmas vigil lights on their homes, and riding horses through the streets on the feast of San Juan and other saint days. As expressions of Tejanos' religious and cultural background, these practices were a public manifestation of their continuing allegiance to their ancestral heritage.

Tejanos also sought to defend the use of Spanish in public schools and to overcome a series of legislative attempts to ban *fandangos*. These actions further illustrate their resistance to efforts that would curtail or suppress their language or culture.

While some evidence suggests Tejanos' mingling with Anglo-Americans and Germans in social activities, this mingling was usually limited to the more prominent classes, and then only on an occasional basis. The most striking instances of cohesive relations occurred in marriages between wealthy Tejanas and Anglo-Americans, usually resulting in their children's identification with the ethnic group of their Anglo-

American fathers. But these instances were infrequent, accounting for less than 5 percent of Tejana marriages from 1837 to 1860. However, the Anglo-American presence resulted in some loss of Tejano identity when social mingling led to mixed marriages.

Conflicts over particular issues and incidents, along with occasional instances of cohesion, do not constitute the general pattern of Tejano and Anglo-American relations during this period. Unlike the period of the Texas Republic, after U.S. annexation the feast of Our Lady of Guadalupe and other public festivities did not tend to be occasions in which Anglo-Americans (and others) were incorporated into the life of the local Tejano community. Instead, the various groups tended to remain separate from one another, as newcomers from outside the Tejano community could now attend activities of their own. Tejano festivities thence became occasions in which the Tejano community was separated from other nationality groups, thus sharpening the sense that their Mexican Catholic celebrations distinguished them from others. This sense of their own heritage as distinct from that of Anglo-Americans and others is the most critical element of San Antonio Tejanos' response to the advent of ethnic diversity in their city after U.S. annexation.

Protestant and Catholic activity in the city reinforced the social distance between ethnic groups, as Protestants established English- and German-speaking congregations, and Catholics began to form national parishes along ethnic lines. Furthermore, none of the six Protestant congregations founded at San Antonio before 1860 attracted significant Tejano participation. Four Tejanos attended the Sunday school started by John McCullough, but their parents later induced them to desist from going. Several others were students in the day school McCullough founded, but official membership lists indicate that neither these students nor their families joined the Presbyterian Church during the antebellum period. There are some claims of Tejano conversions to Methodism, although the identity of these converts is uncertain. Early members of the Episcopalian and Baptist churches included Tejanas who had married Anglo-American Protestants. Thus, of the three Protestant denominations that attracted Tejano members who endured beyond the antebellum period, at least two did so through mixed marriages, not Protestant ministerial efforts. This suggests that Tejano loyalties remained staunchly Catholic, except in a few isolated cases of mixed marriage which led to Tejana acceptance of their husbands' denominational affiliation.

Several factors account for Tejano retention of their Catholic allegiance. One is the weakness of Protestant initiatives among Tejanos, which were hampered by a lack of personnel and finances, the negative attitudes of some Protestants toward Tejanos and Catholics in general, and the tendency of some Protestant ministers to focus their attention beyond the Tejano community to Mexico. John McCullough, the lone Anglo-American Protestant minister sent to work specifically among San Antonio Tejanos during this period, was deficient in Spanish language ability. Protestant denominations also failed to attract Tejano converts because Catholic ministries were available in Spanish for the Tejano community, and Catholic clergy issued stern warnings about the dangers of Protestant churches and schools. The participation of Catholic priests in Tejano processions and feasts was of particular importance; their presence linked the newly arrived Catholic leadership with the native San Antonians' traditional Mexican Catholic practices. Continuing Tejano affiliation at San Fernando parish also provided a symbolic link with the heritage of their Catholic ancestors. This symbolic link buttressed Tejano allegiance to Catholicism during these years when emerging Protestant congregations tested that allegiance by offering a variety of denominational alternatives.

In the political sphere, Tejanos opposed U.S. annexation, the Mexican War, and slavery, apparently valuing regional autonomy, their Mexican sympathies, and the local approach with regard to slavery more than Anglo-American laws and aspirations. In the heated electoral debates at San Antonio in 1855, Know Nothings, Democrats, and Tejanos themselves consistently identified the Tejano community as native Texans who were staunchly Catholic. This discourse undoubtedly sharpened Tejano identity, especially when local residents formed their first Tejano political organization, publicly defended their Catholic allegiance, and claimed the status of being San Antonio's true native-born citizens. In embracing their Catholic background and the heritage of their ancestors who had founded and developed San Antonio, Tejanos differentiated themselves from Anglo-Americans and other immigrants to their city. They also reinforced their loyalty to their religious and cultural heritage.

The legacy of their Mexican heritage was no longer the only source of Tejano pride. When Anglo-Americans proffered their versions of San Antonio history, they contrasted Tejano decline with Anglo-American progress, often as a justification for U.S. expansion. Tejanos countered by recalling the outstanding achievements of their ancestors in establishing San Antonio and sacrificing their lives for its independence. They also outlined the Tejano suffering caused by Anglo-American "progress." Through legends Tejanos recalled the heroic ventures of their ancestors during the time of San Antonio's founding. Like some Anglo-Americans, they also claimed that divine intervention aided their ancestors' efforts. Their defense against the Know Nothings was based in part on Tejanos' being native-born Texans and descendants of San Antonio's founders, while Know Nothings were recent arrivals to the area. Francisco Antonio Ruiz argued that the issue of U.S. annexation should be decided by Tejanos and others who had participated in the Texas Revolution, not by newcomers to Texas. In these statements, native San Antonians drew on the Tejano history of their city, not their Mexican heritage, in defending themselves against Anglo-American newcomers.

Politically, Tejanos had been separated from Mexico for a decade. During the period of the Texas Republic, they expressed in various ways their identity as a people of Mexican Catholic heritage who were adapting to life among Anglo-Americans. After U.S. annexation, however, Tejanos claimed the status of native Texas citizens and identified themselves as the descendants of a people who had founded San Antonio, developed it, sacrificed their lives for it, and therefore retained legitimate claims for respect as a people within it, despite the Anglo-American takeover. While not denying their Mexican heritage, this view of their history distinguished San Antonio Tejanos from their counterparts still in Mexico. It represented an initial step in the development of a distinct Tejano ethnic identity within a culturally and religiously pluralistic milieu, although that identity continued to retain elements of their Mexican Catholic roots.

†

FIVE

SAN ANTONIO TEJANOS AND UNITED STATES EXPANSION: A STUDY OF RELIGION AND ETHNICITY

In his study of European immigrants to the United States, Oscar Handlin claimed that "the newcomers were on the way toward being Americans almost before they stepped off the boat, because their own experience of displacement had already introduced them to what was essential in the situation of Americans." [1] Handlin argued that the experience of being uprooted from their homes, crossing the ocean, and beginning anew predisposed European immigrants to accept a new way of life in the United States. While his work drew attention to the plight of immigrants as an uprooted people, it also assumed that they would inevitably assimilate into U.S. society.

In a frequently cited passage, Handlin also stated: "Once I thought to write a history of the immigrants in America. Then I discovered that the immigrants *were* American history." [2] Given such a claim, it is not surprising that writers on religion and ethnicity in U.S. society have focused significant attention on the experience of European immigrants who, as Handlin suggests, were initiated into this society after the traumatic experience of being uprooted from their homeland and crossing the ocean.

Tejanos were not immigrants to the United States but residents of the Mexican frontier who were incorporated through U.S. territorial expansion. The Tejano experience provides a different perspective for the study of religion and ethnicity in American life, particularly for examining the issues of assimilation and pluralism.

THE SAN ANTONIO TEJANO EXPERIENCE
AND ASSIMILATION

The San Antonio Tejano experience during the years under consideration in this study differs from that of European immigrants on a number of points. These differences demonstrate that Tejanos were less inclined toward assimilation in American life than many European immigrants. To begin with, as theorists like Handlin have argued, immigrants who crossed the ocean made a decisive break with their past. The traumatic experience of being uprooted from their homelands and crossing the ocean influenced their response to the U.S. milieu. Leaving their ancestral homelands behind disposed them to accept the ways and identity of their adopted homeland. The restrictive immigration legislation of the 1920s further severed ties to Europe by discontinuing the flow of first-generation immigrants who could have reinforced language and culture. This augmented the immigrants' break with their homelands and enhanced the assimilation process.[3]

Tejanos, however, were not in a new land. Their incorporation into the United States did not entail a decisive break with their past, as they continued to reside in their own place of birth and in proximity to Mexico. Even after Texas independence removed Tejanos from Mexican political jurisdiction, some of them retired to Mexico during times of battle and conflict and returned to Texas when hostilities subsided. Census tracts show that Mexicans from south of the Rio Grande continued to cross the border and settle at San Antonio. Tejano contact with their former nation and its people was thus not extensively hampered when Texas severed political ties with Mexico. Examining census records from 1836 to 1986, Terry G. Jordan has shown that the pattern of cultural contact between Tejanos and Mexicans continues today. In Jordan's words:

> Mexicans entering Texas find a familiar place . . . The century and a half of Hispanic rule is the basis of much of the sense of familiarity, providing not just toponyms and a venerable population base upon which to build, but also the unexpressed or even subconscious belief that "this land is rightfully ours." In immigration, no ocean is crossed, and the ancestral homeland remains adjacent, permitting close cultural ties. Too, the volume and duration of Mexican immigration are unrivaled by other ethnic groups and provide continual cultural reinforcement. For all these reasons, Hispanic ethnicity remains vital and acculturation is retarded.[4]

While many descendants of European immigrants made a decisive break with the homelands of their ancestors, Tejanos have retained ties to their Mexican roots because of Mexico's proximity, continuing immigration, and their long-standing history as Texan residents of Mexican descent.

Tejanos also differ from European immigrants in that their incorporation into the United States resulted in economic and political losses rather than gains. Many first-generation European immigrants remained poor, of course, and their influence on U.S. political life was not always that significant. But most immigrants undoubtedly saw themselves as improving their lot in moving to the United States, escaping famines, poverty, revolutions, military conscription, and other undesirable situations. For many, social mobility and the opportunity to start anew in the United States further enhanced the process of assimilation.[5]

In the case of Tejanos, however, the rise of Anglo-American influence was accompanied by a corresponding decline in their status, wealth, and political control. While economic conditions at San Antonio de Béxar were often depressed during the Mexican period, a Tejano elite led trade efforts of which they were the primary beneficiaries. After Texas independence, Anglo-Americans made significant inroads into these mercantile efforts and far outdistanced Tejano buyers in land speculation. Some travelers to San Antonio continued to note the existence of a Tejano elite in the city even after U.S. annexation, but such references were far less frequent than in the period of the Texas Republic. The diminishment of the Tejano elite is confirmed by census tracts, which indicate a significant downward trend in Tejano land holdings and a corresponding upward trend in Tejano labor positions.

San Antonio Tejanos' influence also diminished in the political realm. During the Mexican period the native-born population of San Antonio de Béxar controlled local politics. They also wielded an influence beyond their numbers in state and national affairs, as evidenced, for example, in the importance that Anglo-American colonists like Stephen F. Austin placed on the support of Béxar leaders in presenting concerns to Mexican officials. During the Texas Republic, Tejano representatives continued to promote their people's concerns in the Anglo-American–controlled congress. But often their pleas fell on deaf ears, as in attempts to enact legislation providing relief for the descendants of Tejanos who died in the Alamo battle, defend Tejano land claims, have the laws of Texas translated into Spanish, and secure funding for a Béxar County jail. On the local level, Anglo-American candidates won the mayoral office, while Tejanos continued to control the city council. Although this shift probably indicates Tejano accommodation to a "peace structure" that in some ways benefited them, the loss of the mayoral office also reflects a downward trend of Tejano influence in local politics. After U.S. annexation, Tejano representation in the state legislature was rare, and no Tejanos were elected to the national congress. There were no Tejano mayors, and Tejano representation on the city council decreased from a majority of council members in 1845 to no representatives in 1860.

When Anglo-Americans claimed to be the harbingers of progress, then, it is not surprising that Tejanos found their claims difficult to accept. Their loss of status during U.S. expansion made their experience different from that of European immigrants, many of whom perceived their move to the United States as a step toward self-improvement. As Juan Seguín so aptly put it, the Tejano experience was not immigration to a land of opportunity, but exile as foreigners in their native land.

Nor was the reduced status of Tejanos conducive to accepting the ideology often associated with Americanization. This process involves embracing American political ideology, as well as seeing this nation's democratic experiment as a bold new initiative in human history, resulting in a future orientation in which that initiative can be fulfilled as a sacred trust. In this view, assimilation is not simply a process of losing the language, customs, and perhaps religion of one's national origin. It involves the acceptance of an American ideology, suggesting that one can be a true American long before one's ethnoreligious origins have dissipated.[6]

Some San Antonio Tejanos, however, expressed their disagreement with U.S. annexation, and the small number who enlisted in the U.S. forces during the Mexican War demonstrates Tejano disfavor with that effort. In individual cases, Tejanos counteracted U.S. laws by abetting slave escapes. Far from enthusiastically embracing the American political experiment, these actions elucidate Tejano unease with the new nation which had arrived at their homeland.

But the clearest signs that Tejanos did not readily accept the view of a unique and superior U.S. legacy in history were Tejano renderings of Texas history, Tejano legends, and their response to Know Nothing hostility. When Anglo-American writers argued that their arrival initiated an era of progress in Texas, Tejanos reminded these newcomers that they built on earlier Tejano achievements, often at the expense of native-born Texan residents. They recalled the bold initiatives of their own ancestors in San Antonio's development and in the struggle for Mexican independence, initiatives which some Anglo-Americans discredited or omitted in their presentations of Texas history. Tejano legends about the early settlers of San Antonio contrasted with those suggested by celebrations for

U.S. "founding fathers" on occasions such as the Fourth of July, Thanksgiving, and Washington's birthday. Like some editorials connected with these U.S. holidays and the perspectives expounded by some Anglo-American Protestant ministers, these legends suggested that divine intervention sanctioned and supported the efforts of the Tejanos' ancestors. During the Know Nothing controversies of the mid-1850s, Tejanos claimed the status of native-born Texans whose ancestors founded and built San Antonio.

Many European immigrants more readily acknowledged the view that the founding of the United States marked a critical turning point in the history of civilization and that this nation was destined for continued greatness as it fulfilled the sacred trust which its exalted beginning implied. For Tejanos who never left home, this ideology was less acceptable because it entailed denying or diminishing their own history and status as native Texans.

Within the Catholic fold, yet another difference between Tejanos and European immigrants was the role of institutional Catholicism in their adjustment to American life. For many European Catholic immigrants, the Church played a mediating role in the process of assimilation, particularly through national parishes and the native clergy who staffed them. While initially national parishes provided a safe haven which reinforced language, culture, and Catholic faith, ultimately these parishes enabled immigrants to integrate into U.S. society from a position of strength.[7] This was not the case for San Antonio Tejanos, however. Their process of incorporation into the United States was accompanied by a loss of their native clergy; their parish, San Fernando, did not facilitate the assimilation of newly arrived immigrants, but served as a symbolic focal point of Tejano resistance to the Anglo-American takeover.

The removal of the native clergy, along with changing political conditions, necessitated that Tejano leaders play an increasingly significant role in organizing the celebrations of their Mexican Catholic heritage. As under Spanish rule, during the Mexican period the town council worked in conjunction with the local pastor, military leaders, and other prominent citizens to organize feasts like that of their Guadalupan patroness. Foreign clergy who replaced the native priests beginning in 1840 were unfamiliar with some local traditions, necessitating further Tejano initiative in continuing those traditions. Under the new political system of the Republic of Texas, the city council no longer took on the responsibility for planning these festivities. Instead, Tejano and Tejana leaders organized them outside the structures of municipal government.

Celebrations like those for Our Lady of Guadalupe, San Juan, and other feasts, and Tejano processions for children's funerals were centered at San Fernando parish, which consequently retained a Tejano flavor. Tejano practices like devotion to the Santo Niño were part of Christmas Eve rites in the early 1850s, when members of San Fernando's various ethnic groups were presumably all invited to worship. The Tejano flavor of San Fernando is also confirmed by the participation of foreign clergy in Tejano celebrations at the parish and by the consistent Spanish-language ministry available there throughout this period. In 1852, Bishop Odin himself came to help in the months after Father Dubuis was first appointed pastor because Dubuis did not yet know sufficient Spanish to administer the sacraments.

Perhaps in response to the Tejano flavor of San Fernando, during the 1850s Anglo-American, Irish, German, and Polish Catholics promoted their own national parishes. St. Mary's parish, which initially served English- and German-speaking Catholics, was dedicated in 1857; Polish and German national parishes were built in the following decade. San Fernando already was the Tejano parish, and apparently Tejanos saw no need to establish another parish in order to secure a spiritual home.

Thus the newly arrived immigrants opted to define their own "turf" in establishing national parishes; native San Antonians had a parish which had been theirs for over a century. In the face of declining Tejano influence in the economic and political realms, San Fernando provided a symbolic center for Tejano life and activity. Perhaps fear and anger at their economic and political displacement intensified their religious devotion and commitment to their parish center. The symbolic meaning of this parish center was noted by Frederick Law Olmsted on his 1854 visit to the city:

> Around the plaza are American hotels, and new glass-fronted stores, alternating with sturdy battlemented Spanish walls, and confronted by the dirty, grim, old stuccoed stone cathedral, whose cracked bell is now clunking for vespers, in a tone that bids us no welcome, as more of the intruding race who have caused all this progress, on which its traditions, like its imperturbable dome, frown down.[8]

Built by Spanish subjects during the middle of the eighteenth century, San Fernando was a visible sign of San Antonio's origins. Its prominent location between the two central plazas of the city was a silent reminder of enduring Tejano presence and vitality. For Tejanos, their parish was not an immigrant haven in a strange new land, but the one institution from their past which was not taken over by Anglo-American immigrants to their city. As such, it was not a way station on the road to assimilation, but a focal point for Tejano resistance to the diminishment of their religious and cultural heritage.

THE SAN ANTONIO TEJANO EXPERIENCE AND PLURALISM

After U.S. annexation, ethnic and denominational pluralism emerged as significant elements of life at San Antonio. Once the Anglo-American and German populations began to rival Tejanos in size, public celebrations, social life, and the composition of the city's Catholic and Protestant congregations showed a marked degree of separation between ethnic groups. To be sure, social intermingling did occur, and some Tejanas even married Anglo-Americans. But such instances of cohesion were infrequent and usually limited to the more prominent classes. The more general pattern of social distance between the various groups was a visible sign of nascent denominational and ethnic pluralism in the city.[9]

This pluralism was based not only on the different backgrounds of religious and ethnic groups, but also, in the case of Tejanos and Anglo-Americans, on an underlying disagreement about which group comprised the dominant cultural force or legitimate "host society."[10] As a people who did not cross a border to enter the United States but had the border cross them, San Antonio Tejanos thought of themselves as the host society. Initially, they promoted the assimilation of Anglo-American immigrants into the patterns established under their religious and cultural hegemony. During the Mexican period, these immigrants were required by law to accept Mexican citizenship and the Catholic religion. The public school at Béxar facilitated Anglo-American incorporation into the local Tejano community. When these legal prescriptions were removed after Texas independence in 1836, San Antonio Tejanos welcomed the voluntary participation of Anglo-Americans in communal events like the feast of Our Lady of Guadalupe, as well as *fandangos* and other social festivities.

After U.S. annexation, demographic changes diminished the viability of such a response. Many Anglo-Americans perceived themselves as the host society once U.S. rule was established, claiming precedence as the harbingers of progress to the area. Tejanos resisted Anglo-American pressures and legislative efforts which would have reversed their role from host society to immigrant. Despite Anglo-American inducements for Tejanos to join them in their national sentiments, for example, San

Antonians of Mexican heritage did not adopt U.S. holidays like the Fourth of July as their city's sole public celebrations. They even celebrated Mexican Independence Day both in the period of the Texas Republic and after U.S. annexation. Tejanos also successfully resisted attempts to ban their traditional *fandangos*. Despite Anglo-American criticisms that their religious practices were superficial or even superstitious, they also continued to celebrate the feasts and traditions of their Mexican Catholic heritage. The vast majority of San Antonio Tejanos retained their Catholic affiliation, even in the face of denominational pluralism and Protestant proselytizing efforts. José Ramos de Zúñiga, editor of San Antonio's *El Correo,* argued against monolingual English public schools in an 1858 editorial, criticizing the monolingual English model which infringed on Tejano cultural heritage.

Tejano resistance to efforts that would curtail or suppress their language, culture, or religious heritage does not indicate a static Tejano identity, however. During the shift from Mexican to U.S. rule, Tejano identity at San Antonio was altered in two related ways: a declining emphasis on their Mexican origins and allegiance, along with an increasing emphasis on their Tejano ancestry and legacy. When Mexico won independence from Spain in 1821, San Antonio de Béxar residents publicly proclaimed their allegiance to the Catholic faith and the Mexican nation. But their intertwined allegiances to Catholicism and the Mexican Republic had a regional spirit based on local political and economic interests, common enemies and hardships, their frontier heritage, and patronal feast days which marked them off as distinct from other settlements in the Mexican Republic. After Texas independence severed Tejanos from Mexican political alliance, they increasingly perceived themselves as a people of Mexican Catholic heritage who were adapting to life among Anglo-Americans in the Republic of Texas. This perception was evident in major areas of Tejano life at San Antonio: in the choice between opposing armies, in national and local politics, and in their religious and other communal celebrations. After U.S. annexation and the advent of ethnic and denominational pluralism at San Antonio, Tejanos claimed the status of native Texans in defending themselves against Know Nothing attacks. They also articulated the legacy of their Tejano ancestors in legends and versions of San Antonio history. Such statements further distinguished San Antonio Tejanos from their counterparts still in Mexico. While Tejano identity retained elements of their Mexican Catholic roots, it was more clearly based on a growing sense of their own unique background as native-born residents of the Texas frontier.

The experience of uprooted European immigrants frequently led to transformed ethnic identities for these immigrants and their descendants as they adapted to the American milieu. This parallels the Tejano experience during the time of their incorporation, in which their identity increasingly accented their unique Tejano origins and sense of peoplehood. Unlike that of many European immigrants, however, Tejano identity did not become distinct from that of their original homeland, but more rooted in it.[11] In fact, as Tejanos were separated from Mexican political jurisdiction and incorporated into the United States, they responded by claiming their own history, origin legends, and Texan birthright as the basis for a renewed group identity. This renewed identity fostered religious and ethnic pluralism at San Antonio, as it distinguished native-born Tejanos from recently arrived immigrants and formed the basis of Tejano defense against Anglo-American aspirations for cultural dominance.

THE SAN ANTONIO TEJANO EXPERIENCE, RELIGION, AND ETHNICITY

In September 1854, a Tejano reportedly went into San Antonio's Mission San Juan and began to destroy the images of Jesus and the saints. After some Tejanas stopped his destructive spree, the man explained that "the Mexican Gods could neither eat, walk or talk, and were no Gods at all, consequently he wanted to put them out of the way." He added that "if the Mexicans had worshipped the true and only God, the 'gringos' could never have taken Texas."[12]

Although this man appears to have been disturbed, his theological observations about the Mexican gods reflect the disposition of a conquered and defeated people. During the years of their incorporation into the United States, San Antonio Tejanos were increasingly marginalized in the economic and political realms. Tejanos also suffered from ethnic prejudice. Newspapers referred to them with the racist slur "greaser," and even the Protestant press joined in the wholesale attacks on their character. Protestant ministers and other Anglo-Americans sharply criticized their religious practices, while European Catholic clergy and religious claimed their knowledge of the faith was inadequate. Anglo-American historical accounts of Texas characterized Tejano heritage as morally and intellectually impoverished. In the years following Texas independence, such insults were at times accompanied by the violence Anglo-American volunteers in the Texas army directed at Tejanos. These atrocities included robbery, forced displacement from their homes, rape, and murder. After U.S. annexation, San Antonio was a military base for U.S. operations, first during the Mexican War and then as part of army fortifications in Texas. While this military presence provided some civilian jobs, it was also a visible symbol of the new regime which ruled San Antonio.

Faced with these changes and attitudes which relegated his people to a second-class citizenry, the Tejano who destroyed images at Mission San Juan blamed the upheaval on his own people, claiming that their conquest could have been averted had they worshipped the "true and only God." Many Tejanos did not accept the takeover as a sign of inferiority or religious neglect, however, and clung proudly to their heritage and Catholic faith.

Shifting Tejano identity did not result from the transformed ethnicity of immigrants, but from the heightened religious and ethnic consciousness of native-born residents who never left home. Their experience differed from that of many European immigrants in that it did not involve a decisive break with their past, resulted in economic and political losses rather than gains, and was not conducive to accepting an American ideology. Unlike the national parishes formed by European Catholic immigrants, the San Antonio Tejano parish of San Fernando was not a way station on the road to assimilation, but the symbolic center of a Tejano legacy which endured the U.S. takeover. While Europeans were undeniably immigrants, Tejanos rightly claimed the status of native Texans, a claim that buttressed their resistance to Anglo-American efforts that would curtail or suppress their language, religion, and culture. In a word, ocean crossing was conducive to breaking with the past and forging a new identity in a new land, while Tejanos responded to the U.S. takeover by reformulating their identity in terms of their preconquest heritage.

The effects of the initial Tejano response to U.S. incorporation on following generations is beyond the scope of this study. As was previously mentioned, the demographic studies of Terry Jordan suggest that the Tejano situation continued to counteract the process of assimilation. A more refined study of the continuing evolution of Tejano religious and ethnic identity would add valuable insight to Jordan's work. The study of Tejanos in other areas of Texas and of the Spanish-speaking populations in what is now New Mexico, Arizona, and California would further illuminate the dynamics of religion and ethnicity for those who entered the United States not by immigration, but as the result of U.S. expansion into the former territories of northern Mexico.[13]

The San Antonio Tejano experience during their incorporation into the United States illustrates the inadequacy of unilateral assimilationist theories for understanding the complexities of religion and ethnicity in the American milieu. It also suggests an understanding of pluralism which differs from those of some contemporary theorists. In a recent essay on pluralism in American life, historian Olivier Zunz writes that "pluralism poses the essential question of the relation between the center and the periphery."[14] Pluralism in antebellum San Antonio, however, did not result from a recognizable dominant group tolerating diverse marginal or peripheral groups. Rather, it stemmed primarily from a conflict between Tejanos and Anglo-Americans over what constituted the criteria for occupying the "center" at San Antonio. While Anglo-Americans claimed priority as the harbingers of progress to the area, Tejanos asserted their precedence as native-born descendants of those who founded and built San Antonio.

The San Antonio experience after U.S. annexation is significant for contemporary discussions of pluralism in Church and society. Various contemporary issues illustrate the ongoing pluralism debate, such as the possibilities and limits of interreligious dialogue, the role of Spanish services in churches, prayer in public schools, English-only laws, and continuing immigration controversies. Frequently those who discuss such issues presuppose that the primary question is the degree of diversity which a dominant group can or should tolerate. But the presumption of a consensus dominant group or perspective is not universally accepted any longer. In a recent essay assessing the challenge United States Hispanic theology poses for theological pluralism, for example, Roberto Goizueta argues that "there is a price to be paid for any genuine pluralism—that price many pluralists seem finally either unwilling to pay or unable to see . . . The others are not marginal to our centres but centres of their own."[15] Supportive of this study on San Antonio Tejanos, Goizueta's analysis denies that viable pluralism stems from a dominant group tolerating some diversity on the periphery of their centrist position. Instead, he asserts that genuine pluralism entails the recognition that various groups or perspectives can coexist without one dominating the others.

Such an understanding of pluralism can be problematic for those concerned with the legitimate cry for unity amidst societal and ecclesial diversity. But the plea for unity can easily disguise the demand that others conform to our image and likeness. While the San Antonio Tejano experience from 1821 to 1860 does not elucidate a clear model for harmonious relations among diverse religious and ethnic groups, the Tejano legacy of resistance to Anglo-American dominance demonstrates that attempts to achieve unity through conformity can lead to more conflict than cohesion and that dominated groups can find cultural and religious mechanisms to express their own ethnic legitimation.

ABBREVIATIONS USED

†

BA   Béxar Archives, CAH

CAH   Center for American History, University of Texas, Austin

CASA   Catholic Archives at San Antonio, Chancery Office, Archdiocese of San Antonio

CAT   Catholic Archives of Texas, Austin

IWA   Incarnate Word Archives, Incarnate Word Generalate, San Antonio

LC   Library of Congress, Washington, D.C.

ND   The University of Notre Dame Archives, South Bend, Indiana

QTSHA *Quarterly of the Texas State Historical Association*

SWHQ   *Southwestern Historical Quarterly*

NOTES

†

1. INTRODUCTION

1. This literature is fairly extensive. For works on the region as a whole, see, e.g., Rodolfo Acuña, *Occupied America: A History of Chicanos* (New York: Harper & Row, 1981); David J. Weber, *The Mexican Frontier, 1821–1846: The American Southwest under Mexico* (Albuquerque: University of New Mexico Press, 1982); Weber, *The Spanish Frontier in North America* (New Haven: Yale University Press, 1992). Histories of Hispanics or Latinos in the U.S. Catholic Church include Moisés Sandoval, ed., *Fronteras: A History of the Latin American Church in the USA since 1513* (San Antonio: Mexican American Cultural Center Press, 1983); Sandoval, *On the Move: A History of the Hispanic Church in the United States* (Maryknoll, N.Y.: Orbis, 1990). Among works on Tejano history are Donald E. Chipman, *Spanish Texas, 1513–1821* (Austin: University of Texas Press, 1992) and Arnoldo De León, *The Tejano Community, 1836–1900* (Albuquerque: University of New Mexico Press, 1982). The standard work on the Catholic history of Texas is Carlos E. Castañeda, *Our Catholic Heritage in Texas, 1519–1950* (Austin: Von Boeckmann-Jones, 1936–1958), 7 vols. For a more recent work which encompasses most of the period under study here, see James Talmadge Moore, *Through Fire and Flood: The Catholic Church in Frontier Texas, 1836–1900* (College Station: Texas A&M University Press, 1992). An excellent essay on the historiography of Spanish Texas and the borderlands is Gerald E. Poyo and Gilberto M. Hinojosa, "Spanish Texas and Borderlands Historiography in Transition: Implications for United States History," *Journal of American History* 75 (September 1988): 393–416. A few works have treated the issue of communal identity, e.g. Poyo and Hinojosa's book on Tejano identity in eighteenth-century San Antonio, which is summarized below. See also Ch. 5, note 13.

2. Robert E. Park and Herbert A. Miller, *Old World Traits Transplanted* (New York: Harper, 1921), 184–185.

3. "Tejano" here refers to Texas residents of Spanish or Mexican descent.

While this is an anachronistic use of the term, it is the term many contemporary historians employ to designate the community under study in this volume. Shifting San Antonio Tejano identity is developed throughout the presentation which follows.

4. For Seguín's papers, see Juan N. Seguín, *Personal Memoirs of John N. Seguín from the Year 1834 to the Retreat of General Woll from the City of San Antonio in 1842* (San Antonio: Ledger Book and Job Office, 1858); Jesús F. de la Teja, ed., *A Revolution Remembered: The Memoirs and Selected Correspondence of Juan N. Seguín* (Austin: State House Press, 1991). Navarro's papers have yet to be published in a single collection; many of his documented statements are cited throughout this work. His major writing was a rendering of San Antonio history. See José Antonio Navarro, *Apuntes históricos interesantes de San Antonio de Béxar escritos por el C. Dn. José Antonio Navarro, en noviembre de 1853. Y publicados por varios de sus amigos* (San Antonio: Privately printed, 1869). Half of Navarro's account originally appeared in the *San Antonio Ledger*, 12, 19 December 1857, 2 January 1858. Internal textual evidence indicates that two earlier installments appeared in nos. 27 and 28 of the *Ledger* in December 1853, but I have yet to find these numbers. However, the earlier material is in "Anonymous. Early History of San Antonio," 1 December 1853, in *The Papers of Mirabeau Buonaparte Lamar*, ed. Charles Adams Gulick, Jr., and Katherine Elliott (Austin: Von Boeckmann-Jones, 1973), 4: 5–12. This reference states that the first installment of Navarro's history was published in the *Western Texan* (San Antonio) of December 1, 1853. While the editors cite the author of this work as anonymous, it is clearly an English translation of the historical narrative attributed to Navarro in *Apuntes*. For the memoirs of Rodriguez and Menchaca, see J[osé] M[aría] Rodriguez, *Rodriguez Memoirs of Early Texas* (San Antonio: Passing Show Printing, 1913; reprint, San Antonio: Standard, 1961); Antonio Menchaca, *Memoirs,* with a foreword by Frederick C. Chabot and an introduction by James P. Newcomb (San Antonio: Yanaguana Society, 1937); Menchaca, "The Memoirs of Captain Menchaca" (typescript), ed. James P. Newcomb, Center for American History, University of Texas, Austin (CAH).

5. The term *identity* is not without its ambiguities. It has been employed in various ways by scholars from diverse disciplines. In this study, the notion of identity refers to a common sense of peoplehood, i.e. the perception by a group that they are united by some combination of economic, political, social, cultural, and religious commonalties. For a discussion of this term and its usage by scholars, see Philip Gleason, "Identifying Identity: A Semantic History," *Journal of American History* 69 (March 1983): 910–931. Reprinted in Philip Gleason, *Speaking of Diversity: Language and Ethnicity in Twentieth-Century America* (Baltimore: Johns Hopkins University Press, 1992), 123–149.

6. The phrase "pluralistic ignorance" appeared in Martin Marty's contribution to an article with four sections written by four different authors. Marty was referring to a statement made by Ernest Gellner. Martin E. Marty and others, "Sources of Personal Identity: Religion, Ethnicity, and the American Cultural Situation," *Religion and American Culture: A Journal of Interpretation* 2 (Winter 1992): 9. Abner Cohen treats the influence of group conflict on ethnicity in

his *Custom and Politics in Urban Africa: A Study of Hausa Migrants in Yoruba Towns* (Berkeley: University of California Press, 1969), especially 198–200.

7. The population of San Antonio was overwhelmingly Tejano until the U.S. annexation of Texas in 1845. By 1850, Tejanos numbered less than half of local residents for the first time since the settlement's foundation, and the Anglo-American population began to rival them in size. Interactions between Tejanos and Anglo-Americans are given precedence in this work over Tejano relations with other groups. While Germans, other European immigrants, and Native Americans also interacted with San Antonio Tejanos, their influence on Tejano ethnicity during the period under study was not nearly as substantial as the more populous and politically powerful Anglo-Americans.

8. Noah Smithwick, *The Evolution of a State or Recollections of Old Texas Days,* comp. Nanna Smithwick Donaldson, with a foreword by L. Tuffy Ellis (Austin: University of Texas Press, 1983), 31; Seguín, *Memoirs,* 18, 19. Seguín's account of these events is treated more fully in chapter three.

9. John J. Linn, *Reminiscences of Fifty Years in Texas* (New York: D. & J. Sadlier, 1883; reprint, Austin: State House Press, 1986), 16.

10. Abbe [Emanuel] Domenech, *Missionary Adventures in Texas and Mexico: A Personal Narrative of Six Years' Sojourn in Those Regions,* trans. from French (London: Longman, Brown, Green, Longmans, and Roberts, 1858), 99–100.

11. Milton Gordon articulated the insight that assimilation in the United States occurs at various levels. See especially his influential work *Assimilation in American Life: The Role of Race, Religion, and National Origins* (New York: Oxford University Press, 1964).

12. Jesús Francisco de la Teja, "Land and Society in Eighteenth-Century San Antonio de Béxar: A Community on New Spain's Northern Frontier" (Ph.D. diss., University of Texas, Austin, 1988), 370–377; Gerald E. Poyo and Gilberto M. Hinojosa, eds., *Tejano Origins in Eighteenth-Century San Antonio* (Austin: University of Texas Press, 1991). Modern-day San Antonio was called "San Antonio de Béxar" or simply "Béxar" in common parlance during the Spanish and Mexican periods. The name "Béxar" was in honor of the Duke of Béxar, whose brother was viceroy of Mexico when Spanish subjects established their first permanent settlement in what is now the city of San Antonio. The local designation of "Béxar" as the settlement's name during the Spanish and Mexican eras will be reflected in this and the following chapter.

13. Poyo and Hinojosa, eds., *Tejano Origins in Eighteenth-Century San Antonio,* 140.

14. Ibid.

15. Jacques Lafaye, *Quetzalcoatl and Guadalupe: The Formation of Mexican National Consciousness, 1531–1813* (Chicago: University of Chicago Press, 1976), 86, 226, 254–255. For the recognition of these saints as the local patrons, see Juan Recio de León, Public statement, 6 June 1738, Nacogdoches Archives (typescript), 1: 77–78, CAH; *Cabildo* (town council) of the Villa de San Fernando to Baron de Ripperdá, 7 February 1771, ibid., 5: 30–31; *Cabildo* of the Villa de San Fernando and others, Statements on feast days, 12 February 1772–9

January 1788 ibid., 5: 46a–46s. The latter two references were brought to my attention by Adán Benavides, Jr., whom I gratefully acknowledge.

16. De la Teja, "Land and Society in Eighteenth-Century San Antonio de Béxar," 364–369; Report from *cabildo,* Villa de San Fernando, 27 January 1747, Béxar Archives, CAH (BA); William Edward Dunn, "Apache Relations in Texas, 1718–1750," *Quarterly of the Texas State Historical Association (QTSHA)* 14 (January 1911): 260–262. The 1747 report from the *cabildo* of San Fernando is summarized in Gilbert R. Cruz, *Let There Be Towns: Spanish Municipal Origins in the American Southwest, 1610–1810* (College Station: Texas A&M University Press, 1988), 141–143.

2. SHIFTING REGIONAL IDENTITY:
THE MEXICAN PERIOD, 1821 – 1836

1. Jean Louis Berlandier, *Journey to Mexico during the Years 1826 to 1834,* trans. Sheila M. Ohlendorf, Josette M. Bigelow, and Mary M. Standifer, with an introduction by C. H. Muller (Austin: Texas State Historical Association, 1980), 2: 291. For physical descriptions of Béxar and the environs during the Mexican period, see ibid., 2: 290–300; José María Sánchez, "A Trip to Texas in 1828," trans. Carlos E. Castañeda, *Southwestern Historical Quarterly (SWHQ)* 29 (April 1926): 257–260; J. C. Clopper, "J. C. Clopper's Journal and Book of Memoranda for 1828," *QTSHA* 13 (July 1909): 69–71, 75–76; Benjamin Lundy, *The Life, Travels and Opinions of Benjamin Lundy, Including His Journeys to Texas and Mexico; with a Sketch of Contemporary Events, and a Notice of the Revolution in Hayti* (Philadelphia: William D. Parrish, 1847; reprint, New York: Negro Universities Press, 1969), 47–50, 54–55.

2. Jesús F. de la Teja and John Wheat, "Béxar: Profile of a *Tejano* Community, 1820–1832," *SWHQ* 89 (July 1985): 9–11; Juan N. Almonte, "Statistical Report on Texas, 1835," trans. Carlos E. Castañeda, *SWHQ* 28 (January 1925): 186; William Kennedy, *Texas: The Rise, Progress, and Prospects of the Republic of Texas* (London: R. Hastings, 1841; reprint, Fort Worth: Molyneaux Craftsmen, 1925), 2: 44; Francisco Salazar and Antonio Hernandez, List of foreigners at Béxar, 24 April 1828, BA; Andrew Anthony Tijerina, "*Tejanos* and Texas: The Native Mexicans of Texas, 1820–1850" (Ph.D. diss., University of Texas, Austin, 1977), 18; Carlos Sanchez-Navarro, *La guerra de Tejas: Memorias de un soldado* (Mexico City: Editorial Polis, 1938), 148 (quotation), my translation. Several factors influenced the move to secularize the missions, including a decline in Indian converts, a lack of missionary personnel, and competition with town residents over valuable mission lands. See David J. Weber, *The Mexican Frontier, 1821–1846: The American Southwest under Mexico* (Albuquerque: University of New Mexico Press, 1982), 43–68.

3. For contemporary observers who noted class divisions at Béxar, see Berlandier, *Journey to Mexico,* 2: 290; Clopper, "Journal," 72; Lundy, *Life, Travels and Opinions of Benjamin Lundy,* 48; J[osé] M[aría] Rodriguez, *Rodriguez*

Memoirs of Early Texas (San Antonio: Passing Show Printing, 1913; reprint, San Antonio: Standard, 1961), 34, 37–38; Noah Smithwick, *The Evolution of a State or Recollections of Old Texas Days,* comp. Nanna Smithwick Donaldson, with a foreword by L. Tuffy Ellis (Austin: University of Texas Press, 1983), 18. An analysis of these social class divisions is in Weber, *The Mexican Frontier, 1821–1846,* 207–212. The figures cited are compiled from census tracts in Gifford White, *1830 Citizens of Texas* (Austin: Eakin, 1983), 79–112.

4. De la Teja and Wheat, "Béxar: Profile of a *Tejano* Community," 9–10, 26–31; Berlandier, *Journey to Mexico,* 2: 290–291; Sánchez, "A Trip to Texas in 1828," 258; "Petition Addressed by the Illustrious *Ayuntamiento* of the City of Béxar to the Honorable Legislature of the State: To Make Known the Ills Which Afflict the Towns of Texas and the Grievances They Have Suffered Since Their Union with Coahuila," 19 December 1832, in *Troubles in Texas, 1832: A Tejano Viewpoint from San Antonio with a Translation and Facsimile,* ed. David J. Weber, trans. Conchita Hassell Winn and David J. Weber (Dallas: Wind River, 1983), 17–18. Fiscal problems in the national government resulted in cutbacks not just at Béxar, but throughout the military establishments of northern Mexico. These establishments were responsible to national leaders and relied on funding from Mexico City for their operation. In addition to conflicts with Native Americans, Berlandier attributed the lack of agricultural progress to the indolence of local residents.

5. Antonio Martínez to *Ayuntamiento* of Béxar, 18 July 1821, BA; José Sandoval to *Ayuntamiento* of Béxar, 21 July 1821, BA. The description presented here is based on the summary of Félix D. Almaráz, Jr., *Governor Antonio Martínez and Mexican Independence in Texas: An Orderly Transition* (San Antonio: Béxar County Historical Commission, 1979), 9–11. Originally published in the *Permian Historical Annual* 15 (December 1975).

6. Almaráz, *Governor Antonio Martínez and Mexican Independence in Texas,* 7. The Plan of Iguala provided for Mexican independence, support of the Catholic religion, and the union and order of the new Mexican nation. These are the three guarantees which Béxar residents pledged to uphold in the July 19 allegiance ceremony. Recollections of the cruel episodes at Béxar during 1811–1813 were later recorded by various San Antonians. See, e.g., Antonio Menchaca, *Memoirs,* with a foreword by Frederick C. Chabot and an introduction by James P. Newcomb (San Antonio: Yanaguana Society, 1937), 13–19; Rodriguez, *Memoirs,* 59; José Antonio Navarro, "José Antonio Navarro, Béxar, [Texas]," 18 May 1841, in *The Papers of Mirabeau Buonaparte Lamar,* ed. Charles Adams Gulick, Jr., and Katherine Elliott (Austin: Von Boeckmann-Jones, 1973), 3: 525–527; Navarro, "José Antonio Navarro San Antonio de Béxar? [Texas], Autobiographical Notes," "[1841?]," in ibid., 3: 597–598; Navarro, *Apuntes históricos interesantes de San Antonio de Béxar escritos por el C. Dn. José Antonio Navarro, en noviembre de 1853. Y publicados por varios de sus amigos* (San Antonio: Privately printed, 1869), 4–20. Half of Navarro's account in the latter work originally appeared in the *San Antonio Ledger,* 12, 19 December 1857, 2 January 1858. The other half is in "Anonymous. Early History of San Antonio," 1 Decem-

ber 1853, in Gulick and Elliott, eds., *Papers of Lamar*, 4: 5–12. While the editors cite the author of this work as anonymous, it is clearly an English translation of the historical narrative attributed to Navarro in *Apuntes*.

7. For over a century, Béxar residents had expressed their national and Catholic loyalties at key moments in the settlement's history: at its naming by the Terán expedition, at the announcement of a new Spanish monarch, at peace treaties, at the election of a new town council, and on major religious feasts. Mattie Austin Hatcher, "The Expedition of Don Domingo Terán de los Rios into Texas," *Preliminary Studies of the Texas Catholic Historical Society* 2 (January 1932): 14, 55; Report from *cabildo*, Villa de San Fernando, 27 January 1747, BA; William Edward Dunn, "Apache Relations in Texas, 1718–1750," *QTSHA* 14 (January 1911): 260–262; Jesús Francisco de la Teja, "Land and Society in Eighteenth-Century San Antonio de Béxar: A Community on New Spain's Northern Frontier" (Ph.D. diss., University of Texas, Austin, 1988), 363–369. The 1747 report from the *cabildo* of San Fernando is summarized in Gilbert R. Cruz, *Let There Be Towns: Spanish Municipal Origins in the American Southwest, 1610–1810* (College Station: Texas A&M University Press, 1988), 141–143. The dual loyalties of Spanish subjects in Texas are discussed in Félix D. Almaráz, Jr., "Wilderness Duality: Cross and Crown in Spanish Texas," in *Hispanicism and Catholicism: Great Forces in Motion* (San Antonio: Mexican American Cultural Center Press, 1992).

8. Sánchez, "A Trip to Texas in 1828," 260; De la Teja and Wheat, "Béxar: Profile of a *Tejano* Community," 12; Almonte, "Statistical Report on Texas, 1835," 184, 186, 198, 206.

9. Howard Miller, "Stephen F. Austin and the Anglo-Texan Response to the Religious Establishment in Mexico, 1821–1836," *SWHQ* 91 (January 1988): 291.

10. Ibid., 285–290, 315; Mary Angela Fitzmorris, "Four Decades of Catholicism in Texas, 1820–1860" (Ph.D. diss., Catholic University of America, Washington, D.C., 1926), 14–20, 38. Official documents promulgating and reinforcing the prescription of Catholicism can be found in J. P. Kimball, trans., *Laws and Decrees of the State of Coahuila and Texas, in Spanish and English. To Which Is Added the Constitution of Said State: Also: The Colonization Law of the State of Tamaulipas, and Naturalization Law of the General Congress* (Houston: Telegraph Power Press, 1839); H. P. N. Gammel, comp., *The Laws of Texas, 1822–1897* (Austin: Gammel Book Co., 1898), vol. 1. In 1834, the state legislature of Coahuila y Tejas decreed that "no person shall be molested for political and religious opinions, provided, he shall not disturb the public order." This law, enacted the year before the outbreak of the Texas Revolution, allowed for religious freedom but left ambiguous the issue of public worship. Another law enacted three weeks earlier discouraged the establishment of local congregations by decreeing that "the founding of edifices built by charitable donations under any denomination whatever is hereby absolutely prohibited." Decree No. 263, Article 2; Decree No. 272, Section 1, Article 10, in Kimball, trans., *Laws and Decrees of the State of Coahuila and Texas*, 240, 248; Gammel, comp., *Laws of Texas*, 1: 350, 358.

11. The pertinent section of the Texas Constitution is in Gammel, comp., *Laws of Texas*, 1: 1082. For Tejano cultural influence on Anglo-Americans, see Tijerina, *"Tejanos* and Texas."

12. Sánchez, "A Trip to Texas in 1828," 283 (first quotation); Berlandier, *Journey to Mexico*, 2: 291, 1: 145 (second and third quotations); John Duff Brown, "Reminiscences of Jno. Duff Brown," *QTSHA* 12 (April 1909): 299; Smithwick, *Evolution of a State*, 18; Menchaca, *Memoirs*, 21; Rodriguez, *Memoirs*, 56; Frederick Charles Chabot, *With the Makers of San Antonio. Genealogies of the Early Latin, Anglo-American, and German Families with Occasional Biographies, Each Group Being Prefaced with a Brief Historical Sketch and Illustrations* (San Antonio: Artes Gráficas, 1937), 201, 244, 274; Cleburne Huston, *Deaf Smith: Incredible Texas Spy* (Waco: Texian Press, 1973), 15–16.

13. Chabot, *With the Makers of San Antonio*, 120–122. For original correspondence between Seguín and Austin, see Eugene C. Barker, ed., *The Austin Papers* (Washington, D.C.: U.S. Government Printing Office, 1924–1928), vols. 1–2.

14. The correspondence between Navarro and Austin is in Barker, ed., *Austin Papers*. See, e.g., Stephen F. Austin to José Antonio Navarro, 27 February 1827, 1: 1609–1610; Navarro to Austin, 17 May 1828, 2: 40–41; Navarro to Austin, 27 November 1828, 2: 147–148; Navarro to Austin, 8 January 1829, 2: 156–157; Austin to Navarro, 23 July 1829, 2: 233–235; Austin to Navarro, 19 October 1829, 2: 271–273. For an overview of Tejano and Anglo-American cooperation on political issues during this period, see Eugene C. Barker, "Native Latin American Contribution to the Colonization and Independence of Texas," *SWHQ* 46 (January 1943): 317–335.

15. Eugene C. Barker, ed., "Minutes of the *Ayuntamiento* of San Felipe de Austin, 1828–1832," *SWHQ* 21 (January 1918): 311; Ramón Músquiz to Austin, 17 April 1828, in Barker, ed., *Austin Papers*, 2: 31. This law was passed by the state legislature on May 5, 1828. Gammel, comp., *Laws of Texas*, 1: 213.

16. The proceedings of the San Felipe Convention are recorded in Gammel, comp., *Laws of Texas*, 1: 475–503.

17. Weber, ed., *Troubles in Texas*, 1–11. The interpretation presented here draws heavily on Weber's analysis.

18. M[úsquiz] to [Juan Martín de Veramendi], 10 January 1833, BA. This letter is also in Barker, ed., *Austin Papers*, 2: 912–913.

19. "Minutes of the City Council of the City of San Antonio, 1830 to 1835, Spanish Minute Book Two" (typescript), 30 May, 31 October 1833, CAH; *Ayuntamiento* of Béxar to Austin, 31 October 1833, in ibid., 7 November 1833 (quotation); Eugene C. Barker, *The Life of Stephen F. Austin: Founder of Texas, 1793–1836* (Austin: University of Texas Press, 1969), 373–376, 388. The letter from the Béxar *Ayuntamiento* to Austin is also in Barker, ed., *Austin Papers*, 2: 1012–1013.

20. William Stuart Red, *The Texas Colonists and Religion, 1821–1836* (Austin: E. L. Shettles, 1924), 70–84, 99; H[enderson] Yoakum, *History of Texas, from Its First Settlement in 1685 to Its Annexation to the United States in 1846* (New York: Redfield, 1855), 2: 220–222, 536–538, 542–543. Reminiscences

of Protestant ministries in Texas during the period of the Mexican Republic are in Mary S. Helm, *Scraps of Early Texas History* (Austin: B. R. Warner, 1884), 47; Rosa Kleberg, "Some of My Early Experiences in Texas," *QTSHA* 1 (April 1898): 300; A. J. Lee, "Rev. J. W. Kenney," *Texas Methodist Historical Quarterly* 1 (July 1909): 48–50; Lee, "Some Recollections of Two Texas Pioneer Women," *Texas Methodist Historical Quarterly* 1 (January 1910): 209; Z. N. Morrell, *Flowers and Fruits from the Wilderness; or, Thirty-six Years in Texas and Two Winters in Honduras* (Boston: Gould and Lincoln, 1872), 32, 72–73, 385; T. J. P., "First Sunday School in Texas," in *A Texas Scrap Book Made Up of the History, Biography and Miscellany of Texas and Its People,* comp. D. W. C. Baker (New York: A. S. Barnes, 1875; reprint, Austin: Steck, 1935), 74–76; John Rabb to Brother Richardson, 18 September 1850, in "The Texas Wesleyan Banner," *Texas Methodist Historical Quarterly* 1 (July 1909): 80–84.

21. J. B. Link, ed., *Texas Historical and Biographical Magazine* 1 (1891): 23; *Southwestern Presbyterian,* 31 March 1892, in R. Douglas Brackenridge, *Voice in the Wilderness: A History of the Cumberland Presbyterian Church in Texas,* with an introduction by Thomas H. Campbell (San Antonio: Trinity University Press, 1968), 19–20; *Cumberland Presbyterian,* 3 February 1836, in R. Douglas Brackenridge and Francisco O. García-Treto, *Iglesia Presbiteriana: A History of Presbyterians and Mexican Americans in the Southwest* (San Antonio: Trinity University Press, 1974), 3 (quotation); Thomas H. Campbell *History of the Cumberland Presbyterian Church in Texas* (Nashville: Cumberland Presbyterian Publishing House, 1936), 16–18.

22. Brackenridge, *Voice in the Wilderness,* 20.

23. David Ayers, "Reminiscences of David Ayers," *Texas Methodist Historical Quarterly* 1 (July 1909): 39–41. Father Malloy was an Irish Dominican and a land grantee at the Irish settlement of San Patricio. Little is known of his work, except that he was pastor of San Patricio at least from 1834 to 1836 and probably died in the early 1840s. Fitzmorris, "Four Decades of Catholicism in Texas," 22; James Talmadge Moore, *Through Fire and Flood: The Catholic Church in Frontier Texas, 1836–1900* (College Station: Texas A&M University Press, 1992), 3, 37.

24. Stephen F. Austin, "The 'Prison Journal' of Stephen F. Austin," *QTSHA* 2 (January 1899): 189; Morrell, *Flowers and Fruits from the Wilderness,* 32; Orceneth Fisher, *Sketches of Texas in 1840: Designed to Answer, in a Brief Way, the Numerous Enquiries Respecting the New Republic, as to Situation, Extent, Climate, Soil, Productions, Water, Government, Society, Religion, Etc.* (Springfield, Ill.: Walters & Weber, 1841; reprint, Waco: Texian Press, 1964), 43; W. P. Smith to editor of the *Texas Wesleyan Banner,* 12 October 1850, as cited in "The Texas Wesleyan Banner," 84.

25. Clopper, "Journal," 72, 76.

26. Erasmo Seguín to Baron de Bastrop, 24 March 1824, in Barker, ed., *Austin Papers,* 1: 757–758. This quotation is my translation of the text. Seguín's comment about "religious toleration" under the previous administration apparently refers to more permissive legislation enacted during Spanish possession of Louisiana. See Fitzmorris, "Four Decades of Catholicism in Texas," 13.

27. I. J. Cox, "Educational Efforts in San Fernando de Béxar," *QTSHA* 6 (July 1902): 36, 40–49; Refugio de la Garza, Juan Martín de Beramendi, and José María Balmaceda, School Ordinance of Béxar, 13 March 1828, BA. Cox, "Educational Efforts in San Fernando de Béxar," 52–63, has a translation of the Béxar School Ordinance. Information in the following two paragraphs is taken from this document.

28. School Ordinance of Béxar, Ch. 4; Cox, "Educational Efforts in San Fernando de Béxar," 60 (quotation). Apparently the Béxar community celebrated various "observed feast days." In 1840, French Vincentian Jean Marie Odin noted that sixteen holy days of obligation were listed in the Mexican catechism used by Tejanos. Jean Marie Odin to Joseph Rosati, 27 August 1840, Catholic Archives of Texas, Austin (CAT).

29. Brown, "Reminiscences," 300 (quotation). During 1832 and 1833, well under half of the school-age children were enrolled in school. Official school reports for June 1832 indicate a student body of 118 pupils. For December of 1832 the reported number was one hundred, and in December 1833, only sixty. The 1833 Béxar census reports 334 residents between the ages of 7 and 16. Juan Francisco Buchetti, School Report, 31 [*sic*] June 1832, BA; Buchetti, School Report, 31 December 1832, BA; Bruno Huizar, School Report, 31 December 1833, BA; Tijerina, "*Tejanos* and Texas," 21. For a treatment of finances and weekly inspections to the school, see Cox, "Educational Efforts in San Fernando de Béxar," 40–43, 46–49. The 1835 report of Juan Almonte states that the city council had not been able to maintain the school due to a lack of funds. Almonte, "Statistical Report on Texas, 1835," 193.

30. An Anglo-American historian stated in 1855 that "nineteen twentieths of the colonists of Texas neither observed nor believed in the religion prescribed in the Mexican constitution." Yoakum, *History of Texas,* 1: 233. The reminiscences of early settlers report such evasions of the Catholic laws. See Morrell, *Flowers and Fruits from the Wilderness,* 78; Caroline Von Hinueber, "Life of German Pioneers in Early Texas," *QTSHA* 2 (January 1899): 228. Complaints of Presbyterian Sumner Bacon with regard to Father Michael Muldoon and the prescription of Catholicism illustrate Bacon's stance of noncompliance to Catholic laws. Sumner Bacon to Austin, 30 July 1831, in Barker, ed., *Austin Papers,* 2: 683–684. Recollections of "illegal" Protestant ministries are cited above in note 20. At Béxar, over a dozen infant and adult baptisms of Anglo-Americans were recorded in the baptismal register of Béxar's parish church, San Fernando, during the Mexican period. "San Fernando Baptismal Register," books 5 and 6, Catholic Archives at San Antonio, Chancery Office, Archdiocese of San Antonio (CASA). A partial listing of these baptisms is in Chabot, *With the Makers of San Antonio,* 273. Other Anglo-Americans received Catholic baptism before immigrating to Texas and presented certificates of baptism to Mexican officials upon their arrival.

31. Músquiz to *Ayuntamiento* of Nacogdoches, 19 February 1833, Nacogdoches Archives (typescript), 66: 195–197, CAH; J. Villasana Haggard, "Epidemic Cholera in Texas, 1833–1834," *SWHQ* 40 (January 1937): 218–219, 221; Erasmo Seguín to *Ayuntamiento* of Béxar, 3 October 1833, BA; "Minutes

of the City Council of the City of San Antonio, 1830 to 1835," 28 September, 7 October 1833; Pat Ireland Nixon, *The Medical Story of Early Texas, 1528–1853*, with a foreword by Dr. Chauncey D. Leake (Lancaster, Penn.: Lancaster Press, 1946), 137; Lundy, *Life, Travels and Opinions of Benjamin Lundy*, 54 (quotation), 55. Between October 6 and 24, fourteen children who reportedly died of "cough" were buried from San Fernando Church. Only three such deaths were recorded in November and only one in December. "San Fernando Cathedral Deaths," Book 3, 6 October–10 December 1833, CASA.

32. Fane Downs, "The History of Mexicans in Texas, 1820–1845" (Ph.D. diss., Texas Tech University, Lubbock, 1970), 188–191; Haggard, "Epidemic Cholera in Texas, 1833–1834," 225–229; Nixon, *Medical Story of Early Texas,* 138–140; Juan Nepomuceno Seguín to Citizens of Béxar, 26 June 1834, BA; Juan Seguín to [José Antonio Salinas], 29 October 1834, BA; Músquiz to *Ayuntamiento* of Béxar, 1 July 1834, BA; *Ayuntamiento* of Béxar to Juan Seguín, 7 July 1834, BA; "Minutes of the City Council of the City of San Antonio, 1830 to 1835," 7, 16 July, 3 October 1834.

33. Salinas to [Juan Seguín], 27 July 1834, BA; José Jesús de Vidaurri to [Juan Seguín], 7 September 1834, BA; Lundy, *Life, Travels and Opinions of Benjamin Lundy,* 124.

34. Refugio de la Garza to Martínez, 24 October 1821, BA; [Martínez] to [De la Garza], 24 October 1821, BA; [Martínez] to [José Angel Navarro], 30 October 1821, BA; [Martínez] to [De la Garza], 30 October 1821, BA; [*Ayuntamiento* of Béxar] to José León Lobo Guerrero, 4 September 1822, BA; Father Francisco Maynes to *Junta Gubernativa* (governing council) of Texas, 5 June 1823, BA; [*Junta Gubernativa*] to *Ayuntamiento* of Béxar, 6 June 1823, BA; [Antonio Elozúa] to *Ministro de Justicia y Negocios Eclesiásticos* (Minister of Justice and Ecclesiastical Affairs), 23 February 1826, BA; Tomás Buentello to José Antonio Saucedo, 20 July 1827, BA; Tomás de Oquillas to Elozúa, 18 August 1827, BA; "Minutes of the City Council of the City of San Antonio, 1830 to 1835," 11 December 1833.

35. Juan José Zambrano to [Mateo Ahumada], 17 March 1826, BA; Ahumada to [Zambrano], 18 March 1826, BA; "Minutes of the City Council of the City of San Antonio, 1830 to 1835," 2–3 December 1830, 1 December 1831 (quotation), 6 December 1832, 5 December 1833; Juan Seguín to Béxar *Alcalde,* 2 December 1834, BA; De la Teja and Wheat, "Béxar: Profile of a *Tejano* Community," 22–23; Tijerina, "*Tejanos* and Texas," 101–102.

36. Minutes of the junta for the Independence Day celebration, 12 September 1829, BA; Program for Independence Day celebration, 10 September 1830, BA; Committee for decorating church, 10 September 1830, BA; Report of committee on decorations and receipts of expenditures, 12–19 September 1830, BA; Report of expenditures, 31 December 1830, BA; De la Teja and Wheat, "Béxar: Profile of a *Tejano* Community," 22; Carlos Castañeda, *Our Catholic Heritage in Texas, 1519–1936* (Austin: Von Boeckmann-Jones, 1936–1958), 6: 352–353; "Minutes of the City Council of the City of San Antonio, 1830 to 1835," 13 September 1832, 12 September 1833; Clopper, "Journal," 73. The presentation of patriotic

speeches reflects Father de la Garza's political activities, which are treated in chapter three.

37. Minutes of the junta for the Independence Day celebration, 12 September 1829; De la Teja and Wheat, "Béxar: Profile of a *Tejano* Community," 22. A similar celebration was held in 1830. Program for Independence Day celebration, 10 September 1830; Castañeda, *Our Catholic Heritage in Texas*, 6: 352–353; Tijerina, "*Tejanos* and Texas," 102–103.

38. Just a few months before the outbreak of these hostilities, a "grand Independence celebration" was held at Béxar. Rena Maverick Green, ed., *Samuel Maverick, Texan: 1803–1870. A Collection of Letters, Journals, and Memoirs* (San Antonio: Privately printed, 1952), 29. See also receipts of expenditures for Independence Day celebration, 27 August–7 September, 1835, BA.

39. Weber, ed., *Troubles in Texas*, 11.

3. BETWEEN TWO WORLDS: THE PERIOD OF THE TEXAS REPUBLIC, 1836 – 1845

1. William A. McClintock, "Journal of a Trip through Texas and Northern Mexico in 1846–1847," *SWHQ* 34 (October 1930): 146–147. McClintock's description was written in 1846. Similar descriptions from the period of the Texas Republic are in Thomas W. Bell to [William Adam Bell], 31 March 1842, in "Thomas W. Bell Letters," ed. Llerena Friend, *SWHQ* 63 (April 1960): 589–590; W. Eugene Hollon and Ruth Lapham Butler, eds., *William Bollaert's Texas* (Norman: University of Oklahoma Press, 1956), 216–217, 219; George Wilkens Kendall, *Narrative of the Texan Santa Fe Expedition, Comprising a Description of a Tour through Texas, and across the Great Southwestern Prairies, the Camanche [sic] and Caygua Hunting-Grounds, with an Account of the Sufferings from Want of Food, Losses from Hostile Indians, and Final Capture of the Texans, and Their March, as Prisoners, to the City of Mexico. With Illustrations and a Map* (New York: Harper & Brothers, 1844; reprint, Ann Arbor, Mich.: University Microfilms, 1966), 1: 51; Andrew Forest Muir, ed., *Texas in 1837: An Anonymous, Contemporary Narrative* (Austin: University of Texas Press, 1988), 98. San Antonio de Béxar was officially incorporated as the City of San Antonio by the Texas Congress on December 14, 1837. The official name for the city will be used in this and the following chapter.

2. *Houston Telegraph and Texas Register*, 19 May 1838. See also ibid., 15 March 1843; J[osé] M[aría] Rodriguez, *Rodriguez Memoirs of Early Texas* (San Antonio: Passing Show Printing, 1913; reprint, San Antonio: Standard, 1961), 17. The 1840 Texas census is in Gifford White, ed., *The 1840 Census of the Republic of Texas*, with a foreword by James M. Day (Austin: Pemberton, 1966). Over a dozen travelogues and travelers' accounts from this period include population estimates of San Antonio. These sources are cited in the attached bibliography.

3. V. K. Carpenter, comp., *The State of Texas Federal Population Schedules*

Seventh Census of the United States, 1850 (Huntsville, Ark.: Century Enterprises, 1969), 1: 141, entry no. 509. Other entries on the 1850 San Antonio census tract (ibid., 1: 111–189) which indicate families who moved back and forth from Texas to Mexico include nos. 42, 152, 201, 252, 260, 317, 334, 376, and 438.

4. Herman Ehrenberg, *With Milam and Fannin: Adventures of a German Boy in Texas' Revolution,* ed. Henry Smith, trans. Charlotte Churchill (Dallas: Tardy, 1935), 101–102; Rodriguez, *Memoirs,* 9–10, 16; "Stirring Events Are Remembered by Texas Jurist," *San Antonio Express,* 8 September 1912, 35; "Aged Citizen Describes Alamo Fight and Fire," ibid., 1 July 1906, 11; Charles Merritt Barnes, "Builders' Spades Turn Up Soil Baked by Alamo Funeral Pyres," ibid., 26 March 1911, 26; Barnes, "Men Still Living Who Saw the Fall of the Alamo," ibid., 27 August 1911, 9.

5. Fane Downs, "The History of Mexicans in Texas, 1820–1845" (Ph.D. diss., Texas Tech University, Lubbock, 1970), 44; Charles I. Sellon to Marilla, 6 September 1846, in H. Bailey Carroll, "Texas Collection," *SWHQ* 47 (July 1943): 63; T. E. G. to Editors, December 1846, in *United States Catholic Magazine and Monthly Review* 6 (April 1847): 219; Viktor Bracht, *Texas in 1848,* trans. Charles Frank Schmidt (San Antonio: Naylor, 1931), 174; Sarah L. French, "Mrs. French's Reminiscences of Early Days in Béxar," in S. J. Wright, *San Antonio de Béxar: Historical, Traditional, Legendary* (Austin: Morgan, 1916), 96; *San Antonio Express Annual Review,* March 1890, 1–2. The latter reference contains reminiscences from two 1845 visitors to the city, John A. Green and another who was not identified. This edition of the *Annual Review* was an insert of the *San Antonio Express,* 15 March 1890. A few visitors commented that the population of San Antonio was half Tejano and half Anglo-American; their observations do not concur with the majority of visitors to the city. The movement of U.S. troops through San Antonio during the Mexican War (1846–1848) and the frequent presence of traders and travelers in the city might account for their perception of a larger Anglo-American population. U. S. Grant, *Personal Memoirs of U. S. Grant* (New York: Charles L. Webster, 1894), 1: 47; Ferdinand Roemer, *Texas: With Particular Reference to German Immigration and the Physical Appearance of the Country,* trans. Oswald Mueller (San Antonio: Standard, 1935; reprint, Waco: Texian Press, 1967), 120.

6. Ray F. Broussard, "San Antonio during the Texas Republic: A City in Transition," *Southwestern Studies* 5 (1967): 22; Joseph Milton Nance, *After San Jacinto: The Texas-Mexican Frontier, 1836–1841* (Austin: University of Texas Press, 1963), 78–82.

7. John Bost Pitts III, "Speculation in Headright Land Grants in San Antonio from 1837 to 1842" (M.A. thesis, Trinity University, San Antonio, 1966), 29, 31; White, ed., *1840 Census* 12–18.

8. White, ed., *1840 Census.* The latter figure refers to surveyed land which had been patented with the General Land Office. For references to the local Tejano elite, see "Esparza, the Boy of the Alamo, Remembers," in *Rise of the Lone Star: A Story of Texas Told by Its Pioneers,* ed. Howard R. Driggs and Sarah S. King (New York: Frederick A. Stokes, 1936), 218–219; Hollon and Butler, eds., *William Bollaert's Texas,* 217–218; Muir, ed., *Texas in 1837,* 106; J[ohn] C.

Duval, *Early Times in Texas,* with an introduction by John Q. Anderson (Austin: H. P. N. Gammel, 1892; reprint, Austin: Steck-Vaughn, 1967), 2: 64–65; *Austin City Gazette,* 10 June 1840. The latter reference is also available in Joseph Milton Nance, *Attack and Counter-Attack: The Texas-Mexican Frontier, 1842* (Austin: University of Texas Press, 1964), 454–455. Although some visitors did not notice class divisions in the social life of San Antonio (e.g., J. W. Benedict, "Diary of a Campaign against the Comanches," *SWHQ* 32 [April 1929]: 305), evidence to the contrary is quite substantial.

9. Deposition of Francisco Esparza, 26 August 1859, Court of Claims Voucher File No. 2558, General Land Office, Austin; "Children of the Alamo," *Houston Chronicle,* 9 November 1901, 4; "Another Child of the Alamo," *San Antonio Light,* 10 November 1901, 9; "The Story of Enrique Esparza," *San Antonio Express,* 22 November 1902, 8; "Story of the Massacre of Heroes of the Alamo," ibid., 7 March 1904; 5; "Alamo's Only Survivor," ibid., 19 May 1907, 47; "Alamo's Fall Is Told by Witness in a Land Suit," ibid., 9 December 1908, 20; Rodriguez, *Memoirs,* 15–16; Harbert Davenport, "Captain Jesús Cuellar, Texas Cavalry, Otherwise 'Comanche,'" *SWHQ* 30 (July 1926): 56–62; "Señor Navarro Tells the Story of His Grandfather," in Driggs and King, eds., *Rise of the Lone Star,* 268–269, 272–273; Paul D. Lack, *The Texas Revolutionary Experience: A Political and Social History, 1835–1836* (College Station: Texas A&M University Press, 1992), 165; R[euben] M. Potter, *The Texas Revolution: Distinguished Mexicans Who Took Part in the Revolution of Texas, with Glances at Its Early Events,* 18. The latter work is reprinted from the *Magazine of American History* (October 1878) and is available at CAH and the Library of Congress, Washington, D.C. (LC).

10. Deposition of Francisco Esparza; Deposition of Manuel Flores, 13 December 1858, Court of Claims Voucher File No. 2558, General Land Office; Deposition of Gregorio Hernandez, 27 December 1858, Court of Claims Voucher File No. 2558, ibid.; Deposition of Candelario Villanueva, 26 August 1859, Court of Claims Voucher File No. 2558, ibid.; "Children of the Alamo," 4; "Another Child of the Alamo," 9; "The Story of Enrique Esparza," 8; "Story of the Massacre of Heroes of the Alamo," 5; "Alamo's Only Survivor," 47; "Alamo's Fall Is Told by Witness in a Land Suit," 20; "Esparza Remembers," in Driggs and King, eds., *Rise of the Lone Star,* 229. Citing Enrique Esparza, a 1911 account claims that Gregorio's body was never found and consequently was burned with the others. This claim contradicts earlier testimony by several witnesses, including Enrique Esparza himself. Barnes, "Builders' Spades Turn Up Soil Baked by Alamo Funeral Pyres," 26.

11. Vicente Filisola, *Memorias para la historia de la guerra de Texas, por el Sr. General de División y actual Presidente del Supremo Tribunal de Guerra y Marina de la República Don Vicente Filisola* (Mexico City: R. Rafael, 1849), 2: 405–407. See also Davenport, "Captain Jesús Cuellar," 60. Previously, Salvador Cuellar had advised Mexican General José Urrea about the strength of Texan forces at San Patricio. Carlos E. Castañeda, trans., *The Mexican Side of the Texas Revolution [1836] by the Chief Mexican Participants* (Dallas: P. L. Turner, 1928), 215.

12. "Señor Navarro Tells a Story," in Driggs and King, eds., *Rise of the Lone Star*, 272–275; Potter, *The Texas Revolution*, 18–20; John J. Linn, *Reminiscences of Fifty Years in Texas* (New York: D. & J. Sadlier, 1883; reprint, Austin: State House Press, 1986), 345–346; "San Fernando Cathedral Deaths," Book 3, 7 May 1838, CASA; Frederick Charles Chabot, *With the Makers of San Antonio. Genealogies of the Early Latin, Anglo-American, and German Families with Occasional Biographies, Each Group Being Prefaced with a Brief Historical Sketch and Illustrations* (San Antonio: Artes Graficas, 1937), 203. These accounts have some discrepancies but in general present the incident as recounted here. Despite Eugenio's Mexican allegiance, he reportedly wrote from San Luis Potosí to warn a brother at San Antonio of Santa Anna's imminent Texas invasion during the Texas Revolution. J. C. Neill to the Governor and Council, 23 January 1836, in *Official Correspondence of the Texan Revolution, 1835–1836*, ed. William C. Binkley (New York: D. Appleton-Century, 1936), 1: 328.

13. Henry Smith to Edward Burleson, 9 December 1835, in *Official Correspondence of the Texan Revolution*, ed. Binkley, 1: 177; Amos Pollard to Smith, 16 January 1836, in ibid., 1: 300; William Barret Travis to President of Convention, 3 March 1836, in the *San Felipe de Austin* (later *Houston*) *Telegraph and Texas Register*, 12 March 1836; Gregorio Gomez to brothers in arms and inhabitants, 17 October 1835, in *San Felipe de Austin* (later *Houston*) *Telegraph and Texas Register*, 14 November 1835 (quotation); José María Tornel, *Tejas y los Estados-Unidos de America, en sus relaciones con la Repub. Mexicana* (Mexico City: Ignacio Cumplido, 1837), 47, 57, 90 (translated in Castañeda, trans., *The Mexican Side of the Texas Revolution*, 328, 338, 370); Carlos Sanchez-Navarro, *La guerra de Tejas: Memorias de un soldado* (Mexico City: Editorial Polis, 1938), 117; Carmen Perry, ed. and trans., *With Santa Anna in Texas: A Personal Narrative of the Revolution by José Enrique de la Peña*, with an introduction by Llerena Friend (College Station: Texas A&M University Press, 1975), 4; *Mosquito Mexicano* (Mexico City), 27 September 1842; Antonio Menchaca, "The Memoirs of Captain Menchaca" (typescript), ed. James P. Newcomb, 30, CAH. Travis' letter is also in William Kennedy, *Texas: The Rise, Progress, and Prospects of the Republic of Texas* (London: R. Hastings, 1841; reprint, Fort Worth: Molyneaux Craftsmen, 1925), 2: 186; H. P. N. Gammel, comp., *The Laws of Texas, 1822–1897* (Austin: Gammel Book Co., 1898), 1: 845–846.

14. *Columbia* (later Houston) *Telegraph and Texas Register*, 9 November 1836; Muir, ed., *Texas in 1837*, 107. Mexico's president called for the reconquest of Texas shortly after Santa Anna's defeat at San Jacinto. His statement was printed in the *Houston Telegraph and Texas Register*, 18 April 1838. A report that Mexican authorities sought Tejano support for a reconquest effort is in *Houston Telegraph and Texas Register*, 6 January 1841. This report was based on the testimony of Juan Seguín. See also Juan Seguín to the President of the Republic, 26 December 1840, in *A Revolution Remembered: The Memoirs and Selected Correspondence of Juan N. Seguín*, ed. Jesús F. de la Teja (Austin: State House Press, 1991), 176–178.

15. Arista's proclamation was dated 9 January 1842 and was published in the *Houston Telegraph and Texas Register*, 9 March 1842. See also Juan N. Seguín,

Personal Memoirs of John N. Seguín from the Year 1834 to the Retreat of General Woll from the City of San Antonio in 1842 (San Antonio: Ledger Book and Job Office, 1858), 23. Seguín's memoirs are edited and reprinted in De la Teja, ed., *A Revolution Remembered*, 73–102. For a treatment of the 1842 Mexican occupations of San Antonio, see Nance, *Attack and Counter-Attack*, 9–54, 297–408.

16. *Houston Telegraph and Texas Register*, 30 March, 19, 26 October 1842. For Anglo-American accusations that Tejanos advised the Mexican army about the location of Texas troops, see ibid., 15 June 1842; M. C. Hamilton (by order of President Sam Houston) to Alexander Somervell, 13 October 1842, in *The Writings of Sam Houston, 1813–1863*, ed. Amelia W. Williams and Eugene C. Barker (Austin: University of Texas Press, 1940), 3: 177–178; Thomas J. Green, *Journal of the Texian Expedition against Mier; Subsequent Imprisonment of the Author; His Sufferings, and Final Escape from the Castle of Perote. With Reflections upon the Present Political and Probable Future Relations of Texas, Mexico, and the United States* (New York: Harper & Brothers, 1845), 36; Joseph D. McCutchan, *Mier Expedition Diary: A Texan Prisoner's Account*, ed. Joseph Milton Nance, with a foreword by Jane A. Kenamore (Austin: University of Texas Press, 1978), 14–15.

17. William Preston Stapp, *The Prisoners of Perote, Containing a Journal Kept by the Author, Who Was Captured by the Mexicans, at Mier, December 25, 1842, and Released from Perote, May 16, 1844* (Philadelphia: G. B. Zieber, 1845; reprint, Austin: University of Texas Press, 1977), 20.

18. Jean Marie Odin to Jean-Baptiste Étienne, 17 June 1842, CAT; *Houston Morning Star*, 9 June 1842; *Houston Telegraph and Texas Register*, 15 June 1842; Harvey Alexander Adams, "Diary of Harvey Alexander Adams, in Two Parts: Rhode Island to Texas and Expedition against the Southwest in 1842 and 1843" (typescript), 2: 26, CAH; Odin to Anthony Blanc, 4 July 1842, CAT. Odin's complaint about the volunteers is also expressed in the following letters: Odin to John Timon, 20 June 1842, The University of Notre Dame Archives, South Bend, Indiana (ND); Odin to Timon, 20 August 1842, ND; Odin to Stephen Rousselon, 10 December 1842, CAT; Odin to Propagation of the Faith, Paris, 14 May 1845, CAT. For further descriptions of the Texan volunteers' lawless behavior, see Adams, "Diary," 2: 15, 20; John Holmes Jenkins, III, ed., *Recollections of Early Texas: The Memoirs of John Holland Jenkins,* with a foreword by J. Frank Dobie (Austin: University of Texas Press, 1958; reprint, 1987), 96; Francis S. Latham, *Travels in the Republic of Texas, 1842*, ed. Gerald S. Pierce (Austin: Encino, 1971), 5; Prince Carl of Solms-Braunfels, *Texas 1844–45*, trans. from German (Houston: Anson Jones, 1936), 87; Hamilton to Somervell, 19 November 1842, in Williams and Barker, eds., *Writings of Sam Houston*, 3: 197–199; J. de Cramayel to Anson Jones, March 1843, in *Diplomatic Correspondence of the Republic of Texas*, ed. George P. Garrison (Washington, D.C.: Government Printing Office, 1911), 2: 1424–1426; Hamilton to Jones, 27 June 1843, in ibid., 2: 1453–1455; Somervell to Hamilton, 27 June 1843, in ibid., 2: 1455–1456; *Houston Morning Star*, 28 May, 9 June 1842; *Houston Telegraph and Texas Register*, 15 June 1842. Some sources denied that the Texas militia

behaved so dishonorably, e.g. *Houston Telegraph and Texas Register,* 15 June, 7 September 1842.

19. Reports of Tejano participation in military forces are in W. D. Miller to Houston, 9 March 1842, in Nance, *Attack and Counter-Attack,* 30; *Houston Telegraph and Texas Register,* 30 March, 27 April 1842; W. A. Miskel to Dr. [Francis] Moore, 14 December 1842, in ibid., 21 December 1842; Seguín, *Memoirs,* 24, 27–29; Green, *Journal of the Texian Expedition against Mier,* 31, 35–36; Frederick C. Chabot, *The Perote Prisoners: Being the Diary of James L. Truehart, Printed for the First Time Together with an Historical Introduction* (San Antonio: Naylor, 1934), 94–96; Anderson Hutchinson, "Diary," in "The Béxar and Dawson Prisoners," ed. E. W. Winkler, *QTSHA* 13 (April 1910): 294–295; Rodriguez, *Memoirs,* 17–18; Joseph Milton Nance, ed. and trans., "Brigadier General Adrian Woll's Report of His Expedition into Texas in 1842," *SWHQ* 58 (April 1955): 529, 533–535, 538, 542–544. Assistance offered to the Mexican wounded is described in Adams, "Diary," 2: 7. Assistance to Texan captives is recorded in Chabot, *Perote Prisoners,* 96–100; San Antonio prisoners to the American officers and citizens, 11 September 1842, in *Samuel Maverick, Texan: 1803–1870. A Collection of Letters, Journals, and Memoirs,* ed. Rena Maverick Green (San Antonio: Privately printed, 1952), 173–174; Samuel A. Maverick to Mary A. Maverick, 6 October 1842, in ibid., 197; A. Neill to Anson Jones, 29 January 1843, in Winkler, ed., "The Béxar and Dawson Prisoners," 314.

20. Nance, ed., "Woll's Report," 529; Chabot, *Perote Prisoners,* 93–96, 99; Hutchinson, "Diary," in Winkler, ed., "The Béxar and Dawson Prisoners," 294–295; Menchaca, "Memoirs," 35–37. Some witnesses stated that three Tejano commissioners were sent to treat with Woll, apparently referring to the San Antonio representatives Woll mentions in his official report. Chabot, *Perote Prisoners,* 93; Rodriguez, *Memoirs,* 18; Hutchinson, "Diary," in Winkler, ed., "The Béxar and Dawson Prisoners," 294; William E. Jones to [Mirabeau Buonaparte Lamar], 1 February 1844, in ibid., 321; Miskel to Moore, 14 December 1842, in *Houston Telegraph and Texas Register,* 21 December 1842.

21. De la Teja, ed., *A Revolution Remembered,* 24–34; Seguín to Béxar County Judge, 18 April 1842, in ibid., 179. For Seguín's own rendering of his military service during the Texas Revolution, see Seguín, *Memoirs,* 5–15. Mexican accusations against Seguín are in Perry, ed., *With Santa Anna in Texas,* 4; Vicente Filisola, *Memorias para la historia de la guerra de Tejas* (Mexico City: Ignacio Cumplido, 1849), 1: 238–239.

22. Green, *Journal of the Texian Expedition against Mier,* 35–36. Reports of accusations against Seguín from 1840 are in Jean Marie Odin, "Daily Journal" (photocopy), 16, CAT; Rena Maverick Green, ed., *Memoirs of Mary A. Maverick* (San Antonio: Alamo, 1921), 59; George T. Howard to Branch T. Archer, 16 December 1840, in *Appendix to the Journals of the House of Representatives: Fifth Congress* (N.p.: Gazette Office, n.d.), 374–375 (available at CAH). Other accusatory statements about Seguín are presented in De la Teja, ed., *A Revolution Remembered,* 44–48.

23. Seguín, *Memoirs,* 19 (first quotation), iv (second quotation), 21–29.

24. "A Talk with Mrs. Canterbury," *San Antonio Express Annual Review,* March 1890, 4; Seguín to the President of the Republic, 26 December 1840, in De la Teja, ed., *A Revolution Remembered,* 176–178; George W. Hockley to Seguín, 3 February 1[842], in ibid., 178; *Houston Telegraph and Texas Register,* 6 January, 3 February 1841. The latter edition of the *Telegraph and Texas Register* published Seguín's December 26, 1840, letter to the president.

25. A[ndrew] J[ackson] Sowell, *Early Settlers and Indian Fighters of Southwest Texas* (Austin: Ben C. Jones, 1900; reprint, Austin: State House Press, 1986), 14; Houston to Erasmo Seguín, 6 July 1842, in Williams and Barker, eds., *Writings of Sam Houston,* 4: 125. For the suffering of the Seguín family from Anglo-American lawlessness, see Jenkins, ed., *Recollections of Early Texas,* 96; *Houston Morning Star,* 9 June 1842; *Houston Telegraph and Texas Register,* 15 June 1842.

21. Nance, *Attack and Counter-Attack,* 38 (first quotation), 30 (second quotation). See also Thomas W. Bell to [William Adam Bell], 7 March 1842, in "Thomas W. Bell Letters," *SWHQ* 63 (January 1960): 466.

27. Odin to Timon, 20 June 1842; Odin to Rousselon, 10 December 1842. General Woll also testified that San Antonio Tejanos who accompanied him on his return to Mexico did so because they feared reprisal from the Texan forces. Nance, ed., "Woll's Report," 546–548.

28. *Houston Telegraph and Texas Register,* 24 August 1842; Latham, *Travels in the Republic of Texas,* 38. See also Muir, ed., *Texas in 1837,* 107.

29. *Journals of the Senate, of the Republic of Texas; First Session of the Third Congress, 1838* (Houston: National Intelligencer Office, 1839), 10 (quotation). A contemporary of Navarro's later wrote that he "accepted the appointment [as commissioner of the Santa Fe expedition] with misgiving, and only at the earnest solicitation of the President." He even suggests Navarro "felt that in case of success he might prove a useful protector to a Mexican population brought suddenly under the military control of another race." Potter, *The Texas Revolution,* 21. Some observers claim Navarro prepared a strong pro-Texas speech to deliver at New Mexico, but it appears that he merely translated the document in question. Anonymous, "To the Inhabitants of Santa Fe and Other Towns of New Mexico East of the Rio Grande" (typescript), Daughters of the Republic of Texas Library, San Antonio; "Señor Navarro Tells a Story," in Driggs and King, eds., *Rise of the Lone Star,* 289; Reuben M. Potter to Lamar, 5 June 1841, in *The Papers of Mirabeau Buonaparte Lamar,* ed. Charles Adams Gulick, Jr., and Katherine Elliott (Austin: Von Boeckmann-Jones, 1973), 3: 532–533.

30. Francisco Ruiz to the Congress of the Republic of Texas, 26 November 1836, Memorials and Petitions, Texas State Archives, Austin; Gammel, comp., *Laws of Texas,* 1: 1111–1336.

31. *Houston Telegraph and Texas Register,* 19 May 1838; Thomas Lloyd Miller, "Mexican-Texans at the Alamo," *Journal of Mexican American History* 2 (Fall 1971): 33–44. In the view of at least one historian, Anglo-Americans did not experience as much difficulty in obtaining their claims. Amelia Williams, "A Critical Study of the Siege of the Alamo and of the Personnel of Its Defenders," *SWHQ* 37 (April 1934): 257.

32. *Austin City Gazette,* 5 February 1840, in De la Teja, ed., *A Revolution Remembered,* 174. Also in Harriet Smither, ed., *Journals of the Fourth Congress of the Republic of Texas, 1839–1840* (Austin: Von Boeckmann-Jones, 1929), 1: 103–104. An act providing for translation of Texas laws into Spanish had been passed on January 23, 1839. *Houston Telegraph and Texas Register,* 6 February 1836; Gammel, comp., *Laws of Texas,* 2: 76–77. Seguín wrote a letter to Joseph Waples, Texas' chief clerk and acting secretary of state, on June 21, 1840, asking for a progress report on the promised translations. Waples responded that they still were not available. Joseph Waples to Juan Seguín, 1 July 1840, in De la Teja, ed., *A Revolution Remembered,* 175. During this same session of Congress, the position of translator for the Texas land office was also abolished. Smither, ed., *Journals of the Fourth Congress,* 1: 93, 118, 126, 139, 193, 204, 214. Seguín's funding proposal for a Béxar County jail is in ibid., 1: 132. No such law was passed during that congressional session, nor in the session that followed. Gammel, comp., *Laws of Texas,* 2: 175–672.

33. *Houston Telegraph and Texas Register,* 26 January 1839; William F. Weeks, comp., *Debates of the Texas Convention* (Houston: J. W. Cruger, 1846), 209. No legislation passed during Navarro's term at the Third Congress of the Republic of Texas reflects his 1839 intervention on behalf of Tejano land owners. Gammel, comp., *Laws of Texas,* 2: 3–167.

34. Smither, ed., *Journals of the Fourth Congress,* 1: 139, 206 (quotation). The pertinent legislation is in Gammel, comp., *Laws of Texas,* 2: 235–236, 369.

35. Weeks, comp., *Debates of the Texas Convention,* 235, 158, 473–474.

36. *Columbia* (later *Houston*) *Telegraph and Texas Register,* 20 September, 25 October 1836; John A. Wharton to Juan Seguín, 17 September 1836, in De la Teja, ed., *A Revolution Remembered,* 144–145; Juan Seguín to Houston, 6 December 1836, in ibid., 147; Felix Huston to Houston, 14 November 1836, CAT; Houston to Juan Seguín, 16 January 1837, in De la Teja, ed., *A Revolution Remembered,* 152–153 (also in Williams and Barker, eds., *Writings of Sam Houston,* 2: 33–34); Seguín, *Memoirs,* 15–16; Linn, *Reminiscences,* 294–296. There is some discrepancy in these accounts as to the date of Huston's order. John J. Linn postulated that General Huston's order may have been an attempt to induce local Tejanos to sell their land at reduced prices. Ibid., 295–296. Apparently, Seguín was aware of this or similar plots, as he later claimed that Anglo-Americans "were already beginning to work their dark intrigues against the native families, whose only crime was, that they owned large tracts of land and desirable property." Seguín, *Memoirs,* 18.

37. Election results from these years are summarized in Downs, "History of Mexicans in Texas," 255–257. For original documentation of election results and city council minutes, see "Minutes of the City Council of the City of San Antonio from 1837 to 1849, Journal A" (typescript), CAH.

38. A list of San Antonio mayors is given in William Corner, ed. and comp., *San Antonio de Béxar: A Guide and History* (San Antonio: Bainbridge & Corner, 1890; reprint, San Antonio: Graphic Arts, 1977), 66. Antonio Menchaca was also mayor for a brief period in 1838–1839. He was not elected, however, but served out the term of William H. Dangerfield.

39. David Montejano, *Anglos and Mexicans in the Making of Texas, 1836–1986* (Austin: University of Texas Press, 1987), 34 (quotations), 35; Jane Dysart, "Mexican Women in San Antonio, 1830–1860: The Assimilation Process," *Western Historical Quarterly* 7 (October 1976): 370–371.

40. Dysart, "Mexican Women in San Antonio, 1830–1860," 370; John Duff Brown, "Reminiscences of Jno. Duff Brown," *QTSHA* 12 (April 1909): 299; William F. Gray, *From Virginia to Texas, 1835: Diary of Col. Wm. F. Gray, Giving Details of His Journey to Texas and Return in 1835–1836 and Second Journey to Texas in 1837*, with a preface by A. C. Gray (Houston: Gray, Dillaye & Co., 1909; reprint, Houston: Fletcher, 1965), 165; Chabot, *With the Makers of San Antonio*, 152–153; James Ernest Crisp, "Anglo-Texan Attitudes toward the Mexican, 1821–1845" (Ph.D. diss., Yale University, New Haven, 1976), 351, 398.

41. Mary Maverick to Agatha S. Adams, 25 August 1838, in Green, ed., *Samuel Maverick, Texan*, 77; Green, ed., *Memoirs of Mary A. Maverick*, 53–56.

42. Wesley Norton, "Religious Newspapers in Antebellum Texas," *SWHQ* 79 (October 1975): 147–149, 152. Cumberland Presbyterians split from the Presbyterian Church in the United States of America in 1810. The latter then split into New and Old School branches in 1837. Richard B. Hughes, "Old School Presbyterians: Eastern Invaders of Texas, 1830–1865," *SWHQ* 74 (January 1971): 324.

43. Martin Ruter to Secretary of the Missionary Society of the Methodist Episcopal Church, 1838, in C. C. Cody, "Rev. Martin Ruter, A.M., D.D.," *Texas Methodist Historical Quarterly* 1 (July 1909): 25 (first quotation); Lawrence L. Brown, *The Episcopal Church in Texas, 1838–1874: From Its Foundation to the Division of the Diocese* (Austin: Church Historical Society, 1963), 24–25; Z. N. Morrell, *Flowers and Fruits from the Wilderness; or, Thirty-six Years in Texas and Two Winters in Honduras* (Boston: Gould and Lincoln, 1872), 117 (second quotation). In an 1839 letter, Reverend Abel Stevens stated that San Antonio ought to have a Methodist minister but that thus far none was stationed there. As cited in "The Texas Missions," *Texas Methodist Historical Quarterly* 2 (October 1910): 160.

44. W. C. Blair to John Breckenridge, 5 March 1839, in R. Douglas Brackenridge and Francisco O. García-Treto, *Iglesia Presbiteriana: A History of Presbyterians and Mexican Americans in the Southwest* (San Antonio: Trinity University Press, 1974), 5 (first quotation); Valentine Bennet, "Valentine Bennet Scrapbook," 102, 260, CAH; *Annual Report of the Board of Foreign Missions of the Presbyterian Church in the United States of America* (New York, 1841), 8, in Brackenridge and García-Treto, *Iglesia Presbiteriana*, 6 (second quotation). For a brief summary of Blair's ministry and activities among Tejanos, see ibid., 4–8; William Stuart Red, *A History of the Presbyterian Church in Texas* ([Austin]: Steck, 1936), 25–26.

45. John Wesley DeVilbiss, Sr., "Reminiscences of a Superannuated Preacher," in *Reminiscences and Events in the Ministerial Life of Rev. John Wesley DeVilbiss*, comp. H. A. Graves (Galveston: W. A. Shaw, 1886), 40–41, 50; Josephine Forman, *We Finish to Begin: A History of Travis Park United Meth-*

odist Church, San Antonio, Texas, 1846–1991 (San Antonio: Travis Park United Methodist Church, 1991), 2–4; Nancy Lou McCallum, "History of the Methodist Episcopal Church, South, in San Antonio, Texas" (M.A. thesis, University of Texas, Austin, 1936), 1:3; William Wallace McCullough, Jr., *John McCullough: Pioneer Presbyterian Missionary and Teacher in the Republic of Texas* (Galveston: Privately printed, 1944), 31; McCullough, *John McCullough: Pioneer Presbyterian Missionary and Teacher in the Republic of Texas* (Austin: Pemberton, 1966), 61–62, 66–69; Olin W. Nail, *The First Hundred Years of the Southwest Texas Conference of the Methodist Church, 1858–1958* (San Antonio: Southwest Texas Conference, Methodist Church, 1958), 98, 101–105; Macum Phelan, *A History of Early Methodism in Texas, 1817–1866* (Nashville: Cokesbury, 1924), 238–240; *First Presbyterian Church, San Antonio, Texas, 1846–1946* (N.p.: [1946]), 2–3 (available at CAH); Walter N. Vernon and others, *The Methodist Excitement in Texas: A History* (Dallas: Texas Methodist Historical Society, 1984), 73.

46. Muir, ed., *Texas in 1837*, 102–103; Morrell, *Flowers and Fruits from the Wilderness*, 118; W. L. McCalla, *Adventures in Texas, Chiefly in the Spring and Summer of 1840* (Philadelphia: Privately printed, 1841), 81–83.

47. A. B. Lawrence, "Introduction," in *Texas in 1840, or the Emigrant's Guide to the New Republic; Being the Result of Observation, Enquiry and Travel in that Beautiful Country. By an Emigrant, Late of the United States* (New York: William W. Allen, 1840), xviii–xix. See also ibid., 245.

48. Patrick Foley, "From Linares to Galveston: The Early Development of the Catholic Hierarchy in Texas," paper read at the first Biennial Conference of the Texas Catholic Historical Society, St. Edward's University, Austin, 27 October 1989.

49. For Odin's rendering of the San Antonio priests' removal and the local community's response, see Odin to Timon, 14 July 1840, CAT; Odin to Blanc, 24 August 1840, CAT; Odin to Joseph Rosati, 27 August 1840, CAT; Odin to Étienne, 28 August 1840, CAT; Odin to James Cardinal Fransoni, 15 December 1840, CAT; Odin to Étienne, 11 April 1841, CAT; Odin, "Daily Journal," 6–8. The published complaint against Odin is in the *Austin Texas Sentinel*, 29 August 1840. No newspapers were published in San Antonio at this time, so the Austin press was the nearest available. An excellent treatment of the conflicts between European immigrant Catholics and the U.S. hierarchy is Patrick W. Carey, *People, Priests, and Prelates: Ecclesiastical Democracy and the Tensions of Trusteeism* (Notre Dame, Ind.: University of Notre Dame Press, 1987). In New Mexico, native Catholic response to the removal of their clergy was far more conflictual than at San Antonio. See, e.g., Angélico Chávez, *But Time and Chance: The Story of Padre Martínez of Taos, 1793–1867* (Santa Fe: Sunstone, 1981).

50. José Roberto Juarez, "La iglesia Católica y el Chicano en sud Texas, 1836–1911," *Aztlán* 4 (Fall 1973): 219–221; James Talmadge Moore, *Through Fire and Flood: The Catholic Church in Frontier Texas* (College Station: Texas A&M University Press, 1992), 39–40; J. C. Clopper, "J. C. Clopper's Journal and Book of Memoranda for 1828," *QTSHA* 13 (July 1909): 73; Minutes of the junta for the Independence Day celebration, 12 September 1829, BA; Sanchez-

Navarro, *La guerra de Tejas,* 107; *Austin City Gazette,* 12 August 1840; Thomas W. Bell to brother, 17 August 1840, in "Thomas W. Bell Letters," *SWHQ* 63 (October 1959): 303; Green, ed., *Memoirs of Mary A. Maverick,* 59; Odin to Blanc, 24 August 1840; Odin to Rosati, 27 August 1840; Odin to Étienne, 28 August 1840; Odin to Étienne, 11 April 1841; Odin, "Daily Journal," 6.

51. Odin to Blanc, 16 May 1842, CAT; Odin to Étienne, 17 June 1842; Nance, ed., "Woll's Report," 548 (quotation), 549. In his 1892 history of Texas, John Henry Brown claims that General Woll reinstated De la Garza when he occupied San Antonio from September 11 to 20. However, San Fernando parish records indicate that Father Miguel Calvo, the pastor assigned by Odin, presided at three baptisms on September 17. Thus it does not seem that Calvo was ousted during Woll's stay in the city. John Henry Brown, *History of Texas, from 1685 to 1892* (St. Louis: L. E. Daniell, 1892), 2: 230; "San Fernando Baptismal Register," Book 6, 17 September 1842, CASA.

52. Moore, *Through Fire and Flood,* 40.

53. Juan Seguín, "Affidavit on Parish Priests of Béxar and La Bahía," 5 January 1839, in De la Teja, ed., *A Revolution Remembered,* 172; Timon to Blanc, 17? January 1839, ND; John Timon, "Narrative of the Barrens," 39, Vincentian Archives, St. Mary's of the Barrens, Perryville, Missouri; Carlos Castañeda, *Our Catholic Heritage in Texas, 1519–1936* (Austin: Von Boeckmann-Jones, 1936–1958), 7: 26. Timon's letter and memoirs indicate that both Seguín and Navarro testified against the San Antonio clergy, but Seguín's affidavit appears to be the only written record available.

54. Timon, "Narrative of the Barrens," 39; Odin to Propagation of the Faith, 28 March 1852, CAT.

55. Odin to Étienne, 7 February 1842, CAT; Odin, "Daily Journal," 34; Odin to John Baptist Purcell, 25 June 1861, ND (first quotation); Miguel Joaquín Calvo, Personal file, Archivo Matritense C.M., Madrid (second quotation). The quotation from Calvo's personal file is my translation of the text. Odin's 1842 letter is cited in the *United States Catholic Magazine and Monthly Review* 3 (October 1844): 727–730. Earlier Odin had stated that priests in Texas "will have to speak English, Spanish, and a little German." Odin to Blanc, 12 December 1852, CAT. He also provided Spanish classes for recently arrived seminarians, religious, and priests, at times teaching these classes himself. See, e.g., Odin to Blanc, 6 January 1853, 23 April 1856, CAT; Odin to Propagation of the Faith, 9 January, 1 July 1853, CAT; Odin to Rousselon, 21 January 1853, CAT.

56. Papal recognition had been given to the Guadalupan image in 1754, when Benedict XIV proclaimed her the patroness of New Spain and declared December 12 her feast day.

57. Odin to Étienne, 7 February 1842. In a society that kept women subordinate to men, the relative prominence of Tejanas in the planning of these celebrations is striking. Admittedly, their leadership role was limited to collecting jewelry and other ornaments for the decoration of the church and the Guadalupan image. But, as will be shown below, young Tejanas also exercised an important role in the processions as the immediate attendants of that image, which was the principal ritual object. Such prominence was not evident in other areas of

Tejano life. David J. Weber, *The Mexican Frontier, 1821–1846: The American Southwest under Mexico* (Albuquerque: University of New Mexico Press, 1982), 215–216. For an analysis of women's leadership role in Latin American Catholicism, see Ana María Díaz-Stevens, "The Saving Grace: The Matriarchal Core of Latino Catholicism," *Latino Studies Journal*, 4 (September 1993): 60–78.

58. Odin to Étienne, 7 February 1842; Green, ed., *Memoirs of Mary A. Maverick*, 53–54. For a fuller treatment of these celebrations, see Timothy M. Matovina, "Our Lady of Guadalupe Celebrations in San Antonio, Texas, 1840–41," *Journal of Hispanic/Latino Theology*, 1 (November 1993): 77–96. As was previously mentioned, Mary Maverick was the wife of Samuel Maverick, who was mayor of San Antonio from 1839 to 1840.

59. For the participation of visitors to San Antonio in *fandangos*, along with contemporary descriptions of these festive Tejano dances, see Ehrenberg, *With Milam and Fannin*, 102–105; Muir, ed., *Texas in 1837*, 104–106; Benedict, "Diary of a Campaign against the Comanches," 305; Kendall, *Narrative of the Texan Santa Fe Expedition*, 1: 46; Green, *Journal of the Texian Expedition Against Mier*, 41–42; Auguste Frétellière, "Adventures of a Castrovillian," in Julia Nott Waugh, *Castro-Ville and Henry Castro, Empresario* (San Antonio: Standard, 1934), 93; Samuel E. Chamberlain, *My Confession*, with an introduction and postscript by Roger Butterfield (New York: Harper & Brothers, 1956), 44–45; Roemer, *Texas*, 121–123, 131.

60. "Minutes of the City Council of the City of San Antonio from 1837 to 1849," 13 May 1841; Juan Seguín and others to Lamar, 15 May 1841, in Gulick and Elliott, eds., *Papers of Lamar*, 3: 521; Green, ed., *Memoirs of Mary A. Maverick*, 55–56; *Houston Telegraph and Texas Register*, 9 June 1841; *Columbia* (later *Houston*) *Telegraph and Texas Register*, 28 March, 4 April 1837 (quotation); Juan Seguín to General Albert Sidney Johnston, 13 March 1837, in De la Teja, ed., *A Revolution Remembered*, 161–162. Seguín's speech is also in ibid., 156.

61. Nance, ed., "Woll's Report," 542; Green, ed., *Memoirs of Mary A. Maverick*, 53; Hollon and Butler, eds., *William Bollaert's Texas*, 230 (quotation).

62. "Esparza Remembers," in Driggs and King, eds., *Rise of the Lone Star*, 214–215.

63. Andrew Anthony Tijerina, "*Tejanos* and Texas: The Native Mexicans of Texas, 1820–1850" (Ph.D. diss., University of Texas, Austin, 1977), 259–260.

4. EMERGING ETHNICITY: THE FIRST FIFTEEN YEARS AFTER U.S. ANNEXATION, 1845 – 1860

1. Ferdinand Roemer, *Texas: With Particular Reference to German Immigration and the Physical Appearance of the Country*, trans. Oswald Mueller (San Antonio: Standard, 1935; reprint, Waco: Texian Press, 1967), 119; Seth Eastman, *A Seth Eastman Sketchbook, 1848–1849*, with an introduction by Lois Burkhalter (Austin: University of Texas Press, 1961), xxii; Frederick Law Olmsted, *A Journey through Texas; or, A Saddle-Trip on the Southwestern Frontier:*

With a Statistical Appendix (New York: Dix, Edwards & Co., 1857), 150; J[osé] M[aría] Rodriguez, *Rodriguez Memoirs of Early Texas* (San Antonio: Passing Show Printing, 1913; reprint, San Antonio: Standard, 1961), 34.

2. Terry G. Jordan, "Population Origins in Texas, 1850," *Geographical Review* 59 (January 1969): 85.

3. Olmsted, *A Journey through Texas,* 160. See also *San Antonio Daily Herald,* 13 March 1858. Unless otherwise noted, all other newspapers cited in this chapter were published in San Antonio.

4. When J. C. Clopper visited San Antonio in 1828, for example, he reported both French and Irish residents among the local population. Benjamin Lundy met a French resident of San Antonio during his 1833 visit. Italian Guiseppe Cassini (known in Texas as José Cassiano) also lived in the town before Texas independence. J. C. Clopper, "J. C. Clopper's Journal and Book of Memoranda for 1828," *QTSHA* 13 (July 1909): 71; Benjamin Lundy, *The Life, Travels and Opinions of Benjamin Lundy, Including His Journeys to Texas and Mexico; with a Sketch of Contemporary Events, and a Notice of the Revolution in Hayti* (Philadelphia: William D. Parrish, 1847; reprint, New York: Negro Universities Press, 1969), 54; Frederick Charles Chabot, *With the Makers of San Antonio. Genealogies of the Early Latin, Anglo-American, and German Families with Occasional Biographies, Each Group Being Prefaced with a Brief Historical Sketch and Illustrations* (San Antonio: Artes Graficas, 1937), 223–225. See also Rodriguez, *Memoirs,* 59, 63.

5. A correspondent of the *Boston Evening Post* claimed that U.S. forces leaving San Antonio for Mexico in the fall of 1846 numbered 2,600. As cited in *Chronicles of the Gringos: The U.S. Army in the Mexican War, 1846–1848, Accounts of Eyewitnesses & Combatants,* ed. Winston Smith and Charles Judah (Albuquerque: University of New Mexico Press, 1968), 93. A slightly lower number is given in Francis Baylies, *A Narrative of Major General Wool's Campaign in Mexico, in the Years 1846, 1847 & 1848* (Albany: Little, 1851; reprint, Austin: Jenkins, 1975), 12. Bishop Jean Marie Odin estimated the count at nearly four thousand. Jean Marie Odin to Propagation of the Faith, 9 April 1847, CAT. One U.S. soldier claimed the U.S. force was ten-thousand strong, a figure that undoubtedly was too high. William A. McClintock, "Journal of a Trip through Texas and Northern Mexico in 1846–1847," *SWHQ* 34 (October 1930): 143. See also Rodriguez, *Memoirs* 40. All of these estimates represent a larger military force than San Antonio's 1,500 civilians at the time of U.S. annexation. See note 5, Ch. 3. Pertinent sections from official military reports in the 1850s are in W. G. Freeman, "W. G. Freeman's Report on the Eighth Military Department," ed. M. L. Crimmins, *SWHQ* 51 (October 1947): 168; J. K. F. Mansfield, "Colonel J. K. F. Mansfield's Report of the Inspection of the Department of Texas in 1856," *SWHQ* 42 (October 1938): 135–141. See also Carland Elaine Crook, "Military Foundations," ch. in "San Antonio, Texas, 1846–1861" (M.A. thesis, Rice University, Houston, 1964), 19–37.

6. Ralph A. Wooster, "Foreigners in the Principal Towns of Ante-Bellum Texas," *SWHQ* 66 (October 1962): 209, 211; Gilbert J. Jordan, ed. and trans., "W. Steinert's View of Texas in 1849," *SWHQ* 80 (October 1976): 193. The

article edited by Jordan incorrectly cites the 1850 census in stating San Antonio's free population was 3,488. A slightly higher figure for San Antonio "Mexican Americans" in the 1850 census is given in Richard L. Nostrand, "Mexican Americans Circa 1850," *Annals of the Association of American Geographers* 65 (September 1975): 387.

7. Figures tabulated from "Population Schedules of the Eighth Census of the United States, 1860" (Washington, D.C.: The National Archives, 1967, text-fiche), roll 1288: 1–192a. Frederick Law Olmsted estimated the population of San Antonio in 1856 at 10,500 with four thousand Mexicans, three thousand Germans, and 3,500 Americans. About that same time, John C. Reid placed San Antonio's population at about ten thousand, with Germans, Americans, and Mexicans each comprising approximately a third of that number. The *San Antonio Daily Herald* reported the same figures in 1858. In 1859, Horace Elisha Scudder was told that the city had a population of twelve thousand, with five thousand Mexicans, three thousand Americans, and four thousand others, mainly German and French. While these are rough figures, they indicate that the relative size of the major ethnic groups in the city remained fairly constant. Olmsted, *A Journey through Texas*, 160; John C. Reid, *Reid's Tramp, or a Journal of the Incidents of Ten Months Travel through Texas, New Mexico, Arizona, Sonora, and California Including Topography, Climate, Soil, Minerals, Metals, and Inhabitants; with a Notice of the Great Inter-Oceanic Rail Road* (Selma, Ala.: John Hardy, 1858; reprint, Austin: Steck, 1935), 59–60; *Daily Herald*, 25 June 1858; Ellen Bartlett Ballou, "Scudder's Journey to Texas, 1859," *SWHQ* 63 (July 1959): 8.

8. Wooster, "Foreigners in the Principal Towns of Ante-Bellum Texas," 209; "Population Schedules of the Eighth Census of the United States, 1860," roll 1288: 1–192a. For the 1850 census, see V. K. Carpenter, comp., *The State of Texas Federal Population Schedules Seventh Census of the United States, 1850* (Huntsville, Ark.: Century Enterprises, 1969), 1: 111–189. In what follows, references to San Antonio Tejanos encompass other residents of Mexican heritage who were initiated into the local Tejano community.

9. These figures were tabulated from *State of Texas Federal Population Schedules Seventh Census*, 1: 111–189; "Population Schedules of the Eighth Census of the United States, 1860," roll 1288: 1–192a. In both of these years, the majority of Tejano laborers were cartmen. Contemporary travelers to San Antonio also noted the preponderance of these Tejano hirelings who transported goods. See, e.g., Olmsted, *A Journey through Texas*, 152–153, 160; John Russell Bartlett, *Personal Narrative of Explorations and Incidents in Texas, New Mexico, California, Sonora, and Chihuahua, Connected with the United States and Mexican Boundary Commission, during the Years 1850, '51, '52, and '53* (New York: D. Appleton, 1854; reprint, Chicago: Rio Grande Press, 1965), 1: 40.

10. R. W. Brahan, Jr., to John D. Coffee, 20 January [1855], in Aaron M. Boom, "Texas in the 1850s, as Viewed by a Recent Arrival," *SWHQ* 70 (October 1966): 283. On his visit to Texas shortly after U.S. annexation, Ferdinand Roemer noted that most Tejanos were of the "lower class," with only "a few wealthy and cultured [Tejano] families." Roemer, *Texas*, 11. After his 1856 visit to San

NOTES TO PAGES 52–53

Antonio, John C. Reid wrote that "by far the most numerous class of Mexicans" were those of the "lower order." Reid, *Reid's Tramp,* 69. See also McClintock, "Journal of a Trip through Texas and Northern Mexico in 1846–1847," 142–143; Olmsted, *A Journey through Texas,* 162; *Ledger,* 1 September 1853; *Daily Herald,* 24 September 1858.

11. *Ledger,* 23 June 1853. It is possible that the judge and attorneys only appeared to understand the languages spoken, of course. In any event the ethnic diversity of San Antonio is illustrated by this court case which took place in four languages.

12. *Ledger,* 16 December 1852, 12 December 1857, 18 December 1858; *Alamo Star,* 11, 16 December 1854; "Mrs. French's Reminiscences of Early Days in Béxar," in S. J. Wright, *San Antonio de Béxar: Historical, Traditional, Legendary* (Austin: Morgan, 1916), 98; Catherine McDowell, ed., *Letters from the Ursuline, 1852–1853* (San Antonio: Trinity University Press, 1977), 170, 272, 276. I have found no evidence that Tejanos organized a formal association for planning these Guadalupae celebrations, although it is possible that they did so.

13. "Esparza, the Boy of the Alamo, Remembers," in *Rise of the Lone Star: A Story of Texas Told by Its Pioneers,* ed. Howard R. Driggs and Sarah S. King (New York: Frederick A. Stokes, 1936), 220 (quotation); *Daily Herald,* 25 December 1858; McDowell, ed., *Letters from the Ursuline,* 260–261, 271–273, 283, 312–313; Sarah Brackett King, "Early Days in San Antonio Recalled by a Pioneer Resident of the City," *Light,* 4 February 1917, 14; James P. Newcomb, "Christmas in San Antonio Half a Century Ago," *Express,* 18 December 1904, 26. The recollections of three San Antonio residents state that "los Pastores" were also presented at San Fernando Church, but it is not clear if this practice was extant before 1860. "Esparza Remembers," in Driggs and King, eds., *Rise of the Lone Star,* 219–220; "Mrs. French's Reminiscences," in Wright, *San Antonio de Béxar,* 100; King, "Early Days in San Antonio," 14.

14. M. L. Crimmins, "Robert E. Lee in Texas: Letters and Diary," *West Texas Historical Association Year Book* 8 (June 1932): 19 (quotation); Charles Merritt Barnes, *Combats and Conquests of Immortal Heroes: Sung in Song and Told in Story* (San Antonio: Guessaz & Ferlet, 1910), 121; "Mrs. French's Reminiscences," in Wright, *San Antonio de Béxar,* 98; *Correo,* 8 July 1858; Jordan, "W. Steinert's View of Texas in 1849," *SWHQ* 80 (April 1977): 401; King, "Early Days in San Antonio," 14. A painting entitled "Corrida de la Sandía" (The Watermelon Race) by Theodore Gentilz, is in *Gentilz: Artist of the Old Southwest* (Austin: University of Texas Press, 1974), 85. It depicts a watermelon race in San Antonio, where Gentilz first arrived in 1844. Sarah L. French's reminiscences incorrectly identify the feast of San Juan with Cinco de Mayo (May 5). The "Guidelines for a Texas Mission," written in the late 1780s for San Antonio's Mission Concepción, prescribed the feasts of San Juan, San Pedro, Santiago, and Santa Ana as "the days when the Indians go horseback-riding." While there is no evidence which directly links later Tejano practice and these guidelines, it is interesting to note the correlation between the customs of the San Antonio missions and the later Tejano community. Benedict Leutenegger, trans., *Guidelines for a Texas Mission: Instructions for the Missionary of Mission Concepción in San*

121

Antonio, Texas (San Antonio: Old Spanish Missions Historical Research Library, 1976), 6.

15. Fourth of July celebrations at San Antonio are reported in *Ledger,* 10 July 1851, 1 July 1852, 6 July 1854, 5 July 1856, 4 July 1857, 3 July 1858, 6 July 1859; *Western Texan,* 6 July 1854; *Alamo Star,* 8 July 1854; *Bejareño,* 7 July 1855; *Herald,* 5 July 1856; *Texan,* 2 July 1857; *Daily Herald and Public Advertiser,* 6 July 1857; *Ledger and Texan,* 30 June, 7 July 1860; "Journal of City Council B: January 1849 to August 1856, City of San Antonio," 3 July 1852, City Clerk's Office, San Antonio; "Journal of City Council C, April 1, 1856 to February 21, 1870, City of San Antonio," 2 July 1860, ibid. For Washington's birthday celebrations, see *Daily Herald,* 23, 24 February 1859, 14, 17, 23 February, 1860; *Texan,* 24? February 1859; Ballou, "Scudder's Journey to Texas," 9. Reports of Texas Independence Day festivities are in *Ledger,* 6 March 1858; *Herald,* 3 March 1858, 5 March 1859; *Daily Herald,* 3 March 1860; Ballou, "Scudder's Journey to Texas," 9−10. For Thanksgiving Day ceremonies, see *Daily Ledger,* 24−25 November 1858; *Daily Herald,* 25 November 1858, 24 November 1859; *Ledger and Texan,* 26 November 1859, 1 December 1860. May Day celebration reports are in *Herald,* 1 May 1855, 3 May 1856, 15 May 1858; *Texan,* 1 May 1856; *Bejareño,* 3 May 1856; *Ledger,* 2 May 1857, 15 May 1858; *Daily Herald,* 30 April 1858; *Ledger and Texan,* 19 May 1860. German commemorations of Schiller's birthday are announced in *Daily Herald,* 9, 12 November 1859; *Daily Ledger and Texan,* 10 November 1859. Other Texas anniversaries were not celebrated in the city. Although the anniversary of the Texan victory over Santa Anna at San Jacinto (April 21) was commemorated elsewhere in the state, for example, the local press critiqued San Antonio residents for not doing the same. *Herald,* 1, 15 May 1855: *Ledger,* 8 May 1858; *Daily Herald,* 22 April 1859.

16. *Ledger,* 6 July 1854; *Daily Herald,* 9 March 1859; *Ledger,* 6 March 1851. The Texas commemoration of Thanksgiving Day was on March 6 in 1851; the current practice of celebrating it in November had not yet been established.

17. *Ledger,* 10 July 1851.

18. Ibid., 12 May 1853; Newcomb, "Christmas in San Antonio Half a Century Ago," 26; McDowell, ed., *Letters from the Ursuline,* 272, 276.

19. *Correo,* 26 May 1858.

20. "Minutes of the City Council of the City of San Antonio from 1837 to 1849, Journal A" (typescript), 7 January, 27 December 1847, CAH; King, "Early Days in San Antonio," 14. The funds collected for *fandango* licenses were the largest revenue item on the city financial report for 1847, accounting for more than one third of revenues collected.

21. *Western Texan,* 19 June 1851; McDowell, ed., *Letters from the Ursuline,* 283−284; "Journal of City Council B," 1 February 1853; "Journal of City Council C," 13 September 1858. Editorial critiques of *fandangos* are also in *Western Texan,* 20 July 1854; *Bejareño,* 7 February 1855. Father Dubuis founded a society for young people at San Fernando, whose members he deemed "fighters against the *fandangos,* against the public houses and against the efforts of the public schools." Claude Marie Dubuis to Jean Marie Odin, 10 April 1853, Incar-

nate Word Archives, Incarnate Word Generalate, San Antonio (IWA). This letter and other Dubuis correspondence are also in Mary Hoffman Ogilvie, "Claude Marie Dubuis: Nineteenth-Century Texas Missionary" (M.A. thesis, University of Texas, Austin, 1990).

22. *Daily Ledger*, 19 August 1858; "Journal of City Council B," 15 January 1850. City council actions on *fandangos* are in "Minutes of the City Council of the City of San Antonio, Journal A," 12 January, 4 April 1846; 7 January 1847; 31 May 1848; "Journal of City Council B," 28 February, 7 March 1849; 11 February 1852; 22–23 February, 14 April, 7 June 1853; 30 March, 13 April 1854; 8 January 1855; "Journal of City Council C," 4, 11 August, 22 September 1858.

23. "Journal of City Council B," 1, 22–23 February, 14 April, 7 June 1853; *Ledger* 10, 31 March, 28 April, 7 July 1853.

24. Ordinances prohibiting *fandangos* can be found in the city council minutes for the following dates: 7 March 1849, 7 June 1853, 8 January 1855. Reports of *fandangos* held while these ordinances were in force include *Western Texan*, 9 October 1851; *Ledger*, 23 June, 28 July, 4 August 1853; *Alamo Star*, 22 January 1855; *Herald*, 1 May, 18 September, 9 October 1855; *Bejareño*, 1 September 1855; *Texan*, 15 May 1856. The reported assault of the local constable is in *Alamo Star*, 22 January 1855. The rise and decline of the Know Nothing, or American, Party in local politics is treated below.

25. *Herald*, 14 August, 18 September, 9 October 1855, 3 February 1858; *Ledger*, 6 November 1858. See also Brahan to Coffee, 20 January [1855], in Boom, "Texas in the 1850s," 284; Samuel E. Chamberlain, *My Confession*, with an introduction and postscript by Roger Butterfield (New York: Harper & Brothers, 1956), 45; Wharton J. Green, *Recollections and Reflections: An Auto of Half a Century and More* (N.p.: Edwards and Broughton, 1906), 117; Z. N. Morrell, *Flowers and Fruits from the Wilderness; or, Thirty-six Years in Texas and Two Winters in Honduras* (Boston: Gould and Lincoln, 1872), 167; Reid, *Reid's Tramp*, 38. For a discussion of Anglo-American perceptions of Tejanos, see James Ernest Crisp, "Anglo-Texan Attitudes toward the Mexican, 1821–1845" (Ph.D. diss., Yale University, New Haven, 1976); Arnoldo De León, *They Called Them Greasers: Anglo Attitudes toward Mexicans in Texas, 1821–1900* (Austin: University of Texas Press, 1983); Raymund A. Paredes, "The Origins of Anti-Mexican Sentiment in the United States," *New Scholar* 6 (1977): 139–165; David J. Weber, "'Scarce more than apes.' Historical Roots of Anglo American Stereotypes of Mexicans in the Border Region," in *New Spain's Far Northern Frontier: Essays on Spain in the American West, 1540–1821*, ed. David J. Weber (Albuquerque: University of New Mexico Press, 1979), 295–307.

26. Olmsted, *A Journey through Texas*, 126; "Recollections of Texas. By a Returned Emigrant," *North American Miscellany* 2 (17 May 1851): 114; *Texas Presbyterian* (Houston), 15 January 1848. See also Jon Winfield Dancy, "Diary of Jon Winfield Dancy, November 1, 1837 to January, 1847" (photocopy), 34, CAH; William Russell Story, "Diary of William Russell Story, December 3, 1855–March 16, 1856" (typescript), 26, CAH. The near riot at San Antonio is reported in Olmsted, *A Journey through Texas*, 164.

27. Rodriguez, *Memoirs,* 34–35; *Ledger,* 9 September, 2 December 1852, 22 September 1855; *Herald,* 18 September, 9 October 1855; *Texan,* 24 June 1858; *Ledger,* 26 June 1858, 10 July 1851 (quotation). The 1855 Mexican Independence Day celebration was a month after the most heated Know Nothing election in the city's history and apparently brought together Tejano, Anglo-American, and German allies from that political struggle.

28. *Daily Herald,* 24 September 1858.

29. Jane Dysart, "Mexican Women in San Antonio, 1830–1860: The Assimilation Process," *Western Historical Quarterly* 7 (October 1976): 365–375, 370 (quotation). Dysart's research also identified five marriages between Spanish-surnamed men and Anglo-American women at San Antonio from 1830 to 1860. The relatively small number of marriages involving Anglo-American women and Tejano men is explained in large part by male preponderance among Anglo-American immigrants to San Antonio during this period.

30. Ibid., 374 (quotation).

31. *Alamo Star,* 9 October 1854; *Ledger,* 1 September 1853; *Daily Herald,* 13 March 1858; George G. Smith, *The Life and Times of George Foster Pierce, D.D., LL.D., Bishop of the Methodist Episcopal Church, South, with His Sketch of Lovick Pierce, D.D., His Father,* with an introduction by Atticus G. Haygood (Sparta, Ga.: Hancock, 1888), 375. See also Bartlett, *Personal Narrative,* 1: 40.

32. Rena Maverick Green, ed., *Memoirs of Mary A. Maverick* (San Antonio: Alamo, 1921), 53–56, 97–118; Mary A. Maverick to Agatha S. Adams, 25 August 1838, in *Samuel Maverick, Texan: 1803–1870. A Collection of Letters, Journals and Memoirs,* ed. Rena Maverick Green (San Antonio: Privately printed, 1952), 77; Fane Downs, "The History of Mexicans in Texas, 1820–1845" (Ph.D. diss., Texas Tech University, Lubbock, 1970), 258. In the diaries, journals, memoirs, and reminiscences consulted for this study, eight visitors to San Antonio from 1836 to 1846 recorded that they joined local Tejanos in their *fandangos* (see note 59 in Ch. 3). One observer wrote in 1846 that at San Antonio "*fandangos* take place every night God permits to return and some of the resident Americans have not missed any of them for years." Roemer, *Texas,* 123. After 1846, however, there are no reports in extant sources of Anglo-Americans or other newcomers to San Antonio attending *fandangos.*

33. *Ledger,* 12 December 1857; *Alamo Star,* 11 December 1854.

34. Local newspapers regularly listed a schedule of services for the various congregations, although the times for Catholic services were omitted. See, e.g., *Alamo Express,* 15 October 1860. For a brief overview of denominational growth at San Antonio during this period, see Dorothy Kelly Gibson, "Social Life in San Antonio, 1855–1860," (M.A. thesis, University of Texas, Austin, 1937), 93–106.

35. R. Douglas Brackenridge, *Voice in the Wilderness: A History of the Cumberland Presbyterian Church in Texas,* with an introduction by Thomas H. Campbell (San Antonio: Trinity University Press, 1968), 59; *Ledger and Texan,* 28 July 1860; Ballou, "Scudder's Journey to Texas," 8, 10; Crook, "San Antonio, Texas, 1846–1861," 101; *Alamo Express,* 1 October 1860. The 1859 visitor to the city, Horace Elisha Scudder, did not identify the denomination of the African-

American congregation. It could possibly have been a Presbyterian or Methodist group, or else a completely independent church.

36. Francois Bouchu to uncle, 14 May 1855, CAT; letter of R. F. Bunting, 23 November 1859, in *Ledger and Texan*, 14 July 1860; *Texas Baptist* (Anderson), 2 February 1860; *First Presbyterian Church San Antonio, Texas, 1846–1946* (N.p.: [1946]), 6 (available at CAH); "Eighth Census of the United States, 1860, Schedule Six—Social Statistics" (National Archives, text-fiche), Microcopy No. T1134, Roll No. 0044; *Ledger and Texan*, 3 November 1860. In 1860, German Methodists were meeting at a local public school; the Baptists met in a rented room above a store.

37. Odin to Propagation of the Faith, 9 January 1853, CAT; Bouchu to uncle, 14 May 1855.

38. *Texas Baptist* (Anderson), 2 February 1860.

39. [*Domestic*] *Missionary Chronicle* 7 (1848): 88, in R. Douglas Brackenridge and Francisco O. García-Treto, *Iglesia Presbiteriana: A History of Presbyterians and Mexican Americans in the Southwest* (San Antonio: Trinity University Press, 1974), 9 (quotation); William Wallace McCullough, Jr., *John McCullough: Pioneer Presbyterian Missionary and Teacher in the Republic of Texas* (Galveston: Privately printed, 1944), 32–35; McCullough, *John McCullough: Pioneer Presbyterian Missionary and Teacher in the Republic of Texas* (Austin: Pemberton, 1966), 62–63, 70–73; William S. Red, *A History of the Presbyterian Church in Texas* ([Austin]: Steck, 1936), 71–73, 376; *First Presbyterian Church*, 3–4.

40. [*Domestic*] *Missionary Chronicle* 7 (1848): 381, in Brackenridge and García-Treto, *Iglesia Presbiteriana*, 9–10.

41. McCullough (1944), *John McCullough*, 37; Red, *History of the Presbyterian Church in Texas* 74–75, 376; *First Presbyterian Church*, 4–7; Henry S. Bunting, "Early History of the First Presbyterian Church of San Antonio [and] Biography of Its Founder, the Reverend Franklin Bunting, D.D." (typescript), especially 8–21, CAH.

42. John Wesley DeVilbiss, Sr., "Reminiscences of a Superannuated Preacher," in *Reminiscences and Events in the Ministerial Life of Rev. John Wesley DeVilbiss*, comp. H. A. Graves (Galveston: W. A. Shaw, 1886), 50, 53–59; Josephine Forman, *We Finish to Begin: A History of Travis Park United Methodist Church, San Antonio, Texas, 1846–1991* (San Antonio: Travis Park United Methodist Church, 1991), 5–13a; Nancy Lou McCallum, "History of the Methodist Episcopal Church, South, in San Antonio, Texas" (M.A. thesis, University of Texas, Austin, 1936), 2–11; Olin W. Nail, ed., *The First Hundred Years of the Southwest Texas Conference of the Methodist Church, 1858–1958* (San Antonio: Southwest Texas Conference, Methodist Church, 1958), 99–108; Macum Phelan, *A History of Early Methodism in Texas, 1817–1866* (Nashville: Cokesbury, 1924), 240–241, 311–312, 354; Homer S. Thrall, *A Brief History of Methodism in Texas* (Nashville: Publishing House of the Methodist Episcopal Church, South, 1889; reprint, Greenwood, South Carolina: Attic, 1977), 212.

43. H[amilton] G. H[orton], "Beginnings of the Mexican Work," *Texas Methodist Historical Quarterly* 1 (January 1910): 290; Alfredo Nañez, *History*

of the Rio Grande Conference of the United Methodist Church (Dallas: Bridwell Library, Southern Methodist University, 1980), 39; Walter N. Vernon and others, *The Methodist Excitement in Texas: A History* (Dallas: Texas United Methodist Historical Society, 1984), 107; H. G. Horton, "Mexican Work—Early Days," *Texas Christian Advocate* (Galveston), 7 May 1881, 1 (quotation). In the latter article, Horton also stated that San Antonio Tejanos approached Methodist minister J. S. McGee in the late 1850s to request that he "preach the gospel to our people."

44. Horton, "Beginnings of the Mexican Work," 289–290; Chabot, *With the Makers of San Antonio*, 204–205; "San Fernando Cathedral Deaths," Book 4, 14 January 1871, CASA. In another memoir, Horton incorrectly stated that José Antonio Navarro was a veteran of the battles of San Jacinto and Mier. H. G. Horton, "Mexican work" file, undated, United Methodist Church Southwest Texas Conference Archives, Travis Park United Methodist Church, San Antonio.

45. Harriet Brown Moore, *St. Mark's Church, Travis Park, San Antonio, Texas: A Parish with a Personality* (San Antonio: Naylor, 1944), 4–7; Lawrence L. Brown, *The Episcopal Church in Texas, 1838–1874: From Its Foundation to the Division of the Diocese* (Austin: Church Historical Society, 1963), 37, 42–43, 48, 63–66, 73, 101; DuBose Murphy, *A Short History of the Protestant Episcopal Church in Texas* (Dallas: Turner, 1935), 21–22, 29–30; *Texas Baptist* (Anderson), 7 February 1861; *In the Shadow of His Hand: The First Century of the First Baptist Church of San Antonio, Texas, 1861–1961* (San Antonio: Perry, 1961), 36–40 (available at CAH); J[ames] M[ilton] Carroll, *A History of Texas Baptists: Comprising a Detailed Account of Their Activities, Their Progress and Their Achievements*, ed. J. B. Cranfill (Dallas: Baptist Standard, 1923), 483–491; Zane Allen Mason, *Frontiersmen of the Faith: A History of the Baptist Pioneer Work in Texas, 1865–1885* (San Antonio: Naylor, 1970), 159–160; San Antonio Baptist Association, *A Baptist Century around the Alamo, 1858–1958* (San Antonio: Perry, 1958), 14–16. Tejana membership in San Antonio's Episcopal and Baptist congregations is confirmed in Dysart, "Mexican Women in San Antonio, 1830–1860," 374; *In the Shadow of His Hand*, 39; San Antonio Baptist Association, *A Baptist Century around the Alamo*, 16.

46. August L. Wolff, *The Story of St. John's Lutheran Church, San Antonio, Texas* (N.p.: Paul Anderson, 1937), 11–33; H. C. Ziehe, *A Centennial Story of the Lutheran Church in Texas* (Seguin, Tex.: South Texas Printing, 1951): 1: 51–53, 77–81; *Ledger*, 16 January 1858; *Texan*, 21 January 1858; J. A. G. Rabe, "The Work among the Germans," *Texas Methodist Historical Quarterly* 1 (January 1910): 285–286; *Alamo Express*, 15 October 1860. See also Sterling Fisher, "The Rio Grande Conference," *Texas Methodist Historical Quarterly* 1 (April 1910): 346–348; *Daily Herald*, 4 December 1858.

47. The minutes of the 1859 and 1860 sessions of the Rio Grande Conference are summarized in Nañez, *History of the Rio Grande Conference*, 40–41; Fisher, "The Rio Grande Conference," 346–350. For Amos Stone's brief stay in San Antonio, see *Ledger and Texan*, 28 July 1860; *Banner of Peace*, 3 January, 21 February 1861, in Brackenridge, *Voice in the Wilderness*, 59. This source does not cite the place of publication for the *Banner of Peace*. Baptist delay in forming

a congregation at San Antonio is summarized in Carroll, *A History of Texas Baptists*, 484–486.

48. Melinda Rankin, *Texas in 1850* (Boston: Damrell & Moore, 1850; reprint, [Waco]: Texian Press, 1966), 182; *Daily Herald*, 30 April 1858.

49. *Alamo Star*, 6 May 1854.

50. *Herald*, 12 June 1855.

51. [Domestic] *Missionary Chronicle* 7 (1848): 88, in Brackenridge and García-Treto, *Iglesia Presbiteriana*, 9.

52. [Domestic] *Missionary Chronicle* 7 (1848): 88, in Brackenridge and García-Treto, *Iglesia Presbiteriana*, 9; Smith, *Life and Times of George Foster Pierce*, 377; *Texas Baptist* (Anderson), 7 February 1861. A possible motive for the statements of McCullough and others may have been to impress the members of denominational missionary boards, who seemed more prone to fund such ambitious missionary enterprises. Protestant ministers functioned legally in Texas from Texas independence in 1836 but were not allowed into Mexico until more than two decades later. Despite their later start in Mexico, the first permanent Protestant congregations among the Spanish-speaking were in Mexico, not Texas. Robert E. Wright, "Popular and Official Religiosity: A Theoretical Analysis and a Case Study of Laredo–Nuevo Laredo, 1755–1857" (Ph.D. diss., Graduate Theological Union, Berkeley, Calif., 1992), 280.

53. Odin to Jean-Maurice Verdet, 30 August 1852, CAT; Odin to Anthony Blanc, 22 October, 12 December 1852, CAT. For records of priests who served San Antonio Tejanos in the 1850s, see "San Fernando Baptismal Register," books 6–8, CASA; "San Fernando Marriage Register," Book 1, CASA; "San Fernando Cathedral Deaths," Book 3, CASA.

54. P. F. Parisot, *The Reminiscences of a Texas Missionary* (San Antonio: Johnson Bros., 1899), 38–41; Carlos Castañeda, *Our Catholic Heritage in Texas, 1519–1936* (Austin: Von Boeckmann-Jones, 1936–1958), 7: 291–292; McDowell, ed., *Letters from the Ursuline*, 145, 177–178, 216–217; Sister de Ste. Marie to Blanc, 26 September 1854, ND; Joseph William Schmitz, *The Society of Mary in Texas* (San Antonio: Naylor, 1951), 32–33.

55. Jean Marie Odin, "Daily Journal" (photocopy), 57, CAT; McDowell, ed., *Letters from the Ursuline*, 323. Dubuis and most other priests assigned to San Antonio were French. Most of them also learned to speak English. For German and Polish ministries at San Antonio during the 1850s, see Abbe [Emanuel] Domenech, *Missionary Adventures in Texas and Mexico: A Personal Narrative of Six Years' Sojourn in Those Regions*, trans. from French (London: Longman, Brown, Green, Longmans, and Roberts, 1858), 194–195; Dubuis to Odin, 25 February, 2 April 1851, IWA; Odin to Propagation of the Faith, 20 June 1860, 26 January 1861, CAT; Mary Angela Fitzmorris, "Four Decades of Catholicism in Texas, 1820–1860" (Ph.D. diss., Catholic University of America, Washington, D.C., 1926), 79, 93; Castañeda, *Our Catholic Heritage in Texas*, 7: 215–219; Andrew E. Wueste, comp., *St. Mary's: 1857–1957 Centennial* (San Antonio: Privately printed, [1957]), 15 (available at CAT, CASA); "San Fernando Baptismal Register," Books 6–8; "San Fernando Marriage Register," Book 1; "San Fernando Cathedral Deaths," Book 3. Clerical appointments to San Antonio dur-

ing the 1850s are in *The Metropolitan Catholic Almanac and Laity's Directory* (text-fiche), 1850–1860, CAT. The use of English, French, and German in San Antonio's Catholic schools is attested in Castañeda, *Our Catholic Heritage in Texas,* 7: 291–292; McDowell, ed., *Letters from the Ursuline,* 145, 177–178, 216–217; Sister de Ste. Marie to Blanc, 26 September 1854; Schmitz, *The Society of Mary in Texas,* 32–33.

56. P. F. Parisot and C. J. Smith, *History of the Catholic Church in the Diocese of San Antonio, Texas* (San Antonio: Carrico & Bowen, 1897), 145–147, 151; Wueste, comp., *St. Mary's,* 13, 15–17; *Ledger,* 8 September 1853 (first quotation); Dubuis to Odin, 8 March 1855, IWA (second quotation); Willard B. Robinson, "Early Anglo-American Church Architecture in Texas," *SWHQ* 94 (October 1990): 268–269; Lindsay Baker, *The First Polish Americans: Silesian Settlements in Texas* (College Station: Texas A&M University Press, 1979), 103. St. Michael's was the Polish parish, St. Joseph's the German parish. Baker, *First Polish Americans,* 103–104; Jan Maria Wozniak, "St. Michael's Church: The Polish National Catholic Church in San Antonio, Texas, 1855–1950," (M.A. thesis, University of Texas, Austin, 1964), 32–34; John A. Joyce, *Our Polish Pioneers* (N.p.: Privately printed, 1937), 12–13 (available at CASA); Ray Neumann, *A Centennial History of St. Joseph's Church and Parish 1868 to 1968, San Antonio, Texas* (San Antonio: Clemens, 1968), 1–8, 13–14.

57. Odin to Benoite (his sister), 3 May 1822, in Abbe Bony, *Vie de Mgr. Jean-Marie Odin: Missionaire lazarist, archeveque de la Nouvelle-Orleans, par l'auteur de l'initiateur de voeu nacional* (Paris: Imprimerie de D. Dumoulin, 1896), 39 (first quotation); McDowell, ed., *Letters from the Ursuline,* 163 (second and third quotations); Domenech, *Missionary Adventures in Texas,* 136 (fourth quotation), 137–139; Dubuis to Odin, 22 March (fifth quotation), 10 April, 22 April 1853, IWA; McDowell, ed., *Letters from the Ursuline,* 204, 211, 279, 337; *Daily Herald,* 8 July 1858 (sixth quotation). For a brief discussion of French priests and religious in Texas and the training they received, see Barnabas Diekemper, "French Clergy on the Texas Frontier, 1837–1907," *East Texas Historical Journal* 21 (1983): 31–34; Patrick Foley, "Jean-Marie Odin, C.M., Missionary Bishop Extraordinaire of Texas," *Journal of Texas Catholic History and Culture* 1 (March 1990): 45–46. I am grateful to Dr. Patrick Foley, who advised me of Odin's 1822 letter. Dr. Foley translated the passage from that letter cited here.

58. McDowell, ed., *Letters from the Ursuline,* 211, 395; Odin to Propagation of the Faith, 9 January, 1 July (first quotation) 1853, CAT; Dubuis to Odin, 10 (second quotation), 22 April (third quotation) 1853.

59. Odin to Propagation of the Faith, 14 May 1849, CAT. See also Odin to Propagation of the Faith, 15 May 1849, CAT. Robert E. Wright has argued that Catholic clergy in Texas frequently established Catholic schools to counteract the Protestant presence. Wright, "Popular and Official Religiosity," 280, 286–287, 323–325.

60. Domenech, *Missionary Adventures in Texas,* 11; McDowell, ed., *Letters from the Ursuline,* 198; Odin to Verdet, 13 August 1852, CAT; *Daily Ledger,* 14 September 1858. See also McDowell, ed., *Letters from the Ursuline,* 212–213.

61. McDowell, ed., *Letters from the Ursuline,* 277. The novelty of such practices for European clergy could explain in part their impression that Tejano religion was "superficial." Descriptions of these funeral processions are in ibid., 261, 277. A painting depicting such a procession at San Antonio during this period is in *Gentilz: Artist of the Old Southwest,* 83. See also [Anthony Ganilh], *Mexico Versus Texas, A Descriptive Novel, Most of the Characters of Which Consist of Living Persons* (Philadelphia: N. Siegfried, 1838), 246. The latter is a work of fiction but is based on observations made during a trip to Texas.

62. These figures are compiled from annual election returns recorded in "Minutes of the City Council of the City of San Antonio, Journal A"; "Journal of City Council B"; "Journal of City Council C". Only one other Tejano was elected to the state legislature during the first fifteen years of Texas statehood. Laredo resident Bacilio Benavides represented Webb County in the House of Representatives from 1859 to 1860.

63. Jesús F. de la Teja, ed., *A Revolution Remembered: The Memoirs and Selected Correspondence of Juan N. Seguín* (Austin: State House Press, 1991), 50–51.

64. Jane Dysart claims that, at San Antonio, "Anglo men with family ties in the Mexican community consistently won election to city office during the 1840s and 1850s." Dysart, "Mexican Women in San Antonio, 1830–1860," 370.

65. Richard G. Santos, *José Francisco Ruiz* (Béxar County, Tex.: James W. Knight, County Clerk, 1966), 11 (available at CAH); Juan Seguín to Anson Jones, 24 July 1845, in De la Teja, ed., *A Revolution Remembered,* 180. Ruiz later returned to live in San Antonio. Sam Houston Dixon claimed that Ruiz' father, Francisco Ruiz, was the one opposed to annexation who went to live among the Native Americans. This is incorrect, however, as the elder Ruiz died in 1840. Sam Houston Dixon, *The Men Who Made Texas Free* (Houston: Texas Historical Publishing, 1924), 317–318; "San Fernando Cathedral Deaths," Book 3, 20 January 1840.

66. Proclamation of W. S. Harney, 2 May 1846, in *Diary and Letters of Josiah Gregg: Excursions in Mexico & California, 1847–1850,* ed. Maurice Garland Fulton, with an introduction by Paul Horgan (Norman: University of Oklahoma Press, 1941), 1: 221 (first quotation); John E. Wool, Orders, No. 12, 25 August 1846, in ibid.; Roemer, *Texas,* 157 (second quotation). The latter comment is from Roemer's account of his visit to San Antonio in May 1846. Scholars have debated the position of Harney (and others) that "hostilities" were "commenced by Mexico."

67. Baylies, *A Narrative of Major General Wool's Campaign in Mexico,* 10; "Mrs. French's Reminiscences," in Wright, *San Antonio de Béxar,* 100.

68. Henry W. Barton, *Texas Volunteers in the Mexican War* (Waco: Texian Press, 1970), 118; Downs, "History of Mexicans in Texas," 248. See also Thomas Lloyd Miller, "Mexican-Texans at the Alamo," *Journal of Mexican American History* 2 (Fall 1971): 33–44; Miller, "Mexican Texans in the Texas Revolution," *Journal of Mexican American History* 3 (1973): 105–130; Paul D. Lack, *The Texas Revolutionary Experience: A Political and Social History,*

1835–1836 (College Station: Texas A&M University Press, 1992), 133. The latter reference has a composite profile of the Texas army during the Texas Revolution. This profile shows that at least 199 Texas volunteers came from the Tejano stronghold of the Department of Béxar.

69. For a treatment of the Know Nothing movement at the national level, see Ray Allen Billington, *The Protestant Crusade, 1800–1860: A Study of the Origins of American Nativism* (New York: Macmillan, 1938). For a discussion of the movement in Texas, see Sister Paul of the Cross McGrath, "Political Nativism in Texas, 1825–1860" (Ph.D. diss., Catholic University of America, Washington, D.C., 1930); Ralph A. Wooster, "An Analysis of the Texas Know Nothings," *SWHQ* 70 (January 1967): 414–423; C. W. Raines, ed., *Six Decades in Texas: The Memoirs of Francis R. Lubbock, Confederate Governor of Texas* (Austin: Pemberton, 1968), 197–235. For Texas Catholics and the Know Nothing movement, see James Talmadge Moore, *Through Fire and Flood: The Catholic Church in Frontier Texas, 1836–1900* (College Station: Texas A&M University Press, 1992), 111–118.

70. *Texas State Times* (Austin), 6 January 1855; "Journal of City Council B," 4, 8 January 1855. Some references to the Know Nothing Party appeared in San Antonio newspapers before the 1854 municipal elections, e.g. *Ledger,* 11 May, 20 July 1854; *Western Texan,* 10 October 1854. The *Alamo Star* published an alleged "Roman Catholic Oath" and a series of brief quotations by Catholic authors which suggested Catholics would impose their religion if elected to office. *Alamo Star,* 9 October, 13 November 1854. But none of these reports mentioned actual Know Nothing activity in San Antonio. An Anglo-American wrote a letter in October 1854 which speculated about the presence of Know Nothings in the city, but this correspondent was uncertain about actual Know Nothing activities. Benjamin E. Edwards to Mrs. Benjamin Franklin Edwards (nee Green), 6 October 1854, in *Texas Letters,* ed. Frederick C. Chabot (San Antonio: Yanaguana Society, 1940), 168–169.

71. *Herald,* 10 July 1854; *Sentinel,* 14 July 1855.

72. *Ledger,* 14, 21 (quotation), 28 July, 1 August 1855; *Bejareño,* 7, 21 July 1855.

73. *Texan,* 21, 28 June, 12 July 1855; *Texas State Gazette* (Austin), 25 July 1855. See also *Bejareño,* 23 June, 7 July 1855.

74. *Bejareño,* 7 July 1855. Quotations cited are my translation of the text.

75. Ibid., 21 July 1855; *Ledger,* 14, 21 July 1855. Quotations cited are my translation of the text. The translation in the *Ledger* has several inaccuracies.

76. Odin to Blanc, 29 July 1854, CAT; J[ean] P[errichone], *Vie de Monseigneur Dubuis: l'apotre du Texas* (Lyon: n.p., 1900), 133 (available at CAT); L. V. Jacks, *Claude Dubuis, Bishop of Galveston* (St. Louis: B. Herder, 1947), 139. See also Odin to Propagation of the Faith, 30 May 1855, 14 February, 18 June 1856, CAT; Odin to James Cardinal Fransoni, [n.d.] 1855, CAT. The quotation from Perrichone is my translation of the text.

77. McGrath, "Political Nativism in Texas," 98–102. After the August elections, the *Ledger* published lists of former Know Nothings who had withdrawn

from their ranks and reported that a Know Nothing meeting held shortly before the December municipal elections failed to revive the Party. *Ledger,* 22 September, 8 December 1855. Democrats were victorious in those city elections and then swept the state in the 1856 state and national elections, again winning Béxar County by as much as a three-to-one margin over Know Nothing candidates. *Bejareño,* 5 January 1856; McGrath, "Political Nativism in Texas," 146–147, 152. By 1857 Know Nothing support was so weak in Texas that no state convention was held. McGrath, "Political Nativism in Texas," 157.

78. *Herald,* 14 August 1855; *Sentinel,* 11 August 1855, as cited in the *Ledger,* 25 August 1855, and *Herald,* 14 August 1855; John A. Wilcox letter, *Texas State Gazette* (Austin), 6 October 1855. The first quotation is also in *Bejareño,* 18 August 1855; *Ledger,* 25 August 1855. These Democratic organs printed a Know Nothing article in order to refute it. The article first appeared in the *Texas State Times* (Austin), 11 August 1855.

79. *Bejareño,* 18 August, 1 September 1855; *Ledger,* 25 August 1855.

80. Jean Marie Odin, "Pastoral Letter for the Lent of 1862," 16 February 1862, Rare Book Collection, Catholic University of America, Washington, D.C.; Odin, "Pastoral Letter to the Faithful of Our Metropolitan City," 19 May 1863, ibid.; Gerald M. Capers, *Occupied City: New Orleans under the Federals, 1862–1865* (Lexington: University of Kentucky Press, 1965), 185. Capers spells this priest's name "Maestri." The Vincentian ownership of slaves is attested in John E. Rybolt, ed., *The American Vincentians: A Popular History of the Congregation of the Mission in the United States, 1815–1987* (Brooklyn: New York City Press, 1988), 25, 34, 36–37. An overview of U.S. Catholic attitudes to slavery and secession is in Cyprian Davis, *The History of Black Catholics in the United States* (New York: Crossroad, 1990), 46–66; John Tracy Ellis, *American Catholicism* (Chicago: University of Chicago Press, 1969), 89–100; James Hennesey, *American Catholics: A History of the Roman Catholic Community in the United States* (New York: Oxford University Press, 1981), 143–157.

81. David J. Weber, ed., *The Mexican Frontier, 1821–1846: The American Southwest under Mexico* (Albuquerque: University of New Mexico Press, 1982), 211–215.

82. Olmsted, *A Journey through Texas,* 163. See also *Texas State Times* (Austin), 7 April 1855. For the forced removal of Tejanos from Austin, Seguin, and the counties of Colorado and Matagorda, see *Galveston Weekly News,* 5 September 1854; *Texas State Gazette* (Austin), 2, 9 September, 14, 21, 28 October 1854; *Texas State Times* (Austin), 14, 21 October 1854; *Galveston Tri-Weekly News,* 11 September 1856; Olmsted, *A Journey through Texas,* 502–504; Paul D. Lack, "Slavery and Vigilantism in Austin, Texas, 1840–1860," *SWHQ* 85 (July 1981): 1–20. Reports regarding the 1854 meeting at San Antonio and warnings of Tejanos in the city who might abet slave escapes are in *Texas State Gazette* (Austin), 16 September 1854; *Alamo Star,* 2, 16 September 1854. San Antonio resident José María Rodríguez made observations similar to Olmsted's about Tejano attitudes toward slavery, despite his own family's ownership of slaves. Rodríguez, *Memoirs,* 20. A summary of the Tejano

attitude toward slavery in the antebellum period is in De León, *They Called Them Greasers*, 49–53.

83. *Herald*, 6 February 1858. San Antonio press reports of Tejano assistance to escaped slaves include *Alamo Star*, 26 August 1854; *Ledger*, 21 September 1854, 30 May 1857, 11 December 1858; *Daily Herald*, 7 January, 19 May 1858, 20 August 1859. See also Olmsted, *A Journey through Texas*, 65, 106, 427, 456. Reports of Tejanos returning runaway slaves are in *Texan*, 26 August 1858; *Ranchero* (Corpus Christi), 17 March, 17 November 1860.

84. "Population Schedules of the Eighth Census of the United States, 1860," roll 1309: 1–8.

85. Baylies, *A Narrative of Major General Wool's Campaign in Mexico*, 11. Earlier works on Texas history by Anglo-Americans had already articulated this thesis. See, e.g., C[hester] Newell, *History of the Revolution in Texas, Particularly of the War of 1835 & '36; Together with the Latest Geographical, Topographical, and Statistical Accounts of the Country, from the Most Authentic Sources* (New York: Wiley & Putnam, 1838), 13–14; L. T. Pease, "A Geographical and Historical View of Texas; with a Detailed Account of the Texian Revolution and War," in John M. Niles, *History of South America and Mexico; Comprising Their Discovery, Geography, Politics, Commerce, and Revolutions* (Hartford: H. Huntington, 1838), 1: 252–254; William Kennedy, *Texas: The Rise, Progress, and Prospects of the Republic of Texas* (London: R. Hastings, 1841; reprint, Fort Worth: Molyneaux Craftsmen, 1925), 1: 233–234; Arthur Ikin, *Texas: Its History, Topography, Agriculture, Commerce, and General Statistics. To Which Is Added, a Copy of the Treaty of Commerce Entered into by the Republic of Texas and Great Britain. Designed for the Use of the British Merchant, and as a Guide to Emigrants* (London: Sherwood, Gilbert, and Piper, 1841), 1.

86. *Western Texan*, 14 October 1852. See also *Ledger*, 15 September 1853; *Daily Herald*, 15 July 1858. Contemporary scholars have critiqued the tendency of religious and secular historians to present this one-sided perspective of Mexican decline followed by Anglo-American redemption. See, e.g., Gilberto M. Hinojosa, "The Enduring Hispanic Faith Communities: Spanish and Texas Church Historiography," *Journal of Texas Catholic History and Culture* 1 (March 1990): 20–41; Robert E. Wright, "Local Church Emergence and Mission Decline: The Historiography of the Catholic Church in the Southwest during the Spanish and Mexican Periods," *U.S. Catholic Historian* 9 (Winter/Spring 1990): 27–48.

87. *Ledger*, 15 September 1853.

88. "Anonymous. Early History of San Antonio," 1 December 1853, in *The Papers of Mirabeau Buonaparte Lamar*, ed. Charles Adams Gulick, Jr., and Katherine Elliott (Austin: Von Boeckmann-Jones, 1973), 4: 5, 12 (quotations). This reference states that this installment of Navarro's history was originally published in the *Western Texan*, 1 December 1853. While the editors cite the author of this work as anonymous, it is clearly part of a historical narrative attributed to Navarro: José Antonio Navarro, *Apuntes históricos interesantes de San Antonio de Béxar escritos por el C. Dn. José Antonio Navarro, en noviembre de 1853.*

Y publicados por varios de sus amigos (San Antonio: Privately printed, 1869), 13–20.

89. *Ledger,* 12 December 1857 (first quotation), 2 January 1858 (second quotation). The other section of this account was in the *Ledger,* 19 December 1857. Later these three installments appeared in Navarro, *Apuntes,* 4–12.

90. *Correo,* 8 July 1858. These attacks were apparently part of the Cart War. See, e.g., Gibson, "Social Life in San Antonio," 14–17; J. Fred Rippy, "Border Troubles along the Rio Grande, 1848–1860," *SWHQ* 23 (October 1919): 103–104; John J. Linn, *Reminiscences of Fifty Years in Texas* (New York: D. & J. Sadlier, 1883; reprint, Austin: State House Press, 1986), 352–354.

91. Juan N. Seguín, *Personal Memoirs of John N. Seguín from the Year 1834 to the Retreat of General Woll from the City of San Antonio in 1842* (San Antonio: Ledger Book and Job Office, 1858), iv. Seguín's rendering of the events leading up to his departure from Texas were previously summarized in Ch. 3. His memoirs are edited and reprinted in De la Teja, ed., *A Revolution Remembered,* 73–102.

92. Barnes, *Combats and Conquests of Immortal Heroes,* 76–81. Similar versions of these legends are in Wright, *San Antonio de Béxar,* 121–122, 127–128. The legends are also recounted in Antonio Menchaca, "The Memoirs of Captain Menchaca" (typescript), ed. James P. Newcomb, 51–53, CAH. In this manuscript, the legend accounts are abbreviated, however, and the location of the miracles is not given as San Antonio. Another account states that Margil miraculously discovered a spring near Nacogdoches, although it cites the earlier works of Barnes and Wright, who gave the site as San Antonio. E. G. Littlejohn, "The Holy Spring of Father Margil at Nacogdoches," in *Legends of Texas,* ed. J. Frank Dobie (Austin: Texas Folk-Lore Society, 1924), 204–205.

5. SAN ANTONIO TEJANOS AND UNITED STATES EXPANSION: A STUDY OF RELIGION AND ETHNICITY

1. Oscar Handlin, *The Uprooted: The Epic Story of the Great Migrations that Made the American People* (Boston: Little, Brown, 1951), 305.

2. Ibid., 3.

3. Will Herberg and Harry Stout claim that the ethnic and religious heritage of first-generation immigrants bow to the forces of assimilation in the generational transition following this decisive break with their homelands. Will Herberg, *Protestant-Catholic-Jew: An Essay in American Religious Sociology* (1955; revised, Garden City, N.Y.: Anchor, 1960); Harry Stout, "Ethnicity: The Vital Center of Religion in America," *Ethnicity* 2 (1975): 204–224.

4. Terry G. Jordan, "A Century and a Half of Ethnic Change in Texas, 1836–1986," *SWHQ* 89 (April 1986): 400.

5. Studies such as a recent work of Dean Hoge confirm that social mobility is a critical factor in assimilation. Dean Hoge, "Interpreting Change in American Catholicism: The River and the Floodgate," *Review of Religious Research* 27 (June 1986): 289–300. See also Philip Gleason, "Immigrant Assimilation and

the Crisis of Americanization," in his *Keeping the Faith: American Catholicism Past and Present* (Notre Dame, Ind.: University of Notre Dame Press, 1987), 64–65.

6. Philip Gleason, "American Identity and Americanization," in *Harvard Encyclopedia of American Ethnic Groups* (Cambridge: Harvard University Press, 1980), 31–34. Gleason's presentation is employed in this study as a summary of the work done by earlier scholars. See, e.g., Merle Curti, *The Roots of American Loyalty* (New York: Columbia University Press, 1946); Hans Kohn, *American Nationalism: An Interpretive Essay* (New York: Macmillan, 1957); Benjamin T. Spencer, *The Quest for Nationality: An American Literary Campaign* (Syracuse, N.Y.: Syracuse University Press, 1957); Paul C. Nagel, *This Sacred Trust: American Nationality, 1798–1898* (New York: Oxford University Press, 1971); Michael Kammen, *A Season of Youth: The American Revolution and the Historical Imagination* (Ithaca, N.Y.: Cornell University Press, 1978).

7. Silvano M. Tomasi, *Piety and Power: The Role of Italian Parishes in the New York Metropolitan Area, 1880–1930* (Staten Island, N.Y.: Center for Migration Studies, 1975); Joseph Fitzpatrick, *One Church, Many Cultures: The Challenge of Diversity* (Kansas City, Mo.: Sheed & Ward, 1987), 103–118; Fitzpatrick, "Cultural Change or Cultural Continuity: Pluralism and Hispanic-Americans," in *Hispanics in New York: Religious, Cultural and Social Experiences* (New York: Archdiocese of New York, Office of Pastoral Research and Planning, 1989), 2: 67–68; Stephen J. Shaw, *The Catholic Parish as a Way-Station of Ethnicity and Americanization: Chicago's Germans and Italians, 1903–1939*, with a preface by Martin E. Marty (Brooklyn, New York: Carlson, 1991). Allan Figueroa Deck, "At the Crossroads: North American and Hispanic," in *We Are a People! Initiatives in Hispanic American Theology*, ed. with a preface by Roberto S. Goizueta (Minneapolis: Fortress, 1992), 12–14.

8. Frederick Law Olmsted, *A Journey through Texas; or, A Saddle-Trip on the Southwestern Frontier: With a Statistical Appendix* (New York: Dix, Edwards & Co., 1857), 150.

9. The separation between ethnic groups at San Antonio is consistent with Milton Gordon's findings about the lack of structural assimilation, or intermingling at the level of primary social relationships, in American life. Milton M. Gordon, *Assimilation in American Life: The Role of Race, Religion, and National Origins* (New York: Oxford University Press, 1964).

10. I have borrowed this term from Gordon's influential work on assimilation in American life.

11. Theorists like Nathan Glazer and Daniel P. Moynihan have argued that immigrants lose their previous group identity after arriving in the United States but that a new ethnic identity rises in its place. The transformed ethnicity evident in succeeding generations is not equivalent to the national identity of their immigrant ancestors, nor does it conform to an assimilated American ideal. Timothy L. Smith contends that the very experience of immigration realigned ethno-religious boundaries. Nathan Glazer and Daniel P. Moynihan, *Beyond the Melting Pot: The Negroes, Puerto Ricans, Jews, Italians, and Irish of New York City* (1963; revised, Cambridge, Mass.: M.I.T. Press, 1970); Timothy L. Smith,

"Religion and Ethnicity in America," *American Historical Review* 83 (December 1978): 1155–1185.

12. *Alamo Star* (San Antonio), 2 September 1854.

13. Although not primarily concerned with the interplay between religious and ethnic identity, several studies would be helpful for such a comparative analysis. For works on Tejano communities, see Gilberto Miguel Hinojosa, *A Borderlands Town in Transition: Laredo, 1755–1870* (College Station: Texas A&M University Press, 1983); David Montejano, *Anglos and Mexicans in the Making of Texas, 1836–1986* (Austin: University of Texas Press, 1987); Robert E. Wright, "Popular and Official Religiosity: A Theoretical Analysis and a Case Study of Laredo–Nuevo Laredo, 1755–1857" (Ph.D. diss., Graduate Theological Union, Berkeley, Calif., 1992); and the forthcoming collection of essays on Tejano identity, 1760–1860, ed. Gerald E. Poyo and Jesús F. de la Teja. Other volumes include John R. Chávez, *The Lost Land: The Chicano Image of the Southwest* (Albuquerque: University of New Mexico Press, 1984); Thomas D. Hall, *Social Change in the Southwest, 1350–1880* (Lawrence, Kansas: University Press of Kansas, 1989); Frances Leon Swadesh, *Los Primeros Pobladores: Hispanic Americans of the Ute Frontier* (Notre Dame, Ind.: University of Notre Dame Press, 1974); James E. Officer, *Hispanic Arizona, 1536–1856* (Tucson: University of Arizona Press, 1987); Douglas Monroy, *Thrown among Strangers: The Making of Mexican Culture in Frontier California* (Berkeley: University of California Press, 1990); Michael E. Engh, *Frontier Faiths: Church, Temple, and Synagogue in Los Angeles, 1846–1888* (Albuquerque: University of New Mexico Press, 1992).

14. Olivier Zunz, "The Genesis of American Pluralism," *Tocqueville Review* 9 (1987/1988): 208.

15. Roberto S. Goizueta, "United States Hispanic Theology and the Challenge of Pluralism," in *Frontiers of Hispanic Theology in the United States*, ed. and with an introduction by Allan Figueroa Deck (Maryknoll, N.Y.: Orbis, 1992), 14. Goizueta was citing David Tracy at this point in his presentation.

SELECTED BIBLIOGRAPHY

†

In this bibliography, I have attempted to cite the most accessible published accounts. Dates in brackets for primary sources indicate the time frame treated by a particular reference. Page and volume numbers relate the part of a work which deal with San Antonio. Tejano and some other accounts of the Alamo have been included because of their particular interest for this study. A bibliography which cites other Alamo accounts is in Walter Lord, *A Time to Stand* (New York: Harper & Brothers, 1961). Contemporary newspaper collections are usually incomplete; I have listed the most comprehensive collections first in these citations.

PRIMARY SOURCES FOR SAN ANTONIO HISTORY, 1821–1860

Adams, Harvey Alexander. "Diary of Harvey Alexander Adams, in Two Parts: Rhode Island to Texas and Expedition against the Southwest in 1842 and 1843" (typescript), 2: 7–27. CAH. [1842].
    Diary of a Texas volunteer who passed through San Antonio.
Almonte, Juan Nepomuceno. "The Private Journal of Juan Nepomuceno Almonte, February 1–April 16, 1836." With an introduction by Samuel E. Asbury. *SWHQ* 48 (July 1944): 16–25.
    Diary of a soldier in the Mexican army during the Texas Revolution.
———. "Statistical Report on Texas, 1835." Translated by Carlos E. Castañeda. *SWHQ* 28 (January 1925): 185–197, 221–222.
Ballou, Ellen Bartlett. "Scudder's Journey to Texas, 1859." *SWHQ* 63 (July 1959): 7–10.
Barker, Eugene C. "Descriptions of Texas by Stephen F. Austin." *SWHQ* 28 (October 1924): 110, 118. [1831, 1833].
———, ed. *The Austin Papers*. Washington, D.C.: U.S. Government Printing Office, 1924–1928, 3 vols. [1821–1836].

Barnard, J. H. *Dr. J. H. Barnard's Journal: From December, 1835, Including the Fannin Massacre, March 27th, 1836.* Goliad: Goliad Advance, 1912; reprint, Aransas Pass, Texas: Biography Press, 1985, 35–41. [1836]. Also in John J. Linn, *Reminiscences of Fifty Years in Texas,* 176–182. New York: D. & J. Sadlier, 1883; reprint, Austin: State House Press, 1986.
    Diary entries of a doctor captured at Goliad and taken to San Antonio to help wounded after the Alamo battle.
Barnes, Charles Merritt. "Builders' Spades Turn Up Soil Baked by Alamo Funeral Pyres." *San Antonio Express,* 26 March 1911, 26. [1836].
    Recollections of disposal of corpses after the Alamo battle by San Antonio residents Juan Antonio Chávez, Pablo Díaz, and Enrique Esparza.
———. "Men Still Living Who Saw the Fall of the Alamo." *San Antonio Express,* 27 August 1911, 9.
    Reminiscences of several San Antonio residents.
Bartlett, John Russell. *Personal Narrative of Explorations and Incidents in Texas, New Mexico, California, Sonora, and Chihuahua, Connected with the United States and Mexican Boundary Commission, during the Years 1850, '51, '52, and '53.* New York: D. Appleton, 1854; reprint, Chicago: Rio Grande Press, 1965, 1: 33–45. [1850].
Baylies, Francis. *A Narrative of Major General Wool's Campaign in Mexico, in the Years 1846, 1847 & 1848.* Albany: Little, 1851; reprint, Austin: Jenkins, 1975, 10–12. [1846].
Bell, Thomas W., to [William Adam Bell], 31 March 1842. In "Thomas W. Bell Letters," ed. Llerena Friend. *SWHQ* 63 (April 1960): 589–590.
Benedict, J. W. "Diary of a Campaign against the Comanches." *SWHQ* 32 (April 1929): 304–307. [1839].
Bennet, Valentine. "Valentine Bennet Scrapbook," 99, 102, 257, 260. CAH. [1838–1839].
Berlandier, Jean Louis. *Journey to Mexico during the Years 1826 to 1834.* Translated by Sheila M. Ohlendorf, Josette M. Bigelo, and Mary M. Standifer. With an introduction by C. H. Muller. Austin: Texas State Historical Association, 1980, 2: 290–301. [1828].
Béxar Archives, 1821–1836. CAH. These documents are indexed in *The Béxar Archives (1717–1836): A Name Guide,* ed. and comp. Adán Benavides, Jr. Austin: University of Texas Press, 1989.
    Official documents and records from the Mexican period.
Binkley, William C., ed. *Official Correspondence of the Texan Revolution, 1835–1836.* New York: D. Appleton-Century, 1936, 1: 203, 212–214, 220–221, 235–237, 272–275, 278, 294–295, 300, 328–329, 344–346, 349–351, 381–383, 393–395, 409–410, 416–417, 419–425, 439–441.
    Official correspondence from San Antonio in the months preceding the Alamo battle.
Bonnell, George. *Topographical Description of Texas. To Which Is Added, an Account of the Indian Tribes.* Austin: Clark, Wing, and Brown, 1840; reprint, Waco: Texian Press, 1964, 82–83, 134–136.

Bostick, Sion R. "Reminiscences of Sion R. Bostick." *QTSHA* 5 (October 1901): 88–91. [1835].

   A Texan soldier recalls the 1835 siege of San Antonio.

Bouchu, Francois, to uncle, 14 May 1855, CAT.

   A letter from a Catholic priest reporting on conditions at San Antonio.

Bracht, Viktor. *Texas in 1848*. Translated by Charles Frank Schmidt. San Antonio: Naylor, 1931, 169, 174, 177–179, 182–183, 191. [1846–1847].

Brahan, R. W., Jr., to John D. Coffee, 20 January [1855]. In Aaron M. Boom, "Texas in the 1850s, As Viewed by a Recent Arrival." *SWHQ* 70 (October 1966): 282–285.

Brown, John Duff. "Reminiscences of Jno. Duff Brown." *QTSHA* 12 (April 1909): 299–301. [around 1832–1835].

Buquor, Maride [María de] Jesús. "Witnessed Last Struggle of the Alamo Patriots." *San Antonio Express*, 19 July 1907, 3.

Candelaria Castañon, Andrea. "Alamo Massacre." *San Antonio Light*, 19 February 1899, 6. Reprinted in Maurice Elfer, *Madam Candelaria: Unsung Heroine of the Alamo*. Houston: Rein, 1933.

   Reminiscences of a woman alleged to be in the Alamo when it fell.

Canterbury, Elizabeth. "A Talk with Mrs. Canterbury." *San Antonio Express Annual Review*, March 1890, 4. [1841–1844]. This edition of the *Annual Review* was an insert of the *San Antonio Express*, 15 March 1890.

Carl, Prince of Solms-Braunfels. *Texas 1844–45*. Translated from German. Houston: Anson Jones, 1936, 63–64.

Carpenter, V. K., comp. *The State of Texas Federal Population Schedules Seventh Census of the United States, 1850*. Huntsville, Ark.: Century Enterprises, 1969, 1: 111–189.

Castañeda, Carlos E., trans. *The Mexican Side of the Texan Revolution [1836] by the Chief Mexican Participants*. Dallas: P. L. Turner, 1928; reprint, Austin: Graphic Ideas, 1970, 11–15, 101–104, 107–108, 152–153.

   Accounts of the Alamo battle by eyewitnesses Antonio López de Santa Anna and Ramón Martínez Caro.

Chabot, Frederick C. *The Perote Prisoners: Being the Diary of James L. Truehart, Printed for the First Time Together with an Historical Introduction*. San Antonio: Naylor, 1934, 91–103. [1842].

   Eyewitness description of General Woll's 1842 conquest of San Antonio.

———, ed. *Texas Letters*. San Antonio: Yanaguana Society, 1940, 19, 32–33, 168–169. [1845–1854].

   Various letters written from San Antonio.

Chamberlain, Samuel E. *My Confession*. With an introduction and postscript by Roger Butterfield. New York: Harper & Brothers, 1956, 38–46. [1846].

   Reminiscences of a U.S. soldier who fought in the war with Mexico.

Chapman, Thomas F., to a friend, 25 October 1846. In *San Antonio Express*, 21 February 1886, 15.

Chariton, Wallace O. *100 Days in Texas: The Alamo Letters*. Plano, Texas: Wordware, 1990.

Collection of correspondence and diary entries from before and after the Alamo battle.

Clopper, J. C. "J. C. Clopper's Journal and Book of Memoranda for 1828." *QTSHA* 13 (July 1909): 69–76.

Coleman, Thomas W., to William Harrison, 23 April 1849. CAH.

Corner, William, ed. and comp. *San Antonio de Béxar: A Guide and History.* San Antonio: Bainbridge & Corner, 1890; reprint, San Antonio: Graphic Arts, 1977, 107–108, 112–114, 117–123.

Reminiscences of various San Antonio residents.

Court of Claims Voucher Files nos. 2557, 2558, 3416, 5026, 6073. General Land Office, Austin.

Depositions and other documentation for land claims made by family members of Tejanos who died in the Alamo battle.

Crimmins, M. L. "Robert E. Lee in Texas: Letters and Diary." *West Texas Historical Association Year Book* 8 (June 1932): 18–20. [1860].

Includes a brief description of a San Juan Day celebration among the Tejano community.

———, ed. "John W. Smith, the Last Messenger from the Alamo and the First Mayor of San Antonio." *SWHQ* 54 (January 1951): 344–346.

Obituary of John W. Smith reprinted from the *Texas National Register,* 18 January 1845.

Dancy, Jon Winfield. "Diary of Jon Winfield Dancy, November 1, 1837 to January, 1847" (photocopy), 31–34, 112–118. CAH. [1838, 1842].

Dantzler, L. N. "Visits San Antonio After Long Absence." *San Antonio Semi-Weekly Express,* 16 December 1904, 5. [1854].

Day, James M., comp. *The Texas Almanac, 1857–1873: A Compendium of Texas History.* With an introduction by Walter Moore. Waco: Texian Press, 1967.

Includes several reminiscences and other accounts from contemporary sources.

De Cordova, J. *Texas: Her Resources and Her Public Men. A Companion for J. De Cordova's New and Correct Map of the State of Texas.* Philadelphia: J. B. Lippincott, 1858, 268–269.

De la Garza, Refugio, Juan Martín de Beramendi, and José María Balmaceda. School Ordinance of Béxar, 13 March 1828. BA. Translated in I. J. Cox. "Educational Efforts in San Fernando de Béxar." *QTSHA* 6 (July 1902): 52–63.

De la Teja, Jesús F., ed. *A Revolution Remembered: The Memoirs and Selected Correspondence of Juan N. Seguín.* Austin: State House Press, 1991. [1833–1860].

DeShields, James T. *Tall Men with Long Rifles: The Glamorous Story of the Texas Revolution, as Told by Captain Creed Taylor, Who Fought in That Heroic Struggle from Gonzales to San Jacinto.* San Antonio: Naylor, 1935, 51–69. [1835].

A Texan soldier recalls the 1835 siege of San Antonio.

DeVilbiss, John Wesley, Sr. "Reminiscences of a Superannuated Preacher." In *Reminiscences and Events in the Ministerial Life of Rev. John Wesley De-*

Vilbiss, comp. H. A. Graves, 40–41, 50, 53–59. Galveston: W. A. Shaw, 1886. [1844–1847].

Reminiscences of the first resident Methodist minister assigned to San Antonio.

Díaz, Juan. "As a Boy, Juan Díaz, Venerable San Antonian Witnessed the Attack on the Alamo." *San Antonio Light*, 1 September 1907, 13.

Díaz, Pablo. "Aged Citizen Describes Alamo Fight and Fire." *San Antonio Express*, 1 July 1906, 11.

Recollections of the 1835 siege of San Antonio and the Alamo battle.

———. "This Man Heard Shots Fired at Battle of Alamo." *San Antonio Light*, 31 October 1909, 10.

Dielmann, Henry B. "Emma Altgelt's Sketches of Life in Texas." *SWHQ* 63 (January 1960): 368–370. [1854].

Domenech, Abbe [Emanuel]. *Missionary Adventures in Texas and Mexico: A Personal Narrative of Six Years' Sojourn in Those Regions*. Translated from French. London: Longman, Brown, Green, Longmans, and Roberts, 1858, 37–41, 82–86, 94–97, 99–100, 174–177, 194–195. [1848–1850].

Dubuis, Claude Marie. Correspondence, 1851–1859. IWA, CAT.

A series of letters from a Catholic priest reporting on conditions at San Antonio. See also Mary Hoffman Ogilvie. "Claude Marie Dubuis: Nineteenth-Century Texas Missionary [Correspondence with Bishop Odin]." M.A. thesis, University of Texas, Austin, 1990, 47–143.

Duval, J[ohn] C. *Early Times in Texas*. With an introduction by John Q. Anderson. Austin: H. P. N. Gammel, 1892; reprint, Austin: Steck-Vaughn, 1967, 2: 64–74. [1843]. The 1843 date is given in J. W. Wilbarger. *Indian Depredations in Texas*, 290–295. Austin: Hutchings, 1889; reprint, Austin: State House Press, 1991.

Eastman, Seth. *A Seth Eastman Sketchbook, 1848–1849*. With an introduction by Lois Burkhalter. Austin: University of Texas Press, 1961, xxi–xxiv, 43–47, 61. [1848–1849].

Edward, David B. *The History of Texas; Or, The Emigrant's, Farmer's, and Politician's Guide to the Character, Climate, Soil, and Productions of that Country: Geographically Arranged from Personal Observation and Experience*. Cincinnati: J. A. James, 1836, 32.

Ehrenberg, Herman. *With Milam and Fannin: Adventures of a German Boy in Texas' Revolution*. Edited by Henry Smith and translated by Charlotte Churchill. Dallas: Tady, 1935, 35–119. [1835].

A Texan soldier recalls the 1835 siege of San Antonio and life in the town afterwards.

Elfer, Maurice. *Madam Candelaria: Unsung Heroine of the Alamo*. Houston: Rein, 1933.

Reminiscences of a woman alleged to be in the Alamo when it fell. Based on earlier newspaper accounts in the San Antonio, Dallas, and Houston press. See especially *San Antonio Light*, 19 February 1899, 6.

Esparza, Enrique. "Alamo's Fall Is Told by Witness in a Land Suit." *San Antonio Express*, 9 December 1908, 20.

————. "Alamo's Only Survivor." *San Antonio Express,* 12 May 1907, 14; 19 May 1907, 47.
  Reminiscences of the Alamo battle by an eyewitness.
————. "Another Child of the Alamo." *San Antonio Light,* 10 November 1901, 9. Also appeared as "Children of the Alamo." *Houston Chronicle,* 9 November 1901, 4.
  Alamo reminiscences.
————. "Esparza, The Boy of the Alamo, Remembers." In *Rise of the Lone Star: A Story of Texas Told by Its Pioneers,* ed. Howard R. Driggs and Sarah S. King, 213–231. New York: Frederick A. Stokes, 1936.
  Description of Alamo battle and other reminiscences.
————. "The Story of Enrique Esparza." *San Antonio Express,* 22 November 1902, 8. Reprinted as "Story of The Massacre of Heroes of the Alamo." *San Antonio Express,* 7 March 1904, 5.
  Alamo reminiscences.
"Extracts from a Traveller's Journal." *Houston Morning Star,* ·13 May 1839; reprint, *Houston Telegraph and Texas Register,* 15 May 1839. [5, 7, 8 August 1838].
  Includes an early Anglo-American account of the battles at San Antonio during the Texas Revolution.
Falconer, Thomas. *Letters and Notes on the Texan Santa Fe Expedition, 1841– 1842.* New York: Dauber & Pine, 1930, 71–74.
Filisola, Vicente. *Memorias para la historia de la guerra de Tejas.* Mexico City: Ignacio Cumplido, 1849, 1: 3–48. [1836].
  A Mexican general's memoirs of the Alamo battle and its aftermath in San Antonio.
Fisher, Orceneth. *Sketches of Texas in 1840: Designed to Answer, in a Brief Way, the Numerous Enquiries Respecting the New Republic, as to Situation, Extent, Climate, Soil, Productions, Water, Government, Society, Religion, Etc.* Springfield, Ill.: Walters & Weber, 1841; reprint, Waco: Texian Press, 1964, 36.
Folsom, George. *Mexico in 1842: A Description of the Country, Its Natural and Political Features; with a Sketch of Its History, Brought Down to the Present Year.* New York: Charles J. Folsom, 1842, 204.
Freeman, W. G. "W. G. Freeman's Report on the Eighth Military Department." Edited by M. L. Crimmins. *SWHQ* 51 (October 1947): 167–174. [1853].
French, Sarah L. "Mrs. French's Reminiscences of Early Days in Béxar." In S. J. Wright. *San Antonio de Béxar: Historical, Traditional, Legendary,* 96–101. Austin: Morgan, 1916. [1846–1860].
Frétellière, Auguste. "Adventures of a Castrovillian." In Julia Nott Waugh. *Castro-Ville and Henry Castro, Empresario,* 91–94. San Antonio: Standard, 1934. [1844].
Froebel, Julius. *Seven Years' Travel in Central America, Northern Mexico, and the Far West of the United States.* London: Richard Bentley, 1859, 424–427, 436–442. [1852, 1853].
Fulton, Maurice Garland, ed. *Diary and Letters of Josiah Gregg: Excursions in*

Mexico & California, 1847–1850. With an introduction by Paul Horgan. Norman: University of Oklahoma Press, 1941, 1: 214–252. [1846].

G., T. E., to Editors, 1 November, December 1846. In the *United States Catholic Magazine and Monthly Review* 6 (1847): 52–54, 218–220.

Gentilz: Artist of the Old Southwest. Austin: University of Texas Press, 1974.
   A collection of paintings by an artist who first came to San Antonio in 1844.

Grant, U. S. *Personal Memoirs of U. S. Grant.* New York: Charles L. Webster, 1894, 1: 47. [1845].

Green, John A. "A Talk about the San Antonio of the Earlier Days." *San Antonio Express Annual Review,* March 1890, 2–3. [1845]. This edition of the *Annual Review* was an insert of the *San Antonio Express,* 15 March 1890.

Green, Rena Maverick, ed. *Memoirs of Mary A. Maverick.* San Antonio: Alamo, 1921. [1838–1842, 1847–1859].

———. *Samuel Maverick, Texan: 1803–1870. A Collection of Letters, Journals, and Memoirs.* San Antonio: Privately printed, 1952, 24–44, 63–68, 76–77, 88–91, 98–102, 138–140, 173–175, 194–195, 271. [1835–1844].

Green, Thomas J. *Journal of the Texian Expedition against Mier; Subsequent Imprisonment of the Author; His Sufferings, and Final Escape from the Castle of Perote. With Reflections upon the Present Political and Probable Future Relations of Texas, Mexico, and the United States.* New York: Harper & Brothers, 1845, 25–37, 41–51. [1842].

Green, Wharton J. *Recollections and Reflections: An Auto of Half a Century and More.* N.p.: Edwards and Broughton, 1906, 116–123. [1855].

Gulick, Charles Adams, Jr., and Katherine Elliott, eds. *The Papers of Mirabeau Buonaparte Lamar.* Austin: Von Boeckmann-Jones, 1973, 6 vols. [1821–1857]. These papers are indexed in *Calendar of the Papers of Mirabeau Buonaparte Lamar,* ed. and comp. Michael R. Green. Austin: Texas State Library, 1982.

Hammond, George P. and Edward H. Howes, eds. *Overland to California on the Southwestern Trail, 1849: The Diary of Robert Eccleston.* Berkeley: University of California Press, 1950, 22–27.

Harby, Lee C. "The Last Survivor of the Alamo, Señora Candelaria." *Times-Democrat* (New Orleans), 22 April 1894, 28.
   Interview of Andrea Candelaria Castañon, a woman alleged to be in the Alamo when it fell.

Haydon, George W., to Anthony Blanc, 13 March 1840. CAT.
   Description of a brief visit to San Antonio by a Catholic priest.

Holley, Mary Austin. *Texas.* Lexington, Ky.: J. Clarke, 1836; reprint, Austin: Texas State Historical Association, 1985, 112–113.

Hollon, W. Eugene, and Ruth Lapham Butler, eds. *William Bollaert's Texas.* Norman: University of Oklahoma Press, 1956, 216–241, 251, 257–258. [1843].

"How the Alamo Looked Nine Years after Its Fall." *San Antonio Express,* 9 April 1905, 9. [1845].
   Description from the memory of a contemporary observer.

Hughes, George W., to Capt. I. H. Prentiss, 20 September 1846 (photocopy). San Antonio Public Library. See also George W. Hughes. *Memoir Description of the March of a Division of the United States Army, Under the Command of Brigadier General John E. Wool, from San Antonio de Béxar, in Texas, to Saltillo, in Mexico,* 9–12. [Washington, D.C.?], 1846.

Hunt, Richard S., and Jesse F. Randel. *Guide to the Republic of Texas: Consisting of a Brief Outline of the History of Its Settlement; a General View of the Surface of the Country; Its Climate, Soil, Productions; Rivers, Counties, Towns and Internal Improvements; the Colonization and Land Laws; List of Courts and Judicial Officers; Tariff and Ports of Entry &c. Accompanied by a New and Correct Map.* New York: J. H. Colton, 1839, 47.

Ikin, Arthur. *Texas: Its History, Topography, Agriculture, Commerce, and General Statistics. To Which Is Added, a Copy of the Treaty of Commerce Entered into by the Republic of Texas and Great Britain. Designed for the Use of the British Merchant, and as a Guide to Emigrants.* London: Sherwood, Gilbert, and Piper, 1841, 31–32, 72.

Jenkins, John H., ed. *The Papers of the Texas Revolution, 1835–1836.* Austin: Presidial, 1973, 10 vols.

Jenkins, John Holmes, III, ed. *Recollections of Early Texas: The Memoirs of John Holland Jenkins.* With a foreword by J. Frank Dobie. Austin: University of Texas Press, 1958; reprint, 1987, 95–99, 219–220. [1842].
    Reminiscences of the two Mexican invasions at San Antonio in 1842.

Jordan, Gilbert J., ed. and trans. "W. Steinert's View of Texas in 1849." *SWHQ* 80 (1976–1977): 191–194, 200, 287, 399–401, 405–406.

"Journal of City Council B, January 1849 to August 1856, City of San Antonio." City Clerk's Office, San Antonio.

"Journal of City Council C, April 1, 1856 to February 21, 1870, City of San Antonio." City Clerk's Office, San Antonio.

Kendall, George Wilkens. *Narrative of the Texan Santa Fe Expedition, Comprising a Description of a Tour through Texas, and across the Great Southwestern Prairies, the Camanche [sic] and Caygua Hunting-Grounds, with an Account of the Sufferings from Want of Food, Losses from Hostile Indians, and Final Capture of the Texans, and Their March, as Prisoners, to the City of Mexico. With Illustrations and a Map.* New York: Harper & Brothers, 1844; reprint, Ann Arbor, Mich.: University Microfilms, 1966, 1: 45–52. [1841].

Kennedy, William. *Texas: The Rise, Progress, and Prospects of the Republic of Texas.* London: R. Hastings, 1841; reprint, Fort Worth: Molyneaux Craftsmen, 1925, 1: 173, 2: 44.
    Citation from volume two is Dr. John Charles Beales' diary account of his 1834 visit to San Antonio.

King, Sarah Brackett. "Early Days in San Antonio Recalled by a Pioneer Resident of the City." *San Antonio Light,* 4 February 1917, 14. [1846–1860].

Latham, Francis S. *Travels in the Republic of Texas, 1842.* Edited by Gerald S. Pierce. Austin: Encino, 1971, 3–5, 33–38. Latham's description of San Antonio appeared in the *Houston Telegraph and Texas Register,* 17 August 1842.

LeClerc, Frederic. *Texas and Its Revolution.* Translated by James L. Shepherd. Houston: Anson Jones, 1950, 38–39, 140.

Linn, John J. *Reminiscences of Fifty Years in Texas.* New York: D. & J. Sadlier, 1883; reprint, Austin: State House Press, 1986, 176–182, 294–296, 345–346. [1836–1838].

Lundy, Benjamin. *The Life, Travels and Opinions of Benjamin Lundy, Including His Journeys to Texas and Mexico; with a Sketch of Contemporary Events, and a Notice of the Revolution in Hayti.* Philadelphia: William D. Parrish, 1847; reprint, New York: Negro Universities Press, 1969, 47–56, 124. [1833, 1834].

Mansfield, J. K. F. "Colonel J. K. F. Mansfield's Report of the Inspection of the Department of Texas in 1856." *SWHQ* 42 (October 1938): 133–143.

Maverick, Mary A. "How They Saw San Antonio a Half Century Ago." *San Antonio Express Annual Review,* March 1890, 3–4. [1838–1842]. This edition of the *Annual Review* was an insert of the *San Antonio Express,* 15 March 1890.

McClintock, William A. "Journal of a Trip through Texas and Northern Mexico in 1846–1847." *SWHQ* 34 (1930): 36–37, 141–149. [1846].

McCullough, John. "Annual Report." *[Domestic] Missionary Chronicle* 7 (1848): 88, 376. In R. Douglas Brackenridge and Francisco O. García-Treto. *Iglesia Presbiteriana: A History of Presbyterians and Mexican Americans in the Southwest,* 9–10. San Antonio: Trinity University Press, 1974.

———. "'Reminiscences." In William Wallace McCullough, Jr. *John McCullough: Pioneer Presbyterian Missionary and Teacher in the Republic of Texas,* 34–36. Galveston: Privately printed, 1944. [1846–1849]. Also in William Wallace McCullough, Jr. *John McCullough: Pioneer Presbyterian Missionary and Teacher in the Republic of Texas,* 70–73. Austin: Pemberton, 1966.
    Account of the Presbyterian minister whose congregation built the first Protestant church in San Antonio.

McCutchan, Joseph D. *Mier Expedition Diary: A Texan Prisoner's Account.* Edited by Joseph Milton Nance. With a foreword by Jane A. Kenamore. Austin: University of Texas Press, 1978, 9–15. [1842].

McDowell, Catherine, ed. *Letters from the Ursuline, 1852–1853.* San Antonio: Trinity University Press, 1977.
    Series of letters from two Irish nuns who came to San Antonio in 1852.

Menchaca, Antonio. *Memoirs.* With a foreword by Frederick C. Chabot and an introduction by James P. Newcomb. San Antonio: Yanaguana Society, 1937, 20–24. [1822–1836].

———. "The Memoirs of Captain Menchaca" (typescript). Edited and annotated by James P. Newcomb, 22–38. CAH. [1836–1846].

"Minutes of the City Council of the City of San Antonio, 1830 to 1835, Spanish Minute Book Two" (typescript). CAH. Also at City Clerk's Office, San Antonio.

"Minutes of the City Council of the City of San Antonio from 1837 to 1849, Journal A" (typescript). CAH. Also at City Clerk's Office, San Antonio.

Moore, Francis, Jr. *Map and Description of Texas, Containing Sketches of Its*

History, Geology, Geography and Statistics: With Concise Statements, Relative to the Soil, Climate, Productions, Facilities of Transportation, Population of the Country; and Some Brief Remarks Upon the Character and Customs of Its Inhabitants. Philadelphia: H. Tanner Jr., 1840; reprint, Waco: Texian Press, 1965, 26, 48–49.

Morrell, Z. N. *Flowers and Fruits from the Wilderness; or, Thirty-six Years in Texas and Two Winters in Honduras.* Boston: Gould and Lincoln, 1872, 117–118. [1839].

    Comments of a Baptist minister based on a two-day visit to San Antonio.

Muir, Andrew Forest, ed. *Texas in 1837: An Anonymous, Contemporary Narrative.* Austin: University of Texas Press, 1988, 96–116, 123.

Nance, Joseph Milton, ed. and trans. "Brigadier General Adrian Woll's Report of His Expedition into Texas in 1842." *SWHQ* 58 (April 1955): 523–552.

Navarro, José Antonio. *Apuntes históricos interesantes de San Antonio de Béxar escritos por el C. Dn. José Antonio Navarro, en noviembre de 1853. Y publicados por varios de sus amigos.* San Antonio: Privately printed, 1869.

Navarro Alsbury, Juana. "Mrs. Alsbury's Recollections of the Alamo." In "John S. Ford Memoirs" (unpublished manuscript), 102–104. CAH.

Newcomb, James P. "Christmas in San Antonio Half a Century Ago." *San Antonio Express,* 18 December 1904, 26.

    More of a description of life at San Antonio in the 1850s than of the city's Christmas celebrations during that period.

Newell, C[hester]. *History of the Revolution in Texas, Particularly of the War of 1835 & '36; Together with the Latest Geographical, Topographical, and Statistical Accounts of the Country, from the Most Authentic Sources.* New York: Wiley & Putnam, 1838, 147–149.

Nuñez, Felix. "Fall of the Alamo." *San Antonio Express,* 30 June 1889, 3. See also "The Felix Nuñez Account and the Siege of the Alamo: A Critical Appraisal," ed. Stephen L. Hardin. *SWHQ* 94 (July 1990): 65–84.

Odin, Jean Marie. "Daily Journal" (photocopy), 6–12, 33–34, 57–58. CAT. [1840–1841, 1844].

———. Correspondence, 1840–1860. CAT, ND. See especially Odin to Anthony Blanc, 24 August 1840, CAT; Odin to Joseph Rosati, 27 August 1840, CAT; Odin to Jean-Baptiste Étienne, 28 August 1840, 11 April 1841, 7 February 1842, CAT.

    Select correspondence by the first Catholic bishop of Texas. Cited letters treat pastoral visits to San Antonio.

Olmsted, Frederick Law. *A Journey through Texas; or, A Saddle-Trip on the Southwestern Frontier: With a Statistical Appendix.* New York: Dix, Edwards & Co., 1857, 148–160, 164–165, 433–439. [1854]. Olmsted's account is reprinted in *Journey through Texas: A Saddle-Trip on the Southwestern Frontier,* ed. James Howard. Austin: Von Boeckmann-Jones, 1962.

Page, Frederic Benjamin. *Prairiedom: Rambles and Scrambles in Texas or New Estremadura.* New York: Paine & Burgess, 1845, 125–136. [1844?].

Parisot, P. F. *The Reminiscences of a Texas Missionary.* San Antonio: Johnson Bros., 1899, 38–41. [1857–1858].

Parker, A. A. *Trip to the West and Texas. Comprising a Journey of Eight Thousand Miles, through New York, Michigan, Illinois, Missouri, Louisiana and Texas, in the Autumn and Winter of 1834–1835. Interspersed with Anecdotes, Incidents and Observations. With a Brief Sketch of the Texian War.* Concord, New Hampshire: White & Fisher, 1835, 157.

Pease, L. T. "A Geographical and Historical View of Texas; with a Detailed Account of the Texian Revolution and War." In John M. Niles. *History of South America and Mexico; Comprising Their Discovery, Geography, Politics, Commerce, and Revolutions,* 1: 288–297. Hartford: H. Huntington, 1838.

    Reports and official documents related to the Texan capture of San Antonio in December 1835.

Perry, Carmen, ed. and trans. *With Santa Anna in Texas: A Personal Narrative of the Revolution by José Enrique de la Peña.* With an introduction by Llerena Friend. College Station: Texas A&M University Press, 1975, 37–62. [1836].

    A Mexican soldier's account of the Alamo battle and its aftermath in San Antonio.

"Petition Addressed by the Illustrious *Ayuntamiento* of the City of Béxar to the Honorable Legislature of the State: To Make Known the Ills Which Afflict the Towns of Texas and the Grievances They Have Suffered Since Their Union with Coahuila," 19 December 1832. In *Troubles in Texas, 1832: A Tejano Viewpoint from San Antonio with a Translation and Facsimile,* ed. David J. Weber and trans. Conchita Hassell Winn and David J. Weber, 15–32. Dallas: Wind River, 1983.

"Population Schedules of the Eighth Census of the United States, 1860." Washington, D.C.: The National Archives, 1967, rolls 1288: 1–192a, 1309: 1–8. Text-fiche.

Potter, R[euben] M. *The Texas Revolution: Distinguished Mexicans Who Took Part in the Revolution of Texas, with Glances at Its Early Events,* 18–20. Reprinted from the *Magazine of American History,* October 1878. Available at CAH, LC.

    Recollection of a fatal affray [1838] between Eugenio Navarro and an Anglo-American named Tinsley.

Rankin, Melinda. *Texas in 1850.* Boston: Damrell & Moore, 1850; reprint, [Waco]: Texian Press, 1966, 181–185.

    Assessment of the prospects for evangelization in San Antonio by a Protestant missionary.

"Recollections of Texas. By a Returned Emigrant." *North American Miscellany* 2 (17 May 1851): 113–116.

Reid, John C. *Reid's Tramp, or a Journal of the Incidents of Ten Months Travel through Texas, New Mexico, Arizona, Sonora, and California including Topography, Climate, Soil, Minerals, Metals, and Inhabitants; with a Notice of the Great Inter-Oceanic Rail Road.* Selma, Ala.: John Hardy, 1858; reprint, Austin: Steck, 1935, 59–72, 80–83. [1856].

Rodríguez, J[osé] M[aría]. *Rodriguez Memoirs of Early Texas.* San Antonio: Passing Show Printing, 1913; reprint, San Antonio: Standard, 1961. [1835–1860].

————. "Stirring Events Are Remembered by Texas Jurist." *San Antonio Express,* 8 September 1912, 35. [1835–1842].

Roemer, Ferdinand. *Texas: With Particular Reference to German Immigration and the Physical Appearance of the Country.* Translated by Oswald Mueller. San Antonio: Standard, 1935; reprint, Waco: Texian Press, 1967, 11, 119–133, 156–159. [1846].

Ruiz, Francis Antonio. "Fall of the Alamo, and Massacre of Travis and His Brave Associates." In *The Texas Almanac for 1860,* trans. J. A. Quintero, 80–81. Houston: James Burke, 1859. Also in *The Texas Almanac, 1857–1873: A Compendium of Texas History,* comp. James M. Day, 356–358. With an introduction by Walter Moore. Waco: Texian Press, 1967. See also *Alamo Express* (San Antonio), 25 August 1860, 1.

San Antonio Express Annual Review, March 1890, 1–2. [1845]. This edition of the *Annual Review* was an insert of the *San Antonio Express,* 15 March 1890.
    Reminiscences of San Antonio from an anonymous source.

"San Fernando Baptismal Register." Books 5–8. CASA.

"San Fernando Cathedral Deaths." Book 3. CASA.

"San Fernando Marriage Register." Book 1. CASA.

Sánchez, José María. "A Trip to Texas in 1828." Translated by Carlos E. Castañeda. *SWHQ* 29 (April 1926): 257–260.

Sanchez-Navarro, Carlos. *La guerra de Tejas: Memorias de un soldado.* Mexico City: Editorial Polis, 1938, 96–123, 148–158. [1835, 1836].
    A Mexican soldier's memoirs of the 1835 Texan siege of San Antonio and the battle of the Alamo.

Seguín, Juan N. *Personal Memoirs of John N. Seguín from the Year 1834 to the Retreat of General Woll from the City of San Antonio in 1842.* San Antonio: Ledger Book and Job Office, 1858. [1834–1842]. These memoirs are edited and reprinted in *A Revolution Remembered: The Memoirs and Selected Correspondence of Juan N. Seguín,* ed. Jesús F. de la Teja, 73–102. Austin: State House Press, 1991.

Sellon, Charles I., to Marilla, 6 September 1846. In H. Bailey Carroll. "Texas Collection." *SWHQ* 47 (July 1943): 63.

"Señor Navarro Tells the Story of His Grandfather." In *Rise of the Lone Star: A Story of Texas Told by Its Pioneers,* ed. Howard R. Driggs and Sarah S. King, 267–275. New York: Frederick A. Stokes, 1936.
    Family traditions about incidents involving the Navarros around the time of the Texas Revolution.

Sister de Ste. Marie to Anthony Blanc, 26 September 1854, ND. Report of an Ursuline sister assigned to San Antonio.

Smith, George G. *The Life and Times of George Foster Pierce, D.D., LL.D., Bishop of the Methodist Episcopal Church, South, with His Sketch of Lovick Pierce, D.D., His Father.* With an introduction by Atticus G. Haygood. Sparta, Ga.: Hancock, 1888, 373–377. [1859].

Smith, Ophia D. "A Trip to Texas in 1855." *SWHQ* 59 (July 1955): 36–37.

Smithwick, Noah. *The Evolution of a State or Recollections of Old Texas Days.*

Compiled by Nanna Smithwick Donaldson. With a foreword by L. Tuffy Ellis. Austin: University of Texas Press, 1983, 18. [ca. 1827].

Stapp, William Preston. *The Prisoners of Perote, Containing a Journal Kept by the Author, Who Was Captured by the Mexicans, at Mier, December 25, 1842, and Released from Perote, May 16, 1844.* Philadelphia: G. B. Zieber, 1845; reprint, Austin: University of Texas Press, 1977, 16–23. [1842].

Stiff, Edward. *The Texan Emigrant: Being a Narration of the Adventures of the Author in Texas, and a Description of the Soil, Climate, Productions, Minerals, Towns, Bays, Harbors, Rivers, Institutions, and Manners and Customs of the Inhabitants of That Country; Together with the Principal Incidents of Fifteen Years Revolution in Mexico: And Embracing a Condensed Statement of Interesting Events in Texas, from the First European Settlement in 1692, Down to the Year 1840.* Cincinnati: George Conclin, 1840, 28–29.

Stillman, J. D. B. *Wanderings in the Southwest in 1855 by J. D. B. Stillman.* Edited with an introduction by Ron Tyler. Spokane, Wash.: Arthur H. Clark, 1990, 54, 87–89.

Story, William Russell. "Diary of William Russell Story, December 3, 1855–March 16, 1856" (typescript), 25–37. CAH. [30 December 1855–16 March 1856].

Texas in 1840, or the Emigrant's Guide to the New Republic; Being the Result of Observation, Enquiry and Travel in that Beautiful Country. By an Emigrant, Late of the United States. New York: William W. Allen, 1840, 218–220.

Van Zandt, Isaac, to Daniel Webster, 23 March 1843. In *Diplomatic Correspondence of the Republic of Texas,* ed. George P. Garrison, 2: 156, 158–161. Washington, D.C.: U.S. Government Printing Office, 1911.
    Treats briefly the 1835 siege of San Antonio and General Woll's 1842 occupation of the city.

White, Gifford. *1830 Citizens of Texas.* Austin: Eakin, 1983, 79–112.

———, ed. *The 1840 Census of the Republic of Texas.* With a foreword by James M. Day. Austin: Pemberton, 1966, 12–18.

Williams, Charles Richard, ed. *Diary and Letters of Rutherford Birchard Hayes: Nineteenth President of the United States.* Columbus, Ohio: F. J. Heer, 1922, 1: 261–262, 264. [1849]. See also Claude Michael Gruener. "Rutherford B. Hayes's Horseback Ride through Texas." *SWHQ* 68 (January 1965): 359.

Williams, Samuel. Correspondence. Rosenberg Library, Galveston. See especially letters to Williams from José Antonio Navarro. [1830–1834].

Winkler, E. W., ed. "The Béxar and Dawson Prisoners." *QTSHA* 13 (April 1910): 294–297, 312–315, 320–322. [1842].
    Three accounts of General Woll's 1842 occupation of San Antonio.

Yoakum, H[enderson]. *History of Texas from Its First Settlement in 1685 to Its Annexation to the United States in 1846.* New York: Redfield, 1855, 2 vols.

Yorba, Eulalia. "Another Story of the Alamo." *San Antonio Express,* 12 April 1896, 13.
    Reminiscences of the Alamo battle.

Zirkel, Ray. "The Letters of Juan Manuel Zambrano" (unpublished manuscript), CASA. [1823].
 Also contains an introduction and brief summary of Zambrano's life.

Contemporary Newspapers

Alamo Express (San Antonio). 18 August–5 November 1860. CAH, San Antonio Public Library.
Alamo Star (San Antonio). 25 March 1854–29 January 1855. CAH, San Antonio Public Library.
Austin City Gazette, 10 June 1840. CAH.
Austin Texas Sentinel. 15 January 1840–11 November 1841. CAH.
Bejareño (San Antonio). 7 February 1855–28 June 1856. CAH.
Correo (San Antonio). 28 April, 26 May, 8 July 1858. CAH.
Daily Herald and San Antonio Public Advertiser. 1857. CAH, San Antonio Public Library.
Daily Texan (San Antonio). 18 April–9 August 1859. CAH. Merged with the *San Antonio Daily Ledger* in 1859, forming the *San Antonio Daily Ledger and Texan.*
Houston Morning Star. 1839–1846. CAH, Houston Public Library.
Houston Telegraph and Texas Register. 1835–1848. CAH, Houston Public Library.
 Publication at Houston began in 1837. Previously published for brief periods at San Felipe de Austin, Harrisburg, and Columbia.
Ranchero (San Antonio). 4–28 July 1856. CAH, San Antonio Public Library.
San Antonio Daily Hearld. 1857–1860. Houston Public Library, San Antonio Public Library.
San Antonio Daily Ledger. 1858–1860. CAH, San Antonio Public Library.
 Merged with the *Daily Texan* (San Antonio) in 1859, forming the *San Antonio Daily Ledger and Texan.*
San Antonio Herald. 1855–1856, 1858–1859. CAH, San Antonio Public Library.
San Antonio Ledger. 1851–1860. CAH, LC, San Antonio Public Library.
 Merged with the *Texan* in 1859, forming the *San Antonio Ledger and Texan.*
San Antonio Reporter. 1856. CAH, San Antonio Public Library.
San Antonio Zeitung. 1853–1856. San Antonio Public Library, CAH.
Semi-Weekly Western Texan (San Antonio). 28 June 1852. CAH.
Sentinel (San Antonio). 14 July 1855. San Antonio Public Library.
Texan (San Antonio). See *Western Texan.*
Texas Baptist (Anderson). 2 February 1860, 7 February 1861. CAH.
 Articles on religious conditions at San Antonio, founding of First Baptist Church of San Antonio.
Union (San Antonio). 1859. CAH, San Antonio Public Library.
Western Texan (San Antonio). 1848–1860. CAH, San Antonio Public Library, LC.
 Name changed to *Texan* in 1855. Merged with the *San Antonio Ledger* in 1859, forming the *San Antonio Ledger and Texan.*

SECONDARY SOURCES FOR SAN ANTONIO HISTORY, 1821–1860

Almaráz, Félix D., Jr. *Governor Antonio Martínez and Mexican Independence in Texas: An Orderly Transition.* San Antonio: Béxar County Historical Commission, 1979. Originally published in the *Permian Historical Annual* 15 (December 1975).

Barker, Eugene C. "Native Latin American Contribution to the Colonization and Independence of Texas." *SWHQ* 46 (January 1943): 317–335.

Barnes, Charles Merritt. *Combats and Conquests of Immortal Heroes: Sung in Song and Told in Story.* San Antonio: Guessaz & Ferlet, 1910.

Barr, Alwyn. *Texas in Revolt: The Battle for San Antonio, 1835.* Austin: University of Texas Press, 1990.

Bayard, Ralph. *Lone-Star Vanguard: The Catholic Re-Occupation of Texas (1838–1848).* St. Louis: Vincentian Press, 1945.

Biesele, R. L. "The Texas State Convention of Germans in 1854." *SWHQ* 33 (April 1930): 247–261.

Brackenridge, R. Douglas, and Francisco O. García-Treto. *Iglesia Presbiteriana: A History of Presbyterians and Mexican Americans in the Southwest.* San Antonio: Trinity University Press, 1974.

Broussard, Ray F. "San Antonio during the Texas Republic: A City in Transition." *Southwestern Studies* 5 (1967): 3–40.

Bunting, Henry S. "Early History of the First Presbyterian Church of San Antonio [and] Biography of Its Founder, the Reverend Franklin Bunting, D.D." (typescript). CAH.

Castañeda, Carlos E. *Our Catholic Heritage in Texas, 1519–1936.* Austin: Von Boeckmann-Jones, 1936–1958, vols. 6–7.

Chabot, Frederick Charles. *With the Makers of San Antonio. Genealogies of the Early Latin, Anglo-American, and German Families with Occasional Biographies, Each Group Being Prefaced with a Brief Historical Sketch and Illustrations.* San Antonio: Artes Graficas, 1937.

Cox, I. J. "Educational Efforts in San Fernando de Béxar." *QTSHA* 6 (July 1902): 27–63.

Crisp, James Ernest. "Anglo-Texan Attitudes toward the Mexican, 1821–1845." Ph.D. diss., Yale University, New Haven, 1976.

Crook, Carland Elaine. "San Antonio, Texas, 1846–1861." M.A. thesis, Rice University, Houston, 1964.

Davis, John L. *San Antonio: A Historical Portrait.* Austin: Encino, 1978.

Dawson, Joseph Martin. *José Antonio Navarro: Co-Creator of Texas.* Waco: Baylor University Press, 1969.

De la Teja, Jesús F., and John Wheat. "Béxar: Profile of a *Tejano* Community, 1820–1832." *SWHQ* 89 (July 1985): 7–34.

De León, Arnoldo. *The Tejano Community, 1836–1900.* Albuquerque: University of New Mexico Press, 1982.

———. *They Called Them Greasers: Anglo Attitudes toward Mexicans in Texas, 1821–1900.* Austin: University of Texas Press, 1983.

Diekemper, Barnabas. "French Clergy on the Texas Frontier, 1837–1907." *East Texas Historical Journal* 21 (1983): 29–38.

Downs, Fane. "The History of Mexicans in Texas, 1820–1845." Ph.D. diss., Texas Tech University, Lubbock, 1970.

Dysart, Jane. "Mexican Women in San Antonio, 1830–1860: The Assimilation Process." *Western Historical Quarterly* 7 (October 1976): 365–375.

Everett, Donald E. *San Antonio: The Flavor of Its Past, 1845–1898.* San Antonio: Trinity University Press, 1975.

———. *San Antonio Legacy.* San Antonio: Trinity University Press, 1979.

First Presbyterian Church San Antonio, Texas, 1846–1946. N.p.: [1946]. Available at CAH.

Fitzmorris, Mary Angela. "Four Decades of Catholicism in Texas, 1820–1860." Ph.D. diss., Catholic University of America, Washington, D.C., 1926.

Foley, Patrick. "Beyond the Missions: The Immigrant Church and the Hispanics in Nineteenth Century Texas." In *Hispanicism and Catholicism: Great Forces in Motion.* San Antonio: Mexican American Cultural Center Press, 1992.

———. "From Linares to Galveston: The Early Development of the Catholic Hierarchy in Texas." Paper read at the first Biennial Conference of the Texas Catholic Historical Society, St. Edward's University, Austin, 27 October 1989.

———. "Jean-Marie Odin, C. M., Missionary Bishop Extraordinaire of Texas." *Journal of Texas Catholic History and Culture* 1 (March 1990): 42–60.

Forman, Josephine. *We Finish to Begin: A History of Travis Park United Methodist Church, San Antonio, Texas, 1846–1991.* San Antonio: Travis Park United Methodist Church, 1991.

Gibson, Dorothy Kelly. "Social Life in San Antonio, 1855–1860." M.A. thesis, University of Texas, Austin, 1937.

Haggard, J. Villasana. "Epidemic Cholera in Texas, 1833–1834." *SWHQ* 40 (January 1937): 216–230.

Hinojosa, Gilberto, M. "The Enduring Hispanic Faith Communities: Spanish and Texas Church Historiography." Journal of Texas Catholic History and Culture 1 (March 1990): 20–41.

H[orton], H[amilton] G. "Beginnings of the Mexican Work." *Texas Methodist Historical Quarterly* 1 (January 1910): 289–291.

———. "Mexican Work—Early Days," *Texas Christian Advocate* (Galveston), 7 May 1881, 1.

In the Shadow of His Hand: The First Century of the First Baptist Church of San Antonio, Texas, 1861–1961. San Antonio: Perry, 1961. Available at CAH.

Jordan, Terry G. "A Century and a Half of Ethnic Change in Texas, 1836–1986." *SWHQ* 89 (April 1986): 385–422.

———. "Population Origins in Texas, 1850," *Geographical Review* 59 (January 1969): 83–103.

Juarez, José Roberto. "La iglesia Católica y el Chicano en sud Texas, 1836–1911." *Aztlán* 4 (Fall 1973): 217–255.

Keeth, Kent. "Sankt Antonious: Germans in the Alamo City in the 1850s." *SWHQ* 76 (October 1972): 183–202.

Lack, Paul D. *The Texas Revolutionary Experience: A Political and Social History, 1835–1836.* College Station: Texas A&M University Press, 1992.

Matovina, Timothy M. "Our Lady of Guadalupe Celebrations in San Antonio, Texas, 1840–41." *Journal of Hispanic/Latino Theology* 1 (November 1993): 77–96.

Mayer, Arthur James. "San Antonio: Frontier Entrepot." Ph.D. diss., University of Texas, Austin, 1976.

McCallum, Nancy Lou. "History of the Methodist Episcopal Church, South, in San Antonio, Texas." M.A. thesis, University of Texas, Austin, 1936.

McGrath, Sister Paul of the Cross. "Political Nativism in Texas, 1825–1860." Ph.D. diss., Catholic University of America, Washington, D.C., 1930.

Miller, Howard. "Stephen F. Austin and the Anglo-Texan Response to the Religious Establishment in Mexico, 1821–1836." *SWHQ* 91 (January 1988): 283–316.

Miller, Thomas Lloyd. "Mexican-Texans at the Alamo." *Journal of Mexican American History* 2 (Fall 1971): 33–44.

———. "Mexican Texans in the Texas Revolution." *Journal of Mexican American History* 3 (1973): 105–130.

Montejano, David. *Anglos and Mexicans in the Making of Texas, 1836–1986.* Austin: University of Texas Press, 1987.

Moore, Harriet Brown. *St. Mark's Church, Travis Park, San Antonio, Texas: A Parish with a Personality.* San Antonio: Naylor, 1944.

Moore, James Talmadge. *Through Fire and Flood: The Catholic Church in Frontier Texas, 1836–1900.* College Station, Texas A&M University Press, 1992.

Nance, Joseph Milton. *After San Jacinto: The Texas-Mexican Frontier, 1836–1841.* Austin: University of Texas Press, 1963.

———. *Attack and Counter-Attack: The Texas-Mexican Frontier, 1842.* Austin: University of Texas Press, 1964.

Nañez, Alfredo. *History of the Rio Grande Conference of the United Methodist Church.* Dallas: Bridwell Library, Southern Methodist University, 1980.

———. "Methodism Among the Spanish-Speaking People in Texas and New Mexico." In Walter N. Vernon, Alfredo Nañez, and John H. Graham. *One in the Lord: A History of Ethnic Minorities in the South Central Jurisdiction, The United Methodist Church.* Bethany, Okla.: Cowan, 1977, 50–94.

Nixon, Pat Ireland. *The Medical Story of Early Texas, 1528–1853.* With a foreword by Dr. Chauncey D. Leake. Lancaster, Pa.: Lancaster Press, 1946.

Nostrand, Richard L. "Mexican Americans Circa 1850." *Annals of the Association of American Geographers* 65 (September 1975): 378–390.

Paredes, Raymund A. "The Origins of Anti-Mexican Sentiment in the United States." *New Scholar* 6 (1977): 139–165.

Parisot, P. F., and C. J. Smith. *History of the Catholic Church in the Diocese of San Antonio, Texas.* San Antonio: Carrico & Bowen, 1897.

Peters, Robert K. "Texas: Annexation to Secession." Ph.D. diss., University of Texas, Austin, 1977.

Pitts, John Bost, III. "Speculation in Headright Land Grants in San Antonio from 1837 to 1842." M.A. thesis, Trinity University, San Antonio, 1966.

Posey, Walter Brownlow. *Frontier Mission: A History of Religion West of the Southern Appalachians to 1861.* Lexington: University of Kentucky Press, 1966.

Poyo, Gerald E., and Gilberto M. Hinojosa. "Spanish Texas and Borderlands Historiography in Transition: Implications for United States History." *Journal of American History* 75 (September 1988): 393–416.

———, eds. *Tejano Origins in Eighteenth-Century San Antonio.* Austin: University of Texas Press, 1991.

Red, William Stuart. *The Texas Colonists and Religion, 1821–1836.* Austin: E. L. Shettles, 1924.

Remy, Caroline. "Hispanic-Mexican San Antonio: 1836–1861."*SWHQ* 71 (April 1968): 564–582.

Rippy, J. Fred. "Border Troubles along the Rio Grande, 1848–1860." *SWHQ* 23 (October 1919): 91–111.

San Antonio Baptist Association. *A Baptist Century around the Alamo, 1858–1958.* San Antonio: Perry, 1958.

Sandoval, Moisés. *On the Move: A History of the Hispanic Church in the United States.* Maryknoll, N.Y.: Orbis, 1990.

———, ed. *Fronteras: A History of the Latin American Church in the USA Since 1513.* San Antonio: Mexican American Cultural Center Press, 1983.

Santos, Richard G. *José Francisco Ruiz.* Béxar County, Tex.: James W. Knight, County Clerk, 1966. Available at CAH.

Schmitz, Joseph William. *The Society of Mary in Texas.* San Antonio: Naylor, 1951.

Sheridan, Mary Benignus. "Bishop Odin, John Mary, 1801–1870, and the New Era of the Catholic Church in Texas, 1840–1860." Ph.D. diss., St. Louis University, 1937.

Sibley, Marilyn McAdams. *Travelers in Texas, 1761–1860.* Austin: University of Texas Press, 1967.

Tijerina, Andrew Anthony. "*Tejanos* and Texas: The Native Mexicans of Texas, 1820–1850." Ph.D. diss., University of Texas, Austin, 1977.

Weber, David J. *The Mexican Frontier, 1821–1846: The American Southwest under Mexico.* Albuquerque: University of New Mexico Press, 1982.

———. "'Scarce more than apes.' Historical Roots of Anglo American Stereotypes of Mexicans in the Border Region." In *New Spain's Far Northern Frontier: Essays on Spain in the American West, 1540–1821,* ed. David J. Weber, 295–307. Albuquerque: University of New Mexico Press, 1979.

Wheeler, Kenneth W. *To Wear a City's Crown: The Beginnings of Urban Growth in Texas, 1836–1865.* Cambridge: Harvard University Press, 1968.

Williams, Amelia. "A Critical Study of the Siege of the Alamo and of the Personnel of Its Defenders." *SWHQ* 36–37 (1933–1934).

Wolff, August L. *The Story of St. John's Lutheran Church, San Antonio, Texas.* N.p.: Paul Anderson, 1937.

Wooster, Ralph A. "Foreigners in the Principal Towns of Ante-Bellum Texas." *SWHQ* 66 (October 1962): 208–220.

Wozniak, Jan Maria. "St. Michael's Church: The Polish National Catholic Church in San Antonio, Texas, 1855–1950." M.A. thesis, University of Texas, Austin, 1964.

Wright, Robert E. "Local Church Emergence and Mission Decline: The Historiography of the Catholic Church in the Southwest during the Spanish and Mexican Periods." *U.S. Catholic Historian* 9 (Winter/Spring 1990): 27–48.

Wueste, Andrew E., comp. *St. Mary's: 1857–1957 Centennial*. San Antonio: Privately printed, [1957]. Available at CAT, CASA.

Zavala, Adina de. *History and Legends of the Alamo and Other Missions in and around San Antonio*. San Antonio: Privately printed, 1917.

RELIGION AND ETHNICITY IN AMERICAN LIFE

Abramson, Harold J. *Ethnic Diversity in Catholic America*. New York: John Wiley & Sons, 1973.

Alexander, June Granatir. "Religion and Ethnic Identity in a Slavic Community: Pittsburgh's Slovak Catholics and Protestants." *Studi Emigrazione* 103 (September 1991): 423–441.

Blegen, Theodore C. *Norwegian Migration to America: The American Transition*. Northfield, Minn.: Norwegian-American Historical Association, 1940.

Brown, Francis J., and Joseph S. Roucek, eds. *One America: The History, Contributions, and Present Problems of Our Racial and National Minorities*. 2d ed. Englewood Cliffs, N.J.: Prentice-Hall, 1952.

Charsley, S. R. "The Formation of Ethnic Groups." In *Urban Ethnicity*, ed. Abner Cohen, 337–368. London: Tavistock, 1974.

Curti, Merle. *The Roots of American Loyalty*. New York: Columbia University Press, 1946.

Fitzpatrick, Joseph. "Cultural Change or Cultural Continuity: Pluralism and Hispanic-Americans." In *Hispanics in New York: Religious, Cultural and Social Experiences*, 2: 51–86. New York: Archdiocese of New York, Office of Pastoral Research and Planning, 1989.

———. *One Church, Many Cultures: The Challenge of Diversity*. Kansas City, Mo.: Sheed & Ward, 1987.

Fuchs, Lawrence. "Assimilation in the U.S." *Tocqueville Review* 9 (1987/1988): 181–199.

———. "Cultural Pluralism and the Future of American Unity: The Impact of Illegal Aliens." *International Migration Review* 18 (Fall 1984): 800–813.

Gans, Herbert J. "Symbolic Ethnicity: The Future of Ethnic Groups and Cultures in America." In *On the Making of Americans: Essays in Honor of David Riesman*, ed. Herbert J. Gans, Nathan Glazer, Joseph R. Gusfield, and Christopher Jencks, 193–220. [Philadelphia]: University of Pennsylvania Press, 1979.

Glazer, Nathan. "*Beyond the Melting Pot* Twenty Years After." *Journal of American Ethnic History* 1 (Fall 1981): 43–55.

────. "Ethnic Groups in America: From National Culture to Ideology." In *Freedom and Control in Modern Society,* ed. Morroe Berger, Theodore Abel, and Charles H. Page, 158–173. New York: D. Van Nostrand, 1954.

Glazer, Nathan, and Daniel P. Moynihan. *Beyond the Melting Pot: The Negroes, Puerto Ricans, Jews, Italians, and Irish of New York City.* 2d ed. Cambridge, Mass.: M.I.T. Press, 1970.

Gleason, Philip. "American Identity and Americanization." In *Harvard Encyclopedia of American Ethnic Groups,* 31–58. Cambridge: Harvard University Press, 1980.

────. "Immigrant Assimilation and the Crisis of Americanization." Ch. 3 in *Keeping the Faith: American Catholicism Past and Present.* Notre Dame, Ind.: University of Notre Dame Press, 1987.

────. *Speaking of Diversity: Language and Ethnicity in Twentieth-Century America.* Baltimore: Johns Hopkins University Press, 1992.

Gordon, Milton M. *Assimilation in American Life: The Role of Race, Religion, and National Origins.* New York: Oxford University Press, 1964.

────. "Models of Pluralism: The New American Dilemma." *Annals of the American Academy of Political and Social Science* 454 (March 1981): 178–188.

────. "Toward a General Theory of Racial and Ethnic Group Relations." In *Ethnicity: Theory and Experience,* ed. Nathan Glazer and Daniel P. Moynihan, 84–110. Cambridge: Harvard University Press, 1975.

Greeley, Andrew. *Ethnicity in the United States: A Preliminary Reconnaissance.* New York: John Wiley & Sons, 1974.

────. *Why Can't They Be Like Us? America's White Ethnic Groups.* New York: E. P. Dutton, 1971.

Handlin, Oscar. *Boston's Immigrants: A Study in Acculturation.* Cambridge: Harvard University Press, 1941.

────. *The Uprooted: The Epic Story of the Great Migrations that Made the American People.* Boston: Little, Brown, 1951.

Hansen, Marcus Lee. *The Immigrant in American History.* Edited by Arthur M. Schlesinger. New York: Harper & Row, 1940.

Herberg, Will. *Protestant-Catholic-Jew: An Essay in American Religious Sociology.* Garden City, N.Y.: Doubleday, 1955; revised, Garden City, N.Y.: Anchor, 1960.

Higham, John. "Current Trends in the Study of Ethnicity in the United States." *Journal of American Ethnic History* 2 (Fall 1982): 5–15.

────. "Hanging Together: Divergent Unities in American History." *Journal of American History* 61 (June 1974): 5–28.

────. *Send These to Me: Immigrants in Urban America.* 2d ed. Baltimore: Johns Hopkins University Press, 1984.

Hoge, Dean. "Interpreting Change in American Catholicism: The River and the Floodgate." *Review of Religious Research* 27 (June 1986): 289–300.

Hollinger, David A. "Ethnic Diversity, Cosmopolitanism and the Emergence of the American Liberal Intelligentsia." *American Quarterly* 27 (May 1975): 133–151.

Kallen, Horace M. *Cultural Pluralism and the American Idea: An Essay in Social Philosophy.* Philadelphia: University of Pennsylvania Press, 1956.

———. *Culture and Democracy in the United States: Studies in the Group Psychology of the American Peoples.* New York: Boni and Liveright, 1924.

———. "Democracy Versus the Melting-Pot: A Study of American Nationality." *The Nation* 100 (18, 25 February 1915): 190–194, 217–220.

Kammen, Michael. *A Season of Youth: The American Revolution and the Historical Imagination.* Ithaca, N.Y.: Cornell University Press, 1978.

Kennedy, Ruby Jo Reeves. "Single or Triple Melting-Pot? Intermarriage Trends in New Haven, 1870–1940." *American Journal of Sociology* 49 (January 1944): 331–339.

Kivisto, Peter, and Dab Blanck, eds. *American Immigrants and Their Generations: Studies and Commentaries on the Hansen Thesis after Fifty Years.* Urbana: University of Illinois Press, 1990.

Kodric, Majda. "Religion and Ethnic Identity within the Slovene Community in the United States: The Bases and the Transition to the Second Generation." *Studi Emigrazione* 103 (September 1991): 443–454.

Kohn, Hans. *American Nationalism: An Interpretive Essay.* New York: Macmillan, 1957.

Laumann, Edward O. *Bonds of Pluralism: The Form and Substance of Urban Social Networks.* New York: John Wiley & Sons, 1973.

Mann, Arthur. *The One and the Many: Reflections on the American Identity.* Chicago: University of Chicago Press, 1979.

Marty, Martin. "Ethnicity: The Skeleton of Religion in America." *Church History* 41 (March 1972): 5–21.

Mead, Margaret. *And Keep Your Powder Dry: An Anthropologist Looks at America.* 2d ed. New York: William Morrow, 1965.

Moore, R. Laurence. *Religious Outsiders and the Making of Americans.* Oxford: Oxford University Press, 1986.

Nagel, Paul C. *This Sacred Trust: American Nationality, 1798–1898.* New York: Oxford University Press, 1971.

Newman, William M. *American Pluralism: A Study of Minority Groups and Social Theory.* New York: Harper & Row, 1973.

Novak, Michael. *The Rise of the Unmeltable Ethnics: Politics and Culture in the Seventies.* New York: Macmillan, 1971.

Park, Robert E., and Herbert A. Miller. *Old World Traits Transplanted.* New York: Harper, 1921.

Ross, Edward Alsworth. *The Old World in the New: The Significance of Past and Present Immigration to the American People.* New York: Century, 1914.

Shaw, Stephen J. *The Catholic Parish as a Way-Station of Ethnicity and Americanization: Chicago's Germans and Italians, 1903–1939.* With a preface by Martin E. Marty. Brooklyn, New York: Carlson, 1991.

Smith, Timothy L. "Religion and Ethnicity in America." *American Historical Review* 83 (December 1978): 1155–1185.

Smith, William Carlson. *Americans in the Making: The Natural History of the Assimilation of Immigrants.* New York: D. Appleton-Century, 1939.

Spencer, Benjamin T. *The Quest for Nationality: An American Literary Campaign.* Syracuse, N.Y.: Syracuse University Press, 1957.

Stein, Howard F., and Robert F. Hill. *The Ethnic Imperative: Examining the New White Ethnic Movement.* University Park: Pennsylvania State University Press, 1977.

Stout, Harry. "Ethnicity: The Vital Center of Religion in America." *Ethnicity* 2 (1975): 204–224.

Tomasi, Silvano M. *Piety and Power: The Role of Italian Parishes in the New York Metropolitan Area, 1880–1930.* Staten Island, N.Y.: Center for Migration Studies, 1975.

Vecoli, Rudolph J. "Ethnicity: A Neglected Dimension of American History." In *The State of American History,* ed. and with an introduction by Herbert J. Bass, 70–88. Chicago: Quadrangle, 1970.

Wilson, John F. "Common Religion in American Society." In *Civil Religion and Political Theology,* ed. Leroy S. Rouner, 111–124. Notre Dame, Ind.: University of Notre Dame Press, 1986.

Wittke, Carl. *We Who Built America: The Saga of the Immigrant.* New York: Prentice-Hall, 1939.

Wuthnow, Robert, Martin E. Marty, Philip Gleason, and Deborah Dash Moore. "Sources of Personal Identity: Religion, Ethnicity, and the American Cultural Situation." *Religion and American Culture: A Journal of Interpretation* 2 (Winter 1992): 1–22.

Yancey, William L., Eugene P. Ericksen, and Richard N. Juliani. "Emergent Ethnicity: A Review and Reformulation." *American Sociological Review* 41 (June 1976): 391–403.

Zunz, Olivier. "The Genesis of American Pluralism." *Tocqueville Review* 9 (1987/1988): 201–219.

INDEX

†

feast days, Tejano
Corpus Christi, 6
criticism of, 40, 54–55, 64
distinct ritual calendar, 6, 10, 23, 90
Holy Week, 6, 18, 21
Immaculate Conception, 6, 21, 23
local initiatives to organize, 6,
20–21, 23, 39, 43, 87
minor, 18
Nuestra Señora de la Candelaria, 6
participation of foreign clergy,
43–44, 52–53, 68, 81, 88
San Antonio, 6, 53, 68
San Fernando, 6, 53, 68
San Juan, 53, 68, 79, 87, 121n.14
San Pedro, 53, 68, 121n.14
Sundays and observed, 18–19,
105n.28
See also Christmas, Tejano celebrations; Our Lady of Guadalupe
celebrations
Ferdinand VI, 6
First Baptist Church of San Antonio,
62, 64
Fisher, Rev. Orceneth, 15–16
Flores family, 38
Fourth of July, 53–54, 57, 79, 87, 90
Franciscans, 5, 76, 78
Frederick of York, 21
French, Sarah L., 70

Galveston, diocese of, 41
García family, 38
Garza family, 38
General Land Office (Austin), 26
Germans
in Catholic church, 60, 65, 80, 88,
128n.56
census figures of, 51
and ethnic diversity, 49, 89
and ethnic relations, 52, 57–58, 79,
99n.7
in Protestant churches, 59, 62, 80,
125n.36
public celebrations, 52, 54, 58, 79
voting power of, 69

Glazer, Nathan, 134n.11
Goizueta, Roberto, 93
Goliad. *See* La Bahía
Gordon, Milton, 99n.11, 134nn.9,10
Gregory XVI (Pope), 41

Handlin, Oscar, 83–84
Harney, William Selby, 69
Harris County, 36
Herberg, Will, 133n.3
Hewitt, I. L., 54
Hidalgo, Father Miguel, 22
history, Anglo-American and Tejano
interpretations of, 50, 76–78,
81–82, 86, 90–91, 132n.86
Hoge, Dean, 133n.5
Horton, Rev. H. G., 62, 126n.43
Houston, Sam, 33, 37
Huston, Felix, 37, 46, 114n.36

identity
collective behavior and written
sources illuminate, x, 2–4
dearth of studies on, 1
meaning of term discussed, 98n.5
religion a component of, 4
shifting European immigrant, 84,
90–91, 134n.11
Tejano, 5–6, 9–10, 22–23, 25, 41,
45–48, 79–82, 90–92
intermarriage
cultural influence of, 6, 11–12,
57–58, 79–80
and denominational affiliation, 58,
60, 62, 80
mentioned, 89, 124n.29
political implications of, 38, 46–47
Iturbide, Agustín de, 8–9, 21

Jones, Anson, 69
Jones, Rev. Lucius H., 62
Jordan, Terry G., 84, 92

King, Sarah Brackett, 55
Know Nothing Party, 56, 70–74,
81–82, 86–87, 90, 131n.77